Maurice Tourneur

Maurice Tourneur

The Life and Films

by HARRY WALDMAN

McFarland & Company, Inc., Publishers
Jefferson, North Carolina, and London

ALSO BY HARRY WALDMAN AND FROM MCFARLAND

Nazi Films in America, 1933–1942 (2008)

Missing Reels: Lost Films of American and European Cinema (2000; paper 2008)

Scenes Unseen: Unreleased and Uncompleted Films from the World's Master Filmmakers, 1912–1990 (1991)

Frontispiece: Tourneur in Hollywood, early 1920s

The present work is a reprint of the illustrated case bound edition of Maurice Tourneur: The Life and Films, *first published in 2001 by McFarland.*

LIBRARY OF CONGRESS CATALOGUING-IN-PUBLICATION DATA

Waldman, Harry.
    Maurice Tourneur : the life and films / by Harry Waldman.
      p. cm.
    Includes bibliographical references and index.

    ISBN 978-0-7864-4085-6
    softcover : 50# alkaline paper ∞

    1. Tourneur, Maurice, 1876–1961. I. Title.

PN1998.3.T64 W35   2008
791.43'0233'092 — dc21

                                              2001023433

British Library cataloguing data are available

©2001 Harry Waldman. All rights reserved

No part of this book may be reproduced or transmitted in any form or by any means, electronic or mechanical, including photocopying or recording, or by any information storage and retrieval system, without permission in writing from the publisher.

On the cover: Maurice Tourneur in a 1918 publicity photo

Manufactured in the United States of America

McFarland & Company, Inc., Publishers
  Box 611, Jefferson, North Carolina 28640
    www.mcfarlandpub.com

To Susan L. Morse

CONTENTS

Introduction 1

1. Tourneur at Eclair 3

2. The Films at Eclair, 1912–1914 11

3. Tourneur in America 25

4. The Films in America, 1914–1926 31

5. Tourneur in Europe, 1927–1961 133

6. The Films in Europe, 1927–1948 141

Sources 169

Index 171

Then, gradually, thanks to the work and talent of several men of genius, the intertitles became less numerous: Charlie Chaplin, Gance, King Vidor, Tourneur, René Clair, and several others found the rhythm, the fashion of cutting up the story, the spirit in which it needed to be presented. In short, they invented and raised up on high a new technical resource, an art which they called the Seventh Art.
— *Marcel Pagnol**

Tourneur was a man who had no illusions about working in film. He realized the limitations of Hollywood and the films he was given to direct. However, he brought his considerable talent as a designer to bear on his work, and did not hesitate to experiment. He stylized his sets and was influenced by new movements in the theater, but he also used the effects of nature to heighten his dramas. His awareness of the potentialities of the camera was profound, giving strength to his images.
— *Liam O'Leary*†

---

* *"Cinématurgie de Paris,"* Cahiers du Film 1 *(15 December 1933).*

† *"Maurice Tourneur," in* International Dictionary of Films and Filmmakers, *ed. Laurie Collier Hillstrom (New York: St. James, 1977).*

Introduction

Maurice Tourneur was born in France and worked in early French cinema but he made his name across the Atlantic in the years 1914–1926. No French-born director made better American films or worked longer in America. At the height of his fame in Hollywood, when he took out American citizenship, Tourneur ranked alongside D. W. Griffith. In 1920 he made one of the greatest silents, the breathtaking *The Last of the Mohicans.* His American masterpiece was called "better than Griffith" in a letter from film historian James Card to Henri Langois.

Tourneur left America and Hollywood because he was unhappy in his personal life and ill at ease in a changing Hollywood. When he returned to France in the late 1920s, he was unwelcome in the land of his birth. But after he settled in Paris, no French-American director ever worked longer or better in France. His American experience, efficiency, and frugality helped him — and French cinema — to make the transition to sound in the early 1930s.

Tourneur ended his film career where it had begun. Today his French sound films are appreciated in France, but his American silents, which introduced a new esthetic conception to Hollywood filmmaking, are not. Forgotten is the fact that for a brief time Tourneur's French filmmaking experience influenced American filmmaking; more often than not, it was the other way around.

Here was a French director who favored the macabre and the fantastic walking on the great sidewalk of celebrity in early Hollywood. But even in America, Maurice Tourneur has been all but forgotten. Yet he was one of the first to make crime dramas, fantasies, and pirate films, with a flair and style that made the films memorable.

His early background in French theater and film had prepared him for a career in French and American films. Tourneur acted in and directed little-known French silents in the years 1912–1914 at the Eclair studio in Paris. Before becoming a full-time director, he also served as assistant director to a fine mentor, Emile Chautard (1881–1934). Tourneur's early films are marked by a wide range of subject matter — Grand Guignol, historical romance, adventure, dark police drama, comedy, tales of gamins and waifs, adaptations of works by authors. He later favored the same kinds of subjects in America, first at the Eclair studio in Fort Lee, New Jersey, and later in Hollywood.

The thread of a theme works its way through many of his films. An early "woman's" director, he often presented heroines who resorted to ruses, or were the victims of such, in the search for love. Ruses, or easy deceptions, seemed to be a part of life. Women more often than not were the victims of deceit. They came face-to-face with lovers' tricks and deceptions; they faced familial scandal; and if they were to save themselves and gain love, they had to fight for it. Sometimes they had to kill. They uncovered rogues and snares and traps, and swept them aside to overcome them. Or, in many instances, they had to admit in the end that love was impossible, despite their efforts.

Tourneur made his name by demonstrating a creative eye for beautiful composition and lighting, the innovative use of off-screen space, highly dramatic editing, and visual solutions to difficulties of deep space. He was a director who was willing to share success. Nothing by itself could make a picture, said Tourneur — not the story, the acting, the stars, or the director. It was the combined efforts of cast and crew. He assembled a company of actors and technicians who shared his approach and worked on many of his films.

Maurice Tourneur arrived in the United States in early 1914 to manage productions of the rebuilt French-owned Eclair studios in Fort Lee, New Jersey. After several films, including the highly admired *The Wishing Ring* (1914), he directed *Trilby* (1915), a critical and financial success for Equitable-World. Then for Paramount he directed Mary Pickford in *The Pride of the Clan* (1917) and *The Poor Little Rich Girl* (1917). After these came a string of great films: *The Blue Bird* (1918), *Prunella* (1918), *Woman* (1918), *The Life Line* (1919), and *Victory* (1919).

Within a few years of his arrival in America, the *New York Times* wrote that "Few motion picture directors equal, and fewer surpass ... Tourneur in the art of making scenes for the screen. By his work he stands out prominently, even among the small group of exceptional men who appreciate the particular powers of the camera and know how to employ them."

In 1920, Tourneur reached the peak of his American career with *The Last of the Mohicans*. He later told fellow Hollywood Frenchman Robert Florey: "The cinema is a different medium for hierographically expressing human thoughts using images ... and with a savagery no one means of expression possesses.... It is the most significant instrument for bringing together nations and classes.... More through the cinema than through the efforts of diplomats, men will realize their needs, aspirations and joys and will stop considering others as strangers." Yet in his adaptation of James Fenimore Cooper's classic — and in many of the more than 100 films he directed over 35 years — he showed another side: the ruses we employ on the way to love; and how difficult it is to overcome the ruses that are the emotional, societal, and cultural obstacles to love.

TOURNEUR AT ECLAIR

Born February 2, 1876, in Belleville, France, Tourneur (born Maurice Thomas) graduated in 1894 from the Lycée Condorcet. His classmates included André Citroën, Henri Bernstein, André Maginot, and Jean Joseph-Renaud. After serving three years in the military, Tourneur became a magazine and book illustrator, a poster and fabric designer, then an interior decoration designer. He worked for Auguste Rodin and alongside the muralist Pierre Puvis de Chavannes in the decoration of the Boston Public Library. His training in the decorative arts and his concern with design would be reflected in his films.

In 1900, on the strength of a recommendation by the writer Jean Joseph-Renaud, Tourneur was invited to become an actor at the theater of the Bouffes du Nord in Paris. He began his stage career with a bit part in *La Tour de Nesles*. A year later, having also become a stage manager, he got his first big break: He accompanied the great actress Rejane on a worldwide tour. They performed in England, Spain, Portugal, Italy, North Africa, and South America. At the age of 25, Tourneur was appearing in and handling the greatest comedy and drama of his nation: *La Dame aux camélias*, *Le Demi-Monde*, *Madame Sans-Gêne*, *La Parisienne*, *La Robe rouge*, and *Zaza*. He also learned English.

In 1902 Tourneur made a bold move. He offered his services to another great name of the French stage, the legendary André Antoine (1858–1943). Thus he began a seven-year career as a stage actor and manager at the Théâtre Antoine and at the Odéon.

André Antoine was the famous director of the Théâtre Libre (1887–94), Théâtre Antoine (1897–1900), and Odéon (1900–1914). He produced and directed hundreds of classic plays, including *Les Revenants*, *Les Tisserands*, *Le Voiturier Henschell*, *Les Remplaçants*, *Au Telephone* (1902) by André de Lorde, *La Terre* (1902), after

Emile Zola, and *Julius Caesar* (1906). Antoine favored understatement on the part of actors and naturalism in the theater. He became known for his stand in favor of artistic integrity and against the profit motive. His theaters became homes to an ensemble of actors and to plays which were true to experience. Antoine took risks and encouraged innovation.

Antoine's influence would be felt in cinema within a few years by the presence in the new industry of his protégé, Maurice Tourneur. The two men, however, parted company in 1909, possibly over artistic differences. "I felt a terrible sadness," said Tourneur. "Hardly back home, I bitterly regretted my attitude regarding the man whom I considered the regenerator of the French stage. Antoine welcomed me like a father."

In the years 1910–1912, Tourneur was an actor and set administrator at the Théâtre de Renaissance in Nice under the direction of Abel Tarride. There he made significant artistic contacts by working in the company of Emile Chautard, Léonce Perret, and Henri Roussell. It was at the behest of Chautard that Tourneur subsequently joined the Eclair film studio. His early mentor, Antoine, soon also became a film director, at Pathé. In the period 1915–1922, directing such films as *Le Coupable* (1917), *La Terre* (1921), and *1793* (1921), Antoine exhibited the same spirit of independence and daring as he had in his stage work. He also became a freelance film critic for several publications, campaigning against censorship, encouraging inventive and honest films, attacking the dull and commercial, deploring the ways in which films were cut to standard lengths, and warning against the influence of Hollywood. He was said to be — like his protégé Tourneur — quarrelsome, dictatorial, and obstinate, and a man who abandoned his first wife and child. Even those hurt by Antoine, however, acknowledged his capacity to commit himself to his work, and were won over by the creativity of his imagination.

In mid–1912, Maurice Tourneur began working at the Eclair studio in Paris, which had been founded in 1907. In its first year of operation, the studio had released three films. It followed with forty in 1908, nearly all of which were directed by Victorin Jasset. In 1909, the studio doubled its output, again with Jasset directing most of the films. In 1910, Chautard joined the studio as a director, and that year Eclair produced more than 150 films.

The years 1911–1914 represent the heyday for the film company. With Emile Chautard leading the way, backed by Jasset, Joseph Faivre, and Paul Bertho, Eclair made more than 700 films in all genres. The Great War and emigration, however, then took their toll on the studio. Output declined to sixty films a year in the period 1915–1917, when Emile Cohl and Roger Lion joined the company, then to ten in 1918, six in 1919, and, in its final year of operation, three in 1920.

Because of his theatrical experience, Tourneur was assigned to the studio's artistic film series, called ACAD (Association des Comédiens et Auteurs Dramatiques) whose producer-director was Emile Chautard. "I began working in France," Tourneur said years later, "and there everything is without a schedule." As a director, he'd "go on the set and say to the cameraman, 'Look, come over here, and let's look at it from this point of view.' That's how we worked! I believe great things come from that great reservoir we have within us of ... experience, which is all available."

Since his work for the studio was based on his experience in the theater,

Tourneur's first assignment at Eclair was as assistant director, rather than actor, in an adaptation of a popular play, *Le Bonhomme Jadis/Old Man Jadis* (1912, Emile Chautard). "This work did not interest me much," said Tourneur. But Chautard "had such faith in the future of the cinema that he succeeded in convincing me." Their film is a charming and idyllic little 333-m comedy, set in 1840. It is based on the work by Henri Mürger and the 1905 opera by the Swiss composer Emile Jaques-Dalcroze (1865–1950). The protagonist is sixty-year-old Dazumel Jadis, who has led quite an unorthodox life, and he is the catalyst who uses a ruse to bring two shy lovers together.

In their next collaboration, *Conscience de l'enfant/Child's Conscience* (1912, Emile Chautard), Chautard and Tourneur produced a drama that is a morality tale of another youth's naiveté about love, based on the hugely successful 1899 four-act play by Gaston Devore (1859–1949). It was another example of the studio's adaptations of a contemporary work.

Tourneur had a small role in *La Dame de chez Maxim/The Lady from Maxim's* (1912, Emile Chautard and Raymond Agnel), which was based on the popular 1899 farce by Georges Feydeau (1862–1921), who was called "The King of La Belle Epoque." The three-reeler starred Renée Sylvaire of the Théâtre de la Renaissance. She would become a mainstay in numerous Tourneur films during this time. This film is the earliest screen rendition of the contemporary tale of a prostitute who deceives people into believing she is "the lady from Maxim's," a real married lady of society. She plays the role to everyone's great amazement—and the audience's great amusement. The romantic comedy was a great commercial success.

The film is a representative example of the French film style of the period up to the First World War, which was, in a word, theatrical. Whether or not a production was a literary adaptation, and regardless of whether it was filmed on a set or on location, what mattered to Eclair and its artistic directors were restrained acting, clear photography, and detailed settings. Tourneur, when he became a full-fledged director, would add several elements to the mixture: an emotional connection to the needs of his audience, narrative continuity, and, most important, art. He would, in the process, make his films come alive.

The film team followed their hit with one of the studio's earliest adaptations of a boulevard farce. *Occupe-toi d'Amélie/Keep Your Eyes on Amelie* (1912, Emile Chautard) is based on Georges Feydeau's 1908 play. Here Alice de Tander played Amélie d'Avranches. Replete with ruses, contrivances, intrigues, and misunderstandings, "nothing could be more French," wrote a critic about the story.

Alice de Tander also starred in Chautard and Tourneur's next collaboration, *La Veuve joyeuse/The Merry Widow* (1913, Emile Chautard), the well-known comedy based on Franz Lehár's classic, fascinating, and romantic 1905 three-act operetta, *Die Lustige Witwe*. The film, also part of Eclair's ACAD series, was one of the earliest screen renditions of the light contemporary operetta, the whimsical tale of Missia, a romantically enticing and free-spirited follies girl who becomes the object of attention of two deceitful men who use ruses to try to lure her to love.

Tourneur's stint as assistant director to Emile Chautard—who had been a forceful influence in his life on the stage and the man who had brought him into the world of the cinema—ended in early 1913. When Chautard became head of production at Eclair's Paris studio, Tourneur moved up to become a director at Eclair. He then expanded the range of his subject matter. Besides literary and historical adaptations, he favored stories of gamins in trouble, police and crime dramas, broad comedies, renditions of Grand Guignol, war stories, provincial melodramas, and just plain tales of real issues like adoption, child abuse, and poverty.

Tourneur filmed universal stories about intense family feeling, the sanctity of home and hearth, and the championing of female virtue. He became known as a romanticist, a lover of the bizarre, the fantastic, the adventure that is unusual, and the surprise ending. In many of these films the central element remained the elusive and contradictory nature of love; the appeal of the transparent over the real. He would carry these interests to America, where he made his name as a director with a distinctive style.

Tourneur was the director of sixteen films for the Eclair studio in the years 1913 and 1914. He began, in April 1913, with a drama about a famous sleuth: *Rouletabille Part I: Le Mystère de la chambre jaune/The Mystery of the Yellow Room* (1913, Tourneur and Emile Chautard). French critics wrote that "the novel of M. Gaston Leroux was followed almost from one end to the other by the director who respected the storyline and followed the inquiry by Rouletabille with great precision of detail." A year later Tourneur made the sequel, one of his last prewar silent films in France, *Rouletabille Part II: La Dernière incarnation de Larsan/The Last Incarnation of Larsan* (1914).

Based on the novel by the notorious Gaston Leroux (1868–1927), Part I is a contemporary tale of a young star reporter named Joseph Rouletabille, a man mocked and shunned for his fierce independence and his unusually large head. Leroux's was a groundbreaking novel of the mystery genre, the first of the "locked-room" mysteries. The drama of *The Mystery of the Yellow Room* became known, on the strength of its central puzzle and detection, as one of the classic examples of the genre. Tourneur's film, besides being faithful to Leroux's novel, was said to be precise and clear in detail, with sumptuous settings, excellent production values, and professional acting.

Part II, based on Leroux's sequel to the story, called *Le Parfum de la dame en noir/The Perfume of the Lady in Black*, was released in mid–1914, and was also a great commercial and critical success. In an interview years later with Marie Epstein, Tourneur affirmed that he alone was the director of Part II, a 1,220-m drama set along the Riviera. Between Parts I and II, Tourneur filmed more than a dozen other works and picked up an acting stint or two along the way.

In *Le Miroir d'Ali Maboul/The Mirror of Ali Maboul* (1913, Emile Chautard) Tourneur performed in front of the camera for one of the last times in his career. He played, wrote a critic, "the most nearsighted and ignorant of merchants from Algeria." North Africa would become the locale for several of his later American films and for one of his more important French silents.

Tourneur filmed *Jean de poudre/Powder John* in early 1913 in North Africa. A colonial drama (also called *Jean la Poudre*), it is about the exploits of Marshall Thomas-Robert Bugeaud, Duc D'Isly (1784–1849), who was France's most distinguished military figure during the reign of Louis-Philippe. Bugeaud served during the Napoleonic Wars (at Austerlitz, and in Poland and Spain), but his most important contributions were in connection with the conquest and colonization of Algeria.

Tourneur's film retraces events of 1836–37 in Algeria and the activities of a young Zouave named Jean-La-Frousse (Scaredy-Cat John). During the course of events Jean earns his more incendiary name through acts of daring.

Tourneur followed that serious military work with a lighthearted military tale. *Les Gaîtés de l'escadron/The Gaieties of the Squadron* (1913) is based on the play of the same name by the popular Georges Courteline. Tourneur's 920-m work was considered the director's most important early extant work until *Le Friquet* (1913) was rediscovered. The comedy is filled with esthetic elements rare for the time. Here Tourneur demonstrated his ability to frame and edit a film and displayed an expertise in superimpositions and lateral panoramas. A minimum number of intertitles permits the comedy and theme to come to the fore, especially in the superimposed "dream vision" battle scene that takes place over the heads of "prisoners" as a general is making his inspection. The film was reedited by the studio in 1918, and Tourneur made a grander but still humorous sound version in 1933 when he returned to France.

With *La Dame de Monsoreau* (1913, Tourneur, Emile Chautard, and Charles Krauss) Tourneur helped to film one of the longest productions to date by the Eclair studio. A historical romance, it was one of the earliest to show caped swordsmen. Tourneur and his codirectors gave the French public a romantic, spectacular idea of history, bringing to life a vigorous, intensely romantic drama — the first French screen rendition of Alexandre Dumas' fanciful tale of the 16th century. Critics made note of Tourneur's "sense of composition, for which ... his study of painting had uniquely prepared him."

For *Le Coeur d'une gosse/Heart of a Kid* (1913, Emile Chautard), Tourneur assisted his mentor, Chautard. Their three-reel tale is about a gamine from a poverty-stricken area of a city who is taken under the wing of a wealthy family. It was the first of many films that Tourneur would make about orphans and the helpless. A young girl rises to stardom in the theater; her innocence, or "heart of a kid," saves her from a compromising predicament and allows her to overcome obstacles and wed her lover.

Mademoiselle Cent Millions (1913) starred an actress who would work on and off with Tourneur in silent and sound films, Emmy Lynn. Little is known of this four-reel comedy-drama. It may be based on a novel by the spontaneous and popular writer Charles Paul de Kock (1794–1871), who was held in high esteem by Dumas fils. The film is possibly the romantic historical tale of the amazing life of the Duchess de Mazarin, Hortense de la Porte (1646–1699), born in Rome, who was brought up in the Court of Louis XIV.

Tourneur's next film showed an interest in a subject that shocked people of the day: his love of the macabre. *Le Système du docteur Goudron et du professeur Plume/The System of Dr. Tarr and Professor Fether* (1913) was said to have struck terror into the hearts of the production's actors, and it ranks as one of the first truly original French films, the earliest of the genre and one of the most celebrated — if not the most notorious— of its day.

At 460-m, the "intentionally demonic and demented" tale was adapted from André de Lorde's 1903 one-act Grand-Guignol play. The playwright was inspired by Edgar Allan Poe's "The System of Dr. Tarr and Professor Fether." When produced on stage in Paris, de Lorde's work was described as a "peculiarly revolting spectacle." De Lorde noted that the play was "first presented, received, and even ... rehearsed at Antoine's who, with his usual flair, guessed at a great success. But, since the first rehearsals, the artists, completely bowled over, almost terrorized by the too realistic production ... concluded one could never get to the end of the play."

De Lorde (1871–1942), the son of a physician, was born André de La Tour. He wrote his first play at fifteen and wrote more than 200 dramas in his career. He often collaborated with Alfred Binet, who was director of the psychology laboratory at the Sorbonne. Tourneur, who had worked in the theater, was well aware of the prolific André de Lorde. The dramatist's subjects were anguish, mystery, madness, torture, pseudoscience, apparitions, sadism, the underworld, revenge, revolutionary horrors, murder, and death — all designed to leave an audience in a state of near collapse. De Lorde became known as the "prince of terror," and his works were called a "museum of horror." Tourneur directed several other adaptations of de Lorde's Grand-Guignol dramas *(Figures de cire* [1913], *Obsession* [1934]). The former was released in the United States.

Le Friquet/The Tree Sparrow (1913) was one of Tourneur's most acclaimed films of the era. Recently rediscovered, it is a three-reel tale and one of Tourneur's earliest surviving works, long presumed to be the first film he directed. It stars the well-known vaudeville artiste Polaire (Emile-Marie Bouchard-Zouzé, 1873–1941), a close friend of Colette, in her first film. Just as important to the film is the novel upon which it is based and its author, known as "Gyp."

"Who has not read Gyp?" asked the critics in the late 19th century. Now forgotten, the writer whose pseudonym was Gyp (1849–1932) was born Sibylle Gabrielle Marie Antoinette de Riquetti de Mirabeau, comtesse de Martel de Janville. Her mother was Marie de Gonneville, who separated from her husband, Arundel-Joseph, the last of the Mirabeau counts, and, when widowed, turned to writing novels. Her one child, the comtesse de Martel de Janville, did the same in her marriage, but with greater impact. As Gyp, she pretended to be an army officer with a satirical view of fashionable high society.

In her writing, Gyp employed the *enfant terrible* as narrator. Gyp aroused her enemies, created political excitement, and won the respect of Henry James. She was a combination of fanatical nationalist and right-wing anarchist, calling herself an Anti-Semite. Her influence during the Dreyfus Affair was destructive, and any film based on her work was bound to create a stir. Her novel *Le Friquet* was serialized in *La Revue hebdomadaire* in 1900 and adapted for the stage in 1904. Tourneur adapted several works by the rabble-rousing Gyp before coming to the United States.

Tourneur's first film of a work by the notorious Gyp centers on the young heroine Marie, nicknamed "Le Friquet," who makes a living as a circus performer but who began life as an abandoned waif. The film was one of the earliest by Tourneur to be shown in the United States — though the director was unidentified in the credits.

Tourneur's next few films remain shrouded in mystery. *Le Dernier pardon/The Last Pardon* (1913) has been attributed to Tourneur, and may be based on the 1908 novel *Cloclo* by Gyp, which is the painful story of a ward of an aristocrat who reveals the intrigues of a servant in the wealthy household — and pays a price.

Le Camée (1914), a 600-m drama, starred one of the most popular actors of the period. Alexandre Arquillière (1870–1953) had a physique like the later French star Raimu. He made a name for himself as the notorious master criminal "Zigomar" in Victorin Jasset's series of crime films for Eclair, notably *Zigomar contre Nick Carter* (1911), and later as the costar in Germaine Dulac's *La Souriante madame Beudet/The Smiling Mrs. Beudet* (1922). Tourneur's film, which can be translated as both *The Cameo* and *The Female Drug Addict*, "is of inestimable value which will bring it ten times the amount it cost to make," wrote a critic for *Film-Revue*. "The direction and acting have a claim to excellence.... The photography is perfect.... It will be a great success." Beyond that, the facts are elusive; the film is not extant.

Les Ruses d'amour/Tricks of Love (1914) was one of Tourneur's last films with Eclair in Paris, and one of Tourneur's least-known efforts. It is a one-reel comedy based on the lively, classic, 1736 three-act play by Philippe Poisson (1682–1743) that was adapted for the screen by the would-be director Robert Boudrioz (1887–1949). "The unravelling of events" in this story of romantic deceptions and tricks, wrote a critic, "is one of those that, as unbelievable as it may seem ... works."

With *Figures de cire/Wax Faces* (1914) Tourneur revisited the arena of Grand Guignol. He again turned to that master of the genre, André de Lorde. The son of a physician, de Lorde described Grand Guignol as "the study of the physiological and medical cases which hold the public breathless like all introspective problems and conflicts of the spirit." The genre is characterized by brief and violent action, bloodcurdling situations, a realistic setting, and unexpected endings. This film, which was also called *L'Homme aux figures de cire/Man with Wax Faces*, is now regarded as a forerunner of Paul Leni's expressionistic *Waxworks* (1924).

Monsieur Lecoq (1914) came next. It is based on a well-known 1866 detective novel by Emile Gaboriau (1832–1873), one of the founding fathers of that genre. Tourneur's adaptation became an acutely observed and striking three-reel drama about a mysterious affair. By this time in his career, it is clear, director Tourneur had the freedom to choose his themes, and the themes he chose here were the saving of a woman's honor and the ends justifying the means.

The intriguing tale caught the attention of the critics in America. Again, however, while the film — Tourneur's fourth to be released in America — achieved great success, Tourneur's name as director was absent from the credits wherever the film was shown.

In *Le Corso rouge/The Red Promenade* (1914, Tourneur and Charles Krauss), Tourneur tells a double story of cruelty, deception, and betrayal. The drama is based on a tale by the prolific Pierre Sales (1856–1914), many of whose stories were adapted by Eclair in the years 1912–1920. This film focuses on the fate of an orphan. *Le Puits mitoyen/The Common Well* (1914), which came next, is a three-reel drama about which almost nothing is known, though it may have been based on the exuberant two-act drama *Le Puits* (1902), by Auguste Dorchain (1857–1930).

Soeurette/Little Sister (1915), starring Polaire, was the last French silent Tourneur made until his return to France in the late 1920s. It is based on Gyp's 1902 novel of the same name (reissued in 1930). This two-reel (600-m) drama was released by Eclair a year after director Tourneur had landed in America and was well on the way to establishing himself there.

It is a tale of woe whose prologue shows a woman dying in a hovel while clasping to her breast her seven-year-old daughter. She entrusts the life of her child to a ragpicker neighbor and her young son. The girl, who becomes known as the little sister, saves the life of a young physician. Tourneur's production was labeled a "popular priced film."

The stage and screen actress Polaire, who starred in two silents by Tourneur, was the original gamine. She was a prototype for the great French performer Edith Piaf and for other "tiny, soulful, plebian French *vedettes* who have penciled their brows ... who have been as sentimental about respectability as they were sexually profligate ... and who ... have died broke and disillusioned" (Judith Thurman, *The Secrets of the Flesh: A Life of Colette*).

The Films at Eclair, 1912–1914

Le Bonhomme Jadis/Old Man Jadis

(1912, Emile Chautard). Eclair Film. Assistant Director: Tourneur. Script: Chautard. Design: Hughes Laurent and Dumesnil. Photography: Raymond Agnel. With Gilbert Dalleu (Octave), Renée Pré (Jacqueline), Henri Gouget (Jadis), Suzanne Révonne, Léon Bernard, and Jacques de Féraudy.

Chautard and Tourneur made a charming and idyllic little 333-m comedy set in 1840 based on the popular play by Henri Mürger and the 1905 opera by the Swiss composer Emile Jaques-Dalcroze (1865–1950). Director Chautard asked Tourneur to become his assistant beginning with this production, in June 1912. Tourneur hesitated but agreed to the assignment because the highly experienced Chautard expressed "great faith in the cinema."

The protagonist of this light film, which was part of Eclair's ACAD series, is sixty-year-old Dazumel Jadis, who's led quite an unorthodox life. A widower, he wears old-fashioned clothing and loves to dance. A portrait of his late wife, Jacqueline, hangs on the wall. She often talks to him.

To celebrate his birthday, Jadis invites two people to dinner: 20-year-old Octave, a hard-working but poor young notary's assistant who plays a hunting horn and knows nothing of dancing, smoking, wine, women, or song; and a pretty neighbor named Jacqueline. Octave, it turns out, has the same birthday as Jadis, and is secretly in love with the very proper Jacqueline. Jadis knows this because he has found a love letter that Octave meant for her.

At dinner, Jadis weaves a spell by talking of his youthful conquests and of his exploits as a soldier in Lombardy, in Napoléon's army. He leaves the two turtle doves alone for a while — and they talk of everything and nothing. After Jadis offers them drinks and makes Octave jealous, Octave expresses his feelings for Jacqueline. The generous and open-hearted matchmaker Jadis then gives them the money they need to marry and get started on their new life together.

Conscience de l'enfant/ The Child's Conscience

(1912, Emile Chautard). Eclair Film. Assistant Director: Tourneur. Script: Joseph Faivre. Design: Hughes Laurent and Dumesnil. Photography: Raymond Agnel. With Renée Pré, Georges Saillard, and Suzanne Révonne.

This 209-m "concerned drama" is a morality tale, based on the successful 1899 four-act play by Gaston Devore (1859–1949), and an example of the studio's adaptations of contemporary works.

The film is about the conflicting claims of conscience and love within a maturing young woman. Twenty-year-old Germaine imagines she understands the complex world around her, especially the motives of her father, Montret. He is, however, a man of bold action and strong emotion, and when he loses a fortune, he has an affair. The affair becomes known to his family — and Montret honorably admits his responsibility to wife and daughter.

Germaine, unlike her mother, takes the high moral ground. She judges her father harshly — and expresses her disappointment in him. This causes a considerable amount of tension within the family. Only later does she recognize other truths: that the haste with which she damned her father almost turned her heart to stone; that an apparently virtuous, uncompromising attitude helps neither him nor her. Reconciliation becomes possible only when there is love.

The subject of the tale, wrote a critic, is "both new and interesting."

La Dame de chez Maxim/ The Lady from Maxim's

(1912, Emile Chautard and Raymond Agnel). Eclair Film. With Renée Sylvaire and Maurice Tourneur.

Based on the hugely popular 1899 farce by Georges Feydeau (1862–1921), this was the earliest screen rendition of the contemporary tale of the prostitute who is mistaken for a gentleman's wife. She decides to play the role, to the man's chagrin, his real wife's amazement — and the audience's amusement.

The three-reel (857-m) film, which was part of Eclair's ACAD series of art films, was released in Germany as *Die Dame vom Maxim*. It was a great success wherever it was shown and inspired the studio to adapt other contemporary works.

Occupe-toi d'Amélie/ Keep Your Eyes on Amelie

(1912, Emile Chautard). Eclair Film. With Alice de Tander (Amélie d'Avranches), Hélène Maia, Marcel Simon, G. Leclerc, and Maurice Tourneur.

Based on Georges Feydeau's 1908 play, this was one of the studio's earliest adaptations of a contemporary theatrical work and boulevard farce. As part of Eclair's ACAD series, it is loaded with traditional contrivances, intrigues, and misunderstandings. It starred Alice de Tander from the Théâtre Rejane. "Nothing could be more French," wrote a critic about the story, "not because of its naughtiness, but because of its wit, its brilliance, its pinking of human foibles, and its essential healthiness."

The plot of this 892-m comedy concerns Amélie who, bored with domestic service, establishes a ruse: She becomes a prostitute "by ambition." After agreeing to go through a mock marriage which will permit the handsome Marcel to inherit a fortune from his Uncle van Putzeboum, Amélie is herself deceived. She takes revenge on Marcel by arranging with the mayor to make the marriage real. Only after the ceremony does she reveal that she signed the register under a false name, and that the union is invalid after all.

But there are yet more surprises in the many permutations, twists, turns, and combinations of lovers, mistresses, and unfaithful husbands and wives that make for a dizzying time of it all. The film, which contains the line, "A general ought to be good for something," was released in Germany in 1917 as *Kümmere Dich um Amelie*.

La Veuve joyeuse/ The Merry Widow

(1913, Emile Chautard). Eclair Film. With Alice de Tander (Missia Palmissi) and Maurice Tourneur.

This two-reel (706-m) comedy in Eclair's ACAD series was one of the studio's earliest screen renditions of classic light opera. Based on *Die Lustige Witwe*, Franz Lehár's fascinating and romantic 1905 three-act operetta, it is the whimsical tale of Missia, a romantically enticing and free-spirited folies girl who becomes the object of desire of two conniving princes.

She becomes known as the "merry widow" after the man she does wed, a baron and the richest man in the kingdom, dies on their wedding night. At that point, the princes once again vie for, and duel over, her attention. The story's mazes of courtship were as devious as only the "fabricators of romantic comedy, sorrow, and joys can devise," wrote a critic.

Rouletabille Part I: Le Mystère de la chambre jaune/ The Mystery of the Yellow Room

(1913, Tourneur and Emile Chautard).

Rouletabille Part II: La Dernière incarnation de Larsan/ The Last Incarnation of Larsan

(1914). Eclair Film. Script: Tourneur and Chautard. With Marcel Simon (Rouletabille), Laurence Dulac (Mathilde Stangerson), Paul Escoffier (Detective Larsan/ the husband), Maurice de Féraudy, Van Duren, Jean Garat, Devalence, and André Liabel.

Based on the novel by the notorious Gaston Leroux (1868–1927), Part I was Tourneur's premiere film as a full-fledged director. The author of the novel on which the film was based was a big, bold, audacious man who loved good living, drinking and dressing colorfully. He portrayed himself as larger than life, and many of his novels and stories echoed his own adventures. By 1907, wealthy and secure, Leroux decided to give up his world travel and return to his first love: literature. He used his skills as a reporter, and his sense of adventure and the unknown, to write *The Mystery of the Yellow Room*, which became a major literary success.

In Tourneur's three-reel (905-m) screen rendition, a mysterious man — presumed dead for ten years — has resurfaced in an attempt to murder his former wife Mathilde, who has a fiancé. Hoping to hide the facts of an ignominious past and her shame, Mathilde locks herself in her room. While asleep and dreaming, she actually fires a pistol at an intruder, who then somehow escapes — which brings the police and an inquisitive cub reporter, Rouletabille. "Observers will have to watch the developments with unusual keenness or [they] will be liable to miss the vital point," wrote *Moving Picture World* (9/20/13). "What will most effectively lead [them] astray is the fact that the man for whom the search is being made is the detective himself."

The tale climaxes with the discovery — and then destruction — of the vital marriage certificate, which permits Mathilde to marry her lover. (This is the first of many Tourneur films in which marriage certificates are a key piece of evidence). One special feature of Tourneur's film, wrote the trade journal, "is the celerity with which the premises are established and the story started on its way. At the same time, the fact that Larsan manages to escape punishment in the end and that Mathilde is allowed to proceed with the marriage," wrote a critic, "brings up a question of morals."

"The acting is convincing. The photography is good. The setting and backgrounds are carefully selected. There is an abundance of action," wrote *Moving Picture World*. In Hollywood in 1919, Tourneur's colleague Emile Chautard directed another rendition of the story, also called *The Mystery of the Yellow Room*.

Part II, which was based on Leroux's sequel to the story, called *Le Parfum de la dame en noir/The Perfume of the Lady in Black*, was released in mid–1914, and was also a great commercial and critical success. In an interview years later with Marie Epstein, Tourneur affirmed that he, rather than Chautard, was the director of the film, a 1,220-m drama set along the Riviera.

Part II finds the sad, mysterious lady in black — Mathilde, living secretly in a chateau — afraid that Larsan will track her down. She has reason to fear, because Larsan once again emerges to pursue his prey, and once again sets out on murder. She seeks Rouletabille's protection. During the course of events, the inquisitive reporter is accused of dispatching her fiancé. But Rouletabille manages to prove his innocence by neutralizing a band of criminals in the pay of Larsan, who is finally slain. The film, which contains a thrilling drive from Paris to the coast, was Tourneur's last prewar French silent, although his *Soeurette* was also released after he had arrived in America.

Le Miroir d'Ali Maboul/ The Mirror of Ali Maboul

(1913, Emile Chautard). Eclair Film. With Maud Richard (Saoula), Marcel Simon (Pitou), Maurice Tourneur (Ali Maboul), and César (Toussaint).

In this one-reel (188-m) adaptation of a burlesque tale of Arab life by M. L. Deville, Tourneur is a film actor for one of the last times in his career. He plays, wrote a critic, "the most nearsighted and ignorant of merchants from Algeria."

The comedy, about which little is known, was another in Eclair's ACAD works. It was released commercially in Germany under the title *Ali Mabul und sein Spiegel*.

La Bergère d'Ivry/ The Shepherdess from Ivry

(1913, Tourneur and M. Gabriel). Eclair Film. With Renée Sylvaire (Aimée), Paulette Noizeux (Hortense Fauvel), Henry Roussell (Comte de Granval), and Albert Decoeur (Mr. Fauvel).

This 600-m comedy-drama, released in July 1913, is about the plight of an orphan girl. It was based on the 1866 drama by Lambert Thiboust (1826–1867), who wrote it in collaboration with Adolphe Dennery (1811–1899) and E. Grangé (1810–1887).

From 1848 until his death, Thiboust wrote more than eighty pieces, most of them collaborations—vaudeville, revues, comedies, and dramas. He exhibited a light touch and comic inventiveness. Tourneur's film was part of Eclair's ACAD series of art films. A print of this film, called *Opoffering Eener Pleeddochter/Sacrificing a Foster Daughter*, survives in the Netherlands Filmmuseum in Amsterdam. This appears to be the earliest surviving example of a Tourneur film. Extant.

Jean de poudre/Powder John

(1913). Eclair Film. Script: Jean Joseph-Renaud. With Henri Roussell, Henri Gouget, and Renée Sylvaire.

In the summer of 1913, Tourneur shot this three-part, 874-m colonial drama, also called *Jean la Poudre*, about the exploits of Marshall Thomas-Robert Bugeaud, Duc D'Isly (1784–1849), who was France's most distinguished military figure during the reign of Louis-Philippe. Bugeaud served during the Napoleonic wars (Austria, Poland, Spain), but his most important contributions were in connection with the conquest and colonization of Algeria. The film, part of Eclair's ACAD series, retraces events of 1836–37 in Algeria through the story of a young Zouave named Jean-La-Frousse (Scaredy-Cat John). Part 1 is called "Jean la Poudre"; Part 2, "Episodes from the Conquest of Algeria"; and Part 3, "Summary."

Bugeaud was a commanding personality and a father figure, referred to as "Père Bugeaud" by the officers and Algerians who served under his command. He defended his subordinates in Algeria when they committed terrible deeds, including suffocating tribesmen trapped in caves. In Algeria Bugeaud also promoted the agricultural ideas he had found so effective at home. He sought to control Jewish commercial leaders and, ruling through tribal elites, he tried to create a Muslim agrarian peasantry. Meanwhile, colonial settlement by Europeans as well as the military should encourage orderly progress. He felt that small land holdings would promote the sense of cooperation and community essential to frontier agriculture and respect for local militias. Such programs earned him the local nickname of the "great head gardener." As his tenure as governor-general lengthened, his emphasis on a paternalistic agricultural regime became more authoritarian.

Tourneur's recreation of Algerian events was praised for its beauty, historical accuracy, and sense of the exotic. The "narrative context is scrupulous," wrote an observer. The subject of the film, Bugeaud, enjoyed remarkable military success in North Africa, his greatest triumph—earning him his title and marshal's baton—coming on August 4, 1844, at Isly. This victory assured the final conquest of Algeria. From December 1840 to June 1847 he served as the governor general of Algeria. In the upheavals of 1848 he played a quiet role, succumbing to Bonapartist pleas to remain aloof from presidential politics, thus helping to assure the electoral triumph of Prince Louis Napoleon Bonaparte. The following year he died of cholera.

Les Gaîtés de l'escadron/The Gaieties of the Squadron

(1913, Tourneur and Joseph Faivre). Eclair Film. Script: Tourneur. With Henri Roussell (the General), Devalence, Duquesne (Capt. Hurluret), Jean Garat, Henri Gouget (Sergeant-Major Flick), and Pierre Delmonde.

Based on the play of the same name by the popular Georges Courteline, Tourneur's three-part 920-m work, filmed in November 1913, was considered the director's most significant extant work until *Le Friquet* (1913) was rediscovered. It's a lighthearted, sentimental comedy and barracks revue that satirizes the masculine virtues associated with French military life. Ruses are employed not only to circumvent strict orders but to attain something better. The episodes are entitled "The Story of a Headcheese," "The Heart Under the Epaulettes," and "The Inspection of the General."

Containing hints of sexuality, the film and its ensemble performers present a wide array of vaudeville types: M. Adalbert de la Valmombrée is the middle-class recruit who makes sure he is always properly attired; Potiron is a Fatty Arbuckle–type who would rather do his duty outside the barracks; and Laplotte and Fricot, the defaulters of the unit, often wind up in the brig despite Sergeant-Major Flick's best efforts to help them get around the authoritarian Capt. Hurluret. The arrival, at the end of the film, of an inspecting officer suggests the theme of the production: The Sergeant-Major's aim is to be loved — not feared — by his men. That approach will best help to motivate and inspire the recruits to do their best and their duty.

In this work, which is filled with esthetic elements rare for the time, Tourneur demonstrated his ability to frame and edit a film and displayed a keen ability to use superimpositions and lateral panoramas. He made deft use of close-ups, medium shots, and long shots and a minimum of intertitles to permit the comedy and theme to come to the fore. This is especially true in two superimposed dream sequences.

In the first, an old woman, the barrack's restaurant keeper, recalls a long-ago love affair with a military man, and wipes away a tear at the memory of it all. In the second, a "dream vision" battle scene takes place over the heads of the "prisoners" as an inspecting general is making his rounds. Gouget's performance in the latter role was called remarkable.

Tourneur's film was reedited by the studio in 1918, and in 1932 Tourneur made a grander, sound version (with the English release title *Fun in the Barracks*) when he returned to France. Extant.

Le Dictateur

(1913, Emile Chautard). Eclair Film. Assistant Director: Tourneur. Script: Henri de Brissay. Design: Hughes Laurent and Dumesnil. Photography: Raymond Agnel. With Charles Krauss and André Liabel.

This little-known 536-m tale starring the elegant and urbane Liabel appears to have been a two-part drama whose episodes were called "Rivals of Love" and "Towards the Torment."

La Dame de Monsoreau

(1913, Tourneur, Emile Chautard, and Charles Krauss). Eclair Film. Script: Tourneur. With Marie-Louise Derval (Diane de Méridor), Henry Bosc (Count de Bussy), Paul Guidé (Henri III), Perny (Chicot), Léonce Cargue (Duc d'Anjou), Jean Dulac (Count de Monsoreau), Albert Bras (Baron de Méridor), Garandet (Gorenflot), and Emma Bonnet (Gertrude).

This seven-reel (2,055-m) historical romance was one of the longest by the studio in its ACAD series and one of the earliest showing caped swordsmen in action. Codirector Tourneur helped to give the French public a romantic, spectacular idea of history, bringing to life a vigorous, intense drama centered on friendship, ambition, and love. It was the first French screen rendition of Alexandre Dumas' fictional historical tale (written in 1846) of a strife-torn era in French history.

The story takes place during a period of religious warfare between Catholics and Protestants in France, in the late 1580s. It concerns the sacrifice of the charming Diane de Méridor (The Lady from Monsoreau), the heroism of her lover Bussy d'Amboise, the royal figure of the picturesque Henri III, and the familiar features of the intrepid and witty jester Chicot. The latter could speak his mind fearlessly to his "Henriquet," while the ordinary courtier would cringe obsequiously. Tourneur brought to the screen caped swordsmen and plenty of atmospheric adventure focused on love and intrigue.

A laborious, complex conspiracy is being carried out against Henri III (King of France, 1574–1589) by the Catholic Guises, led by Henri I de Lorraine, 3rd Duc de Guise, who is a rival for the throne. Their plot includes an insider: the Duc d'Anjou, the king's brother. (The Guises, however, have another plan of their own for d'Anjou: they will execute him later.) Amid the conspiracy and intrigues, a love story takes place: that of Diane and de Bussy, who, as a favorite of the king, is the most noble gentleman of the court and a terrific swordsman. Bussy can take on three, four, even five opponents at a time, with blows so fast and violent that all swords in front of him deviate from their targets and are quickly bested.

Diane's beauty, however, has also aroused the passion of another man, the king's brother d'Anjou. For a while she is the plaything between two evil men who are rivals for power. The villainous Count de Monsoreau frees the young girl from the clutches of the prince — in order to marry her himself — but the count dies at the hands, or rather, the sword, of de Bussy. The lovers unite when the plot to assassinate Henri III fails.

Critics called the tale (also known as *La Dame de Montsoreau*) a "grand historical drama," making note of one thing in particular: Tourneur's "sense of composition, for which ... his study of painting had uniquely prepared him."

Le Coeur d'une gosse/ **Heart of a Kid**

(1913, Emile Chautard). Eclair Film. Assistant Director: Tourneur. Script: Joseph Faivre. Design: Hughes Laurent and Dumesnil. Photography: Raymond Agnel. With Maryse Dauvray (Youyou), Renée Sylvaire (Louison), André Liabel (Barthus), Charles Krauss (Armand Delcroix), and Georges Mareck.

The three-reel (830-m) drama appears to have been about a gamine from a poverty-stricken area of a city who is taken under the wing of a wealthy family. She rises to stardom in the theater. Her innocence, or "heart of a kid," saves her from a compromising predicament and allows her to wed her lover. The story is apparently based on the 1908 novel by Julia D. Frankau (1864–1916).

La Fiancée maudite/ **The Accursed Fiancee**

(1913, Emile Chautard and André Liabel). Eclair Film. Assistant Director: Tourneur. Script: Chautard. Design: Hughes Laurent and Dumesnil. Photography: Raymond Agnel. With Josette Andriot (Beauty Love), Renée Sylvaire (Adrienne), Pierre Delmonde, and René d'Auchy.

This little-known three-reel (1,250-m) drama starred Josette Andriot (1886–1942), who often played in tales of daring. She was the sister of the Hollywood photographer

Lucien Andriot. The film is based on a work by the woman writer Michel Morphy (1863–?).

In Germany, the film was shown as *Unter Dämonen/Under the Demon* and as *Verfluchte Braut/Accursed Bride.*

Mademoiselle Cent Millions/ Miss Hundred-Million

(1913) Eclair Film. Script: Tourneur. With André Dubosc, Philippe Damorés, Bahier, Henri Gouget, Bérangère, and Jane Maylianes.

A four-reel (1,250-m) comedy-drama about which little is known. It may have been based on a novel by the spontaneous and popular writer Charles Paul de Kock (1794–1871) — he was held in high esteem by Alexandre Dumas fils — about the amazing Duchess de Mazarin, Hortense de la Porte (1646–1699), born in Rome, who was brought up in the Court of Louis XIV.

Upon inheriting a vast fortune from her uncle, Cardinal Jules Mazarin, the French statesman, on his death in 1661, the Duchess begins a life of adventure. The free-thinking Hortense wears pants, dons the dress of a cavalier, and "befeathered and bewigged" sets off on dangerous journeys through Alsace, Switzerland, Germany, and England. More scandalous, she abandons her husband while taking numerous lovers throughout Europe; her parties become legendary. It was said that "With the beauty of ancient Greece, Hortense combined the virtue of ancient Rome."

The film, which was also titled *Mlle. cent-millions*, was released in Germany as *Hundertmillionenbraut/Hundred-Million Bride.*

Le Système du docteur Goudron et du professeur Plume/ The System of Dr. Tarr and Professor Fether

(1913). Eclair Film. Script: André de Lorde. With Henri Gouget (Goudron), Henri Roussell (the journalist), Renée Sylvaire (the wife), and Bahier.

This startling early effort by Tourneur was said to have struck terror into the hearts of the production's actors. It ranks as one of the first truly original French films — the earliest of the Grand-Guignol genre and one of the most celebrated if not most shocking of its day. At 460-m, the "intentionally demonic and demented" tale was adapted by André de Lorde from his 1903 one-act Grand-Guignol play, which had starred Henri Gouget. The playwright was inspired by Edgar Allan Poe's "The System of Dr. Tarr and Professor Fether." When produced on the stage in Paris, it was described as a "peculiarly revolting spectacle."

"Mystery and terror are two of the ever-ready chords leading to the human heart," wrote a critic for *Moving Picture World* (6/20/14) when the film was released in the U.S. under the title *The Lunatics.* "Any picture that touches these effectively is sure to be popular." The Tourneur film deals with a young reporter, accompanied by his attractive wife, who goes on an assignment to investigate a new and apparently effective approach to treating asylum patients. Just as a terrible storm breaks, the couple arrives at the outer gates of an old mansion, surrounded by a moat. Inside, they quickly realize that the tables have been turned — that the inmates, led by "Dr. Tarr," a big strong man with powerful hands, have taken over.

Telling the visitors that insanity can be "cured" by gouging out a patient's eye and slitting his throat — it takes the two to do the job right — the institution's 45-year-old "director," Dr. Tarr, a man of cunning and grim humor, hurries into another room. He reemerges with blood all over his hands while blood seeps from beneath the door. They also meet the 60-year-old "Prof. Fether," who labors under the impression that he can float.

At this point, a carefully chosen collection of inmates emerge from the shadows. The visitors find it impossible to escape. One of the lunatics wants to begin the treatment on the journalist. The lightning is seen flashing brightly through the tall folding windows, and this so rattles the inmates that they freeze in their tracks. At length the young journalist is grabbed and taken to the table. A gust of wind first blows the big window wide open and then sweeps across the room, tearing at curtains and scattering the papers of the "doctor" to all corners. Again, the lunatics cower. This gives time for the victims — now freed by one of their captors, who has taken a boat around by the moat and carried them out of the barred court — to fetch help.

"The backgrounds are a great aid in making the impression this picture aims at," noted *Moving Picture World*. The setting is "weird and awe-inspiring; just the place for a terrible adventure. The photography ... seems alive. The players ... keep the action convincing." And Tourneur's two-reel "terrible, powerful picture" is "artistic, real, and gripping," concluded the critic.

Le Friquet/The Tree Sparrow

(1913). Eclair Film. Script: Jean Joseph-Renaud. With Polaire (Marie), Henri Roussell (Hubert de Ganges), César (Mafflu), Gilbert Dalleu, and Renée Sylvaire.

One of Tourneur's most acclaimed films of the era was this recently rediscovered three-reel (1,230-m) tale — one of Tourneur's earliest important surviving works — which was long thought to be the first film he directed at Eclair. Scripted by the author-director Jean Joseph-Renaud (1874–?), it stars the well-known vaudeville artist Polaire (Emile-Marie Bouchard-Zouzé, 1873–1941), a close friend of Colette, in her first film. A tale of a young girl seeking love, Tourneur's film takes in the elements of abandonment, abuse, and sacrifice.

This adaptation centers on the young heroine Marie, nicknamed "Le Friquet," who begins life as an abandoned waif. At the start of the film, tree sparrows are pecking at a crust of bread in her hand before she is saved by Mafflu, a sad-eyed circus clown. He introduces her to his itinerant life in the "Great American Circus," where she makes a living as a circus performer. In later years, when Hubert de Ganges, the mayor of a small town, is witness to her emotional and physical collapse as an overworked circus performer, he takes the underfed and emotionally starved girl into his well-furnished home. Marie falls in love with her benefactor, but he is engaged to his cousin. Then a friend of the mayor's falls in love with her. Marie knows that her love for the mayor is a dead end, yet she will not marry the man who declared his love for her. She returns to the circus and to the company of Mafflu. During one of her performances, she sees the mayor with his new bride — and deliberately falls to her death.

The film was one of the earliest by Tourneur to be shown in the United States — where the director was unmentioned in the credits. It is "well staged and photographed," wrote *Moving Picture World* (4/11/14), "and there are charming exteriors and fine interiors." There is also comedy when, for the first time in her life,

Marie encounters a real bed and "toilet accessories," in the home of the mayor. And a moment of real pathos when the young woman, arrayed in a fashionable new gown, sees walking across the lawn of the estate the man she loves arm in arm with his fiancée. Polaire, wrote the trade journal "is strong in the emotional situations." Extant.

Le Dernier Pardon/ The Last Pardon

(1913). Eclair Film. Script: Jean Joseph-Renaud. With Henri Roussell, Emile Kress, and Renée Sylvaire.

The actor Emile Kress attributed this nearly unknown film to Tourneur. It may be based on the 1908 story *Cloclo* by the notorious writer Gyp, which is the painful tale of the ward of a count who reveals the intrigues of a servant in his household—and who pays a price. Debilitated and frightened after a confrontation with the domestic, the girl rejects the marriage proposal of the man she loves and enters a convent.

Le Puits mitoyen/ The Common Well

(1914). Eclair Film. Script: Jean Joseph-Renaud. With Henri Roussell, Renée Sylvaire, M. Manzoni, and Miss Sohèze.

A three-reel (1120-m) drama about which almost nothing is known, though it is possibly based on the exuberant 2-act drama *Le Puits* (1902), by Auguste Dorchain (1857–1930).

The film was released commercially in Germany, where it was called *Der Grenzbrunnen/The Border Well*.

Le Camée/The Cameo

(1914). Eclair Film. Script: Jean Joseph-Renaud. With Emmy Lynn, Henri Roussell, Renée Sylvaire, and Alexandre Arquillière.

In this 600-m drama, Tourneur directed the popular Arquillière (1870–1953) who, with a physique like the later French star Raimu, had made a name for himself as "Zigomar" in Victorin Jasset's series of crime films for Eclair, notably *Zigomar contre Nick Carter* (1911). Much later, Arquillière costarred in Germaine Dulac's *La Souriante madame Beudet/The Smiling Mme. Beudet* (1922).

Tourneur's film, whose title can be translated as both *The Cameo* and *The Female Drug Addict*, "is of inestimable value which will bring it ten times the amount it cost to make," wrote a critic for *Film-Revue*. "The actors' perfection, with Mademoiselle Emmy Lynn and Monsieurs Arquillière and Roussell, rivals the mise-en-scène. Impeccable cinematography and color make *Le Camée* one of the next huge successes on the market."

Les Ruses d'amour/Tricks of Love

(1914, Tourneur and Emile Chautard). Eclair Film. Script: Robert Boudrioz. With Henri Roussell and Renée Sylvaire (Isabelle).

Another of Tourneur's least known efforts is this one-reel (256-m) comedy based on the lively, classic, 1736 three-act play by Philippe Poisson (1682–1743), adapted by the would-be director Boudrioz (1887–1949). It was part of Eclair's ACAD series of films.

Dorimon, a land broker, has promised his daughter Isabelle to Mr. Zero, his miserly and jealous associate. Isabelle, however, loves Clitandre, but the two are prevented from expressing their love openly because of Isabelle's father. Someone suggests a way around the impediment: her young man can don disguises that would allow him to see Isabelle openly, especially in light of the fact that her father is making every effort to give his daughter a proper education.

The ingenious Clitandre jumps at the idea. He takes the opportunity to appear in the guise of a geography teacher and then as a dance instructor freely able to talk to Isabelle in front of her father and the disagreeable Mr. Zero. The latter becomes so irritated at Isabelle's interest in her tutors that he gets rid of all these "teachers."

Clitandre then disguises himself as a woman who faces eviction from her home. "She" is in need of someone to help her quickly find new living quarters. At Dorimon's home "she" relates a tale of woe about an unhappy young woman who sounds suspiciously like Isabelle. She then mentions her "son," named Clitandre, and admits that "she" would like him to meet Isabelle's father, the land broker. At this point, fortune enters in the form of Clitandre's notary, who is negotiating an actual land deal with Dorimon that Clitandre knows nothing about.

Clitandre sets a plan in motion: he asks his valet, Frontin, to disguise himself as the notary's clerk, carrying not a land contract for Dorimon's signature but a marriage certificate between Isabelle and Clitandre. If the plan succeeds, Clitandre will allow Frontin to marry the woman he loves, named Lisette, Isabelle's maid — and Clitandre will get what he wants: Isabelle's hand in marriage.

Of course, when the papers are handed to him, Dorimon pays no heed to what he signs, but then Frontin "discovers" the mistake, and accuses himself of having mixed up the two contracts. Frontin offers to redress the mistake, but when Dorimon witnesses Mr. Zero's outrageously insulting behavior toward Frontin, he agrees to leave his signature on the marriage certificate. He fires Mr. Zero and declares the sales contract unnecessary. The marriage between Isabelle and Clitandre stands.

"The unravelling of events" in this story, wrote a critic, "is one of those that, as unbelievable as it may seem ... works."

Figures de cire/Wax Faces

(1914). Eclair Film. Script: André de Lorde. Henri Roussell, Renée Sylvaire, and Henri Gouget.

For the second Grand-Guignol film in his career, Tourneur again turned to that master of the genre, André de Lorde.

The son of a physician and stepson of Jean Mounet-Sully, the doyen of the Comédie Française, André de Lorde described Grand Guignol as "the study of the physiological and medical cases which hold the public breathless like all introspective problems and conflicts of the spirit." The genre is characterized by brief and violent action, bloodcurdling situations, a realistic setting, and unexpected endings.

The setting for the 280-m film, which is based on de Lorde and Georges Montignac's 1910 play of the same name, is a traveling amusement show. There the impresario has on display wax sculptures of historical figures infamous for their deeds: Jack the Ripper, Ivan the Terrible, and the sultan Harun-al-Rashid (766– 809), who was Caliph of Baghdad (786– 809). To promote the show, the showman has hired a poet to write about their grisly activities. While the young man writes — and the showman's daughter looks on — these wax figures come alive.

This film, which was rereleased in 1918 and was also called *L'Homme aux figures de cire/The Man with Wax Faces*, was a forerunner of Paul Leni's expressionistic work with the same subject matter, *Waxworks* (1924).

Monsieur Lecoq

(1914). Eclair Film. Script: Tourneur and Emile Chautard. With Charles Krauss

(Monsieur Lecoq), Jean Garat (Duke of Sairmuse), Renée Sylvaire (Duchess of Sairmuse), Josette Andriot, Devalence, Georges Tréville, Harry Baur, and Jules Mondos. Based on the well-known detective novel *L'Affaire Lerouge* (1866) by Emile Gaboriau (1832–1873), one of the founding fathers of that genre, Tourneur's adaptation became an acutely observed and striking three-reel (940-m) drama about a resolution to a mysterious affair. By this point in his career it was clear that director Tourneur had the freedom to choose his themes, and the themes he chose here are about saving a good woman's honor and preventing a family scandal. Sometimes, it seems, the ends do justify the means. It is all accomplished through a ruse or two by the eponymous detective.

The tale pits the brilliant detective against an equally brilliant adversary. A reminder of Rouletabille, Monsieur Lecoq makes use of science and deduction. After the Duke of Sairmuse weds a beautiful English girl, Blanche Courtleigh, the new Duchess finds herself in trouble. An unscrupulous few have learned of her brother's background, which includes criminal activity and conviction. They are blackmailing her and she, wild with anxiety, has decided to meet their demands.

Her husband becomes suspicious of her activities, and, disguised as an old man, follows her to the hideout of her blackmailers. He kills them; his wife flees without discovering the killer's identity. Monsieur Lecoq arrives at the scene of the crime to find an old man unwilling to say anything about what has just transpired. Lecoq allows the old man to "escape," and then follows *him*. And then he does some investigating.

When Lecoq meets the Duke again, it is through a ruse of his own. He gains an audience with the Duke by disguising *himself* as *another* old man. When Lecoq strips off his disguise, he reveals himself to the Duke and makes a startling announcement. His sleuthing, he says, has led to a resolution of the mystery of who and why. More important, the Duke's obvious concern for saving his wife from embarrassment and shame has led Lecoq to decide on something else: that he must save the Duke from the gallows and keep the Duchess's name out of the whole mess. To do that, he destroys incriminating evidence. Lecoq's rationale is that Sairmuse has delivered society of three bad men.

The production caught the attention of the critics in America. *Moving Picture World* (9/19/14) wrote: "When you are fortunate enough to sit through a picture ... that is bright, clear and almost devoid of flicker, it is a treat, and you feel like grasping the hand of the director and camera manipulator and giving them a good hearty shake.... They deserve recognition and encouragement.... Many alley and narrow street scenes are embraced in the development of the plot," wrote the trade journal, "in which the light and shadow effect is remarkably well done." One odd note is that while the film — his fourth to be shown in America — achieved great success, Tourneur's name as director was absent from the credits wherever the film was shown.

In Germany it was released under the title *Lecoq, der König der Detektive/Lecoq, the Detective King.*

Le Corso rouge/ The Red Promenade

(1914, Tourneur and Charles Krauss). Eclair Film. Script: Tourneur. With Maryse Dauvray (Comtesse de St. Ermont/Maïna), Emile Keppens (Comte de St. Ermont), Henri Roussell (Montenervo), Renée Sylvaire, Georges Paulais, and Madeleine Grandjean.

Based on a tale by Pierre Sales (1856–1914), many of whose stories were filmed by Eclair, Tourneur's three-reel (870-m) film tells a multilayered story of cruelty, deception, betrayal, and reconciliation. It focuses on one of his favorite subjects, the fate of a lost child.

It begins when the Comtesse de St. Ermont dies grieving over the kidnapping of her young daughter, Maïna. Twenty years go by. Maïna has found sanctuary and has made something of herself: She has become a barebacked circus performer. However, at the height of her fame she is in mortal danger. This time *she* is threatened with death by an outraged lover. But the tale ends happily when the young woman is saved from her fate and reunited at last with her father.

The drama was also called *Le Corseau rouge*, and in Germany it was released commercially as *Der Rote Karneval/The Red Carnival*. Extant.

Soeurette/Little Sister

(1914). Eclair Film. Script: Jean Joseph-Renaud. With Polaire, Henri Roussell, and Renée Sylvaire.

Based on Gyp's 1902 novel of the same name (reissued in 1930), this two-reel (600-m) drama was completed in mid-1914 but released by Eclair in May 1915, a year after director Tourneur landed in America.

The tale of woe opens with a prologue that shows a woman dying in a hovel while clasping to her breast her seven-year-old daughter. She entrusts her child to a ragpicker neighbor and her young son, to whom the girl becomes known as the little sister.

Ten years elapse, during which the girl has become a milliner with a shop of her own. An earnest young doctor named Paul arrives in town, seeking to aid the less fortunate. He falls in love with her just when her real father, who has become wealthy and has remarried, shows up in search of her. His new wife takes an interest in Paul but when he rejects her overtures, she arouses the ire of her jealous husband. He challenges the young doctor to a duel, in which he wounds but does not kill him.

Paul is nursed back to health in the young girl's room where her stepbrother, while looking through her papers, discovers her true identity. In trying to do good by bringing together daughter, father, and stepmother, the stepbrother then gets the innocent young woman into more trouble with her stepmother — and he lands in jail.

The tale, however, ends on a triumphant note when, at a ball given by the father, a "ragpicking fraternity makes a raid upon the place, unmasking the villains and fixing everything happily for the young physician and his future bride," wrote a London critic.

Tourneur's production, which was rereleased in 1917, was labeled a "popular priced film." The actress Polaire, who starred in two silents by Tourneur, became the prototype gamine.

TOURNEUR IN AMERICA

In 1911, Marcel Vandal and Charles Jourjon, co-owners of Eclair in Paris, opened an Eclair branch in Fort Lee, New Jersey. Etienne Arnaud became its head of production after the sudden death of Gaston Larry. Ben Carré, from Gaumont, became the main set designer. On his initial visit to the studio, on Lynnwood Avenue near Main Street, Carré noted that "the glass of the three sides and the roof were diffusing like in Gaumont's in Paris. The stage was small to me, even if it was 60 × 30 feet."

Among the other staff imported to the Fort Lee studio were the cameramen René Guissart, Lucien Andriot, and Georges Benôit. In March 1914, the studio's factory was destroyed in a fire. Eclair's factory had housed the developing and printing rooms, the machine shop, and the storage vault. Left standing were the outer walls of the building. The studio itself was not damaged, since it was located about 100 feet from the factory building. The fire originated as a short-circuit in the electrical connections, and quickly spread to the film stock. Negatives and positive prints were destroyed. Among the negatives lost were *Protea* (1913) and *Mephistophelia* (1914).

Tourneur was 38 when Eclair decided to expand their production of one- and two-reel films by erecting a fireproof factory and building a larger studio in Fort Lee — and replacing Etienne Arnaud. The hard-working Tourneur had made a name for himself for his "sense of composition, for which," said Jean Mitry, "his study of painting had uniquely prepared him." Tourneur was named producer-director of the expanded facility in Fort Lee.

Just as important as his experience was the fact that Tourneur could speak English. He got the job of producer-director thanks to his old friend Emile Chautard, who had visited Fort Lee in 1913. "I was leaving France," Tourneur said. "Was it for three months, for two years, for ten years? I don't know. It was a great adventure and nothing could assure me that I would succeed. That is why I left behind me all my family, deciding to have them come too if events turned in my favor."

Tourneur arrived in New York in May 1914 (taking up residence at 884 Riverside Drive). "I had always been possessed with a strong desire to come to America," said Tourneur in early 1914. "I always felt there was something lacking in our French qualities and this could only be remedied by a personal study in this country." Shortly after Tourneur took over operations at the studio, the Great War forced a change in ownership. Eclair transferred the new studio to World Pictures, headed by Louis J. Selznick and William A. Brady.

Tourneur began his work in America by directing the kinds of productions he knew best from his French beginnings: adaptations of stage successes, featuring a strong sense of visual composition, continuity editing, and few intertitles. He used the latest cinematic developments—cuts, close-ups, long tracking shots, single-source lighting, and the staging of scenes in depth—in order, he said, "to do something" with films. He put together his own stock company, which included art director Ben Carré (until 1919), cameraman John van den Broek (until 1918), editor and assistant director Clarence Brown (until 1921), script clerk, casting director, and (later) leading man Jack/John Gilbert (until 1920). Later, in France in the 1930s and 1940s, he assembled a similar production unit of his own.

In his capacity as director, Tourneur selected costumes and setting, and was not above suggesting how actors were to wear their hair. "It is true," he said, "that I dictate the smallest detail of the action of the players, but it is not because that is my ideal of working. I have to use these methods," he said, "because there are very few cinema actors who have a sufficient grasp and understanding of their work.... This, no doubt, is due to the relative newness of the art of the screen."

Tourneur made four films in his first year in America at the newly named Eclair-Brady World: *Mother*, *The Man of the Hour*, the masterful *The Wishing Ring*, and *The Pit*. Each is concerned with the search for love, however painful and difficult to attain it might be. These early films, wrote *Moving Picture World*, "have shown us the talent of this director under ... entirely different lights ... dramatic emotion ... power, strength and ... high class comedy."

After leaving Eclair-Brady, Tourneur increased his output to seven films in a year at Equitable-World; six in 1916 as production head at Paragon-World; and in 1917 he made ten films, working with the likes of Mary Pickford in *The Pride of the Clan* and *The Poor Little Rich Girl* and Elsie Ferguson in *A Doll's House*.

Critics found the sets and the camerawork just as impressive as the film stars, if not more so. This suited Tourneur, for he loved shooting interiors and was not a big fan of Hollywood's star system. The critics made note of Tourneur's visual style: his "photographic effects, settings, lighting, and pictorial compositions ... are always artistic."

Although Tourneur developed a reputation as a taskmaster who shared success, his work brought the identity of the director to public attention and esteem. Long before the word "auteur" was ever applied to a film director, Tourneur exemplified the idea. In addition, there were other firsts for Tourneur. Before F. W. Murnau established his name, Tourneur had begun to make "plastic beauty" an essential element of film. Tourneur's silent films, before those by Josef von Sternberg, Erich von Stroheim, and F. W. Murnau, were among the rare films whose style is evident after one has seen but a few images.

Among the many American filmmakers, Tourneur became one of the few to make use of, and profit from, his European background. He was able to incorporate his experience into his American cinematic activity. His later French sound films—notably *Avec le sourire* (1936), also contain qualities that are particularly American—although by then it had become more difficult to single out a Tourneur film.

In America, Tourneur maintained his prolific pace, forming his own production company in 1918 and distributing films through Paramount. He espoused a filmic maxim: What matters most in film is the effect on the audience. To achieve the desired effects, he would search for what was original.

But that wasn't easy. "There have been great strides in the development of the photographic and other technical phases of the cinema," noted Tourneur. "But I still bemoan," he said before he set off for Hollywood, "the lack of original scenario writers. Those who write for the camera have not yet acquired the 'film mind'.... In order to acquire this facility men must devote their lives to the work. I have no patience with those writers who grind out a number of scenarios when they have 'nothing better to do.'"

In 1918, Tourneur left the film confines of the East. By the time he became an American citizen in 1921, he had directed forty American films and garnered the acclaim of Hollywood through such fantasies as *The Blue Bird* and *Prunella* (both 1918); the astonishing, episodic *Woman* (1918); the exciting *Sporting Life* (1918) and *My Lady's Garter* (1919); and tales of deception and dangerous love, *The White Heather* (1919), *The Life Line* (1919) and *Victory* (1919).

In an interview after the release of *Sporting Life* (1918), which was his first independent production, Tourneur said, "I am not telling [you] the incidents, twists of plot or surprises. I want audiences to come expectant and go away pleasantly surprised.... I fear for the photoplay unless we jealously guard the element of surprise."

The decade ended with a further string of successes: *The Great Redeemer* (1920), the classic *Treasure Island* (1920), and the magnificent *The Last of the Mohicans* (1920). By now famous, Tourneur was called a "sincere and thoughtful craftsman" by Louis Delluc (1890–1924), who was one of the earliest critics to treat cinema seriously. A critic who sought a cinema that was an expression of its authors and that stressed the emotional lives of its characters, Delluc favored lyrical images and natural settings. He called Tourneur a director "who fashions for himself that kind of atmosphere that gives form, style, and superior quality to a work. He does not transform a given theme. He rises above it. Its merits only shine the more."

Tourneur claimed that "action does not mean melodrama; that movement does not mean speed; that there is as much drama in the glance of an eye as in the burning of a city; and that mental conflict is superior to physical."

Clarence Brown, his longtime assistant who directed *The Great Redeemer* under Tourneur's supervision, noted another aspect of the director. He said that Tourneur was "great on tinting and toning. We never made a picture unless every scene was colored. Night scenes were blue, day scenes amber, sunsets blue-tone pink or blue-tone green. The most beautiful shots I ever saw on the screen were in Tourneur's pictures."

However, there was a change in Tourneur's fortunes after he settled in Hollywood (residing at 2124 N. Commonwealth Ave.). He found it necessary to resist the moguls and film distributors who demanded assembly-line productions. Tourneur thus joined forces with Thomas Ince, Mack Sennett, Marshall Neilan, Alan Dwan, and George Loane Tucker to form Associated Producers in 1920, hoping to avoid what he loathed the most — a bad script assigned by a producer. Tourneur made no secret of his views. "American producers will have to change entirely their machine-made stories and come to a closer and truer view of humanity," he warned repeatedly, "or the foreign market is going to sweep us out with their pictures, made in an inferior way, but carried over by human, possible, different stories."

But just as quickly as he had made his name, Tourneur had quickly reached a troubling time in Hollywood. "I would rather starve and make good pictures if I knew they were going to be shown," he told friends in 1920, "but to starve and make pictures which are thrown into the ash can is above anybody's strength." When rising production costs, rapid staff turnover, and a string of less successful projects sank his production company, Tourneur put himself up for hire. He did well at First National with the exciting historical romantic drama *Lorna Doone* (1922), the tale of desperation called *The Isle of Lost Ships* (1923), and the lively comedy *The Brass Bottle* (1923). At Universal he remade *Sporting Life* (1925). He didn't starve during this period, but his output dropped and the episodic nature of his recent narratives came under attack.

Tourneur had time to appear in the one-reel *Screen Snapshots* (1921), produced by Jack Cohn in cooperation with *Screenland* magazine. The fan publication provided the chance to glimpse Hollywood personalities behind the scenes and at play. In the segment "Till the Sands Grow Cold," Rudolph Valentino acts as make-up assistant to Agnes Ayres before they shoot a scene for *The Sheik* (1922). In "Away from the Studio," Francis X. Bushman, his wife Beverly Bayne, and their son Richard relax on the boardwalk and beach at Atlantic City. In "Every Dog Has Its Day," Tourneur makes an appearance when he, Alice Lake, Ruth Roland, Lottie Pickford, Jack Pickford, and Kathleen Clifford strut their pets' stuff at a dog show in Los Angeles. Three other segments in the 800-ft short are of an auction at a Hollywood home, four-year-old Richard Headrick displaying his swimming skills (shot in slow-motion) and a suntanned Bert Lytell celebrating his birthday with Clara Kimball Young and other stars.

Tourneur also appeared as himself in Jack Cohn's *Mary of the Movies* (1923), the seventy-minute tale of a young woman who hopes to make it big in the film capital. Containing cameos of Hollywood celebrities, the film includes scenes of the famous directors Tourneur, Rex Ingram, and J. W. Kerrigan at their craft.

In 1923, on an assignment for independent producer Samuel Goldwyn, Tourneur sailed to England, where, as a young touring actor, he had learned to speak English. England was now to be the locale for the morality tale *The Christian*. Based on a novel by Hall Caine, *The Christian* tells of a fanatic who tries to turn from the world, the flesh, and the devil only to be brought back by the love of a woman. Ultimately, he dies at the hands of a mob. Tourneur filmed scenes on the Isle of Man, where the novelist based his story.

Critics were enthusiastic. Praised the *New York Times*: "Everyone who has followed Mr. Tourneur's work knows that he can make moving pictures that make you open your eyes and look at them. He has done it in this film. Some of the scenes are beautiful. Others are so sharply significant, or so teeming with headlong action, that they break down all resistance.... *The Christian* is an unusually stirring melodrama." Wrote *Variety*, "If *The Christian* doesn't get money for any theatre at its picture scale, then that theatre might just as well look around for a change of policy."

For the first time since coming to America, Tourneur began to seek opportunities to work abroad. He told *Motion Picture Magazine*, "It is now no more expensive to take a company abroad than it is to keep it at home and build extravagant sets that are merely imitations of the European originals."

Attracted to exotic locales, he went abroad twice in 1925, once for William Randolph Hearst's film company Cosmopolitan, which had ties to Mayer and Thalberg at MGM. Tourneur directed *Never the Twain Shall Meet*, the story of an American's emotional breakdown in the beautiful South Seas. He filmed in the Marquesas in the South Pacific, and brought his 21-year-old son Jacques along as script clerk. During the making of this film, the director experienced serious disagreements with MGM's bosses. After shooting the lush *Aloma of the South Seas* in Puerto Rico, Tourneur came to a crisis point in his life with the 1926 assignment, *Mysterious Island*.

The movie was seen by MGM as its most novel undertaking in years, a film on the scale of *Ben-Hur*, starring Lionel Barrymore and Marceline Day. This adaptation of Jules Verne's famous fantasy would be in technicolor and contain dramatic undersea and submarine scenes. Tourneur had experience filming in the deep. His *The White Heather* (1919) and *Deep Waters* (1920) had proved he could handle himself with undersea equipment and underwater settings. But barely two weeks into the production of *Mysterious Island*— while Tourneur was being hailed in *Moving Picture World* and *Motion Picture News* as one of Hollywood's biggest box-office directors—Tourneur walked off the job. That "hydra-headed aggregation of producers and supervisors," as Josef von Sternberg characterized Hollywood's leadership, had tried once too often to tell Tourneur what to do.

As it turns out, it didn't much matter how he departed. If Tourneur hadn't left of his own volition, he would almost certainly have been fired. Studios had begun to take a tougher policy towards directors, whom they regarded as little more than technicians. Mayer, for instance, could "convince an elephant it was a kangaroo," said Sternberg. In the space of a few months, his studio terminated its contract with Rex Ingram, who was working in France, and fired Sternberg, both of whom were admirers of Tourneur. Next it dumped Frank Capra, William Wellman, and Frank Borzage. Others soon "flushed," as Sternberg characterized it, were Mauritz Stiller, Victor Sjöström, and Stroheim.

Paradoxically, what made Tourneur's Hollywood break more likely was that it coincided with the end of his love life with, and marriage to, the actress Fernande Petit. They had married in 1904, when Petit had acted with André Antoine under the name Fernande Van Doren. The story goes that Tourneur gave his son Jacques, who had been the script clerk on his last six films, $100 and suggested that the young man try to make it on his own in Hollywood. Then Maurice Tourneur — like protagonists of his own 1920s films — bolted from this country to seek work and love elsewhere. With fifty U.S. films under his belt, Tourneur might have imagined that his ranking as an American filmmaker was secure. But as far as Hollywood was concerned, it was out of sight, out of mind — forever. It would be June 1940 before American film critic Lewis Jacobs, writing in the *New York Times*, asked, "Whatever happened to Tourneur?" Jacobs said this about film pioneer Tourneur's time in America, 1914–1926: "Tourneur contributed a healthy influence upon films and filmmakers of that day. His fine taste and stress upon such properties as photography, settings, lighting and pictorial composition, at a time when most movies lacked quality in these attributes, did much to elevate the general standards and gain respect for the new medium."

Louis Delluc observed that Tourneur "is evidently the French director who has worked best in America. He used American technical processes with a brilliant ease and sometimes with virtuosity, which is all the same a compliment. But he stayed French. He conserved the nature and tone of his race. The cocktail mixture of new ingredients added to his personality is completely seductive. This is the only reproach that I will make to Maurice Tourneur: he is always seductive. I do not remember ever having seen something ugly in his films."

THE FILMS IN AMERICA, 1914–1926

Mother

(1914). Eclair-Brady World. Script: Tourneur. Photography: John van den Broek. With Emma Dunn (Mrs. Katherine Wetherell), Priscilla Dean (Ardath) Lillian Cook (Leonora), Belle Adair (Sadie), Henri Desforges (Harry Lake), and Edwin Baker (William).

Tourneur's debut film as a director in America was this hugely sentimental four-reel tale about a widow's struggles to keep her family's integrity intact. The story was adapted from a play by Jules Eckert Goodman. The film's lead, Emma Dunn, said *Variety*, "guarantees the value" because she played the part so well on stage, in 1910.

The first scene opens inside the apparently contented Wetherell home. There the attractive Ardath Wetherell is sewing alongside her younger sister, Leonora. They have four brothers: William Howard, who is married to an ambitious stage actress, Sadie; his younger brother, Walter Thompson, who has abandoned his studies and become secretly engaged to the chorus girl and Sadie's sister, Elizabeth Terhune; and the young twins, James Bingham and John Walton.

Harry Lake, who loves Ardath, has discovered a problem. He has found out that William has embezzled $10,000 from the Lake family bank because, it is said, his wife easily squanders their money. To make good the theft — and avoid going to jail — William has forged his widowed mother's signature on a bank note for a piece of property she owns. When Harry lets Mrs. Wetherell know of her son's activities, "Mother" goes into action. Despite the forgery and William's dismissal from the bank, Katherine stands by the signature and makes good on the promissory note.

Having saved her oldest boy from

disgrace, the mother takes steps to save the second. She tells his fiancée in no uncertain terms that the young man has no money to inherit, but encourages the flashy young woman to marry him anyway. The mother lets the young woman imagine a future in which she is doing the cooking and raising the children. Not surprisingly, the girl bails out of the relationship, denouncing both mother and son on the way out.

The final scene is "perfectly familiar," wrote *Moving Picture World*. It includes the return of the "wayward older boys, which gives the mother back her entire flock, and leaves her watching a brood that is her only love and care." Emma Dunn was praised for acting the part "with much delicacy, great feeling, and an abundance of tenderness, suggested and expressed. She looks the little 'Mother' to perfection.... No one could do more with it."

The Man of the Hour

(1914). Eclair-Brady World. Script: Tourneur. Photography: John van den Broek. With Robert Warwick (Alwyn Bennett), Belle Adair (Dallas Wainwright), Chester Barnett, Ned Burton, Johnny Hines, and Alec B. Francis.

Tourneur's second American film has as its source the popular 1906 play by George Broadhurst, which, critcs pointed out, did the public a good deed. The film was future star Johnny Hines' screen debut.

Emma Dunn, the star of *Mother* (1914), which was Tourneur's first American film, became known as one of the best "portrayers of 'Mother' roles in the profession."

The filmed adaptation is a five-reeler about Alwyn Bennett, a young man of fine instincts with one problem: He has never devoted himself to any pursuit other than the spending of a fortune left to him by his father. Through the protests of Dallas, a young woman who loves him, he comes to realize that he has been idle for far too long and more or less useless in the eyes of the

The Man of the Hour (1914): Belle Adair (as Dallas Wainwright) is the woman whose love turns a nobody into "the man of the hour." Note the mirror in this scene.

world. But all that is about to change: Politics intercedes.

Backed by the political machine because his father was well-known in his day, Alwynn gets himself nominated and then elected mayor of New York. But he has a surprise for his backers: He develops backbone and takes a stand for honesty in the conduct of municipal affairs. But there is another reason for the sudden ambition of the young man: His high office will also enable him to avenge himself upon the New York businessman who ruined his father's life.

Containing flashbacks of the Wild West, where gold mining, horseback riding, fights, and murder are the order of the day, the film was called by *Dramatic Mirror* a "triumph in screen technique; produced clearly and capably." *Moving Picture World* went further in its praise:

> The exteriors are very well chosen and some of them are extremely beautiful. The interiors are also noteworthy for their fidelity to the atmosphere and tone of the story and especially remarkable are the convention hall where the man of the hour makes his campaign speech and the council room of the board of alderman where the fight on the franchise bill is played. Political plays as a rule have on the screen a farcical element due to the fact that the settings ... are manifestly unreal. The undoubted genuineness of the settings in "The Man of the Hour" eliminates this element and forces home

to the spectator in a most telling way the reality of what is being enacted.

Extant.

The Wishing Ring/ An Idyll of Old England

(1914). Eclair-Brady World. Script: Tourneur. Photography: John van den Broek. With Vivian Martin (Sally), Chester Barnett (Giles), Alec B. Francis (Earl of Bateson), and Simeon Wiltse (the parson).

Based on a 1910 play by Owen Davis, Tourneur's exquisite five-reel (4080-ft) work was his first great American film. It reflects both the director's French background and his theatrical experience.

As one of his earliest surviving American films, it is more European than American in atmosphere, with an uncommon use of titles, sunlight for interior spaces, and staging-in-depth. The irresistible film — as charming today as it was then — relates the romance between the effervescent Sally and the mischievous Giles, the son of the Earl of Bateson. Giles has been expelled from college for carousing. In order to be allowed to return to school and receive his father's forgiveness, he has to earn a half-crown.

The tale begins when the graces of

Robert Warwick, the star of *The Man of the Hour* (1914).

Greek mythology open a curtain. They appear at other points in the film to take part in, and comment on, the tale, and at the end bid a good-bye with the close of a curtain. In his godfather's garden, where Giles has been hired to catch the culprit who is stealing the roses, he meets Sally, the poor daughter of a country minister. He woos her under false pretenses, posing as the son of poor but honest parents and of humble occupation. But once Sally

Vivian Martin, in Tourneur's exquisite and hugely entertaining *The Wishing Ring* (1914).

The Pit (1914): Gail Kane portrays Laura Dearborn, the wife who takes a lover but in the end remains true to her money-obsessed husband in this tale of greed.

realizes who Giles is, she not only does not reject him, she seeks to bring together father and son through the use of a gypsy's "wishing ring." Her own charming personality is just as important in setting matters right.

When she wins the Earl's affection, and Giles has paid his father back the half-crown, father and son are reconciled, and the youngsters' love affair is allowed to bloom. The film ends in a harmonious epilogue with sixteen celebrants seated around a table while the camera pans around them. They include the lovers, maidens, soldiers, and gypsies. The last shot is of a dog under the table eating scraps of food.

The film was immediately recognized as a masterpiece. "There isn't a dramatic moment in the story," wrote *Variety*. "There isn't a murder or a fight from first to last, but there are delightful love passages, bits of the most attractive play of humor and a constant succession of lovely, demure, pouting or bubbling crinoline maids. The whole atmosphere of the tale is light and as graceful as a minuet and colored with the nicety of a pastel." Particularly noteworthy also is the tracking shot previously mentioned, during which the protagonists expound on their roles in the drama.

Tourneur's use of the latest cinematic techniques—action cuts, cutaways, close-ups, parallel action, and long tracking shots—paid off. "The picture made an impression," wrote Terry Ramsaye, "starting a career of stardom for Vivian Martin and success for Maurice Tourneur." Tourneur was one of the men who introduced visual beauty to the American screen, wrote Kevin Brownlow. "American pictures of 1914 were often well photographed, but I have seen few to compare for sheer visual elegance with Tourneur's." Richard Koszarski called Tourneur's film, which was rediscovered in the early 1970s, "an extraordinary film — probably the high point of American cinema up to that time." Extant.

The Pit

(1914). Eclair-Brady World. Script: Channing Pollock. Photography: John van den Broek. With Milton Sills (Sheldon Corthell), Hattie Delaro (Mrs. Cressler), Alec B. Francis (Charles Cressler), Gail Kane (Laura Dearborn), and Wilton Lackaye (Curtis Jadwin).

Tourneur's hard-edged five-reeler was his last film with Eclair in America. It is based on Channing Pollock's stage adaptation of Frank Norris' last novel, which William A. Brady produced in New York in 1904. The film was future star Milton Sills' screen debut.

Gail Kane, the star of *The Pit* (1914).

The story is a complex one. It is the chronicle of the lifestyle, self-absorption, and money madness of Curtis Jadwin of Chicago—and of the outrageously greedy actions of the men who work at the "wheat pit" in the Chicago Board of Trade. It is a Zolaesque representation of American life in broad terms, with a plea to workaholics to love their wives before a wicked lover completes the dreaded triangle. Tourneur's film is also a classic case in which a good woman sticks with her man when the going gets rough.

The film opens with a preface, a look at Chicago's wharves and railroads. Then it is on to the harsh world of commodity speculation, where hundreds of men are seen conducting their business on the floor, or pit, of the Chicago Board of Trade. It is within this arena that Curtis Jadwin (played by Wilton Lackaye, who recreated his stage role) learns his trade with the help of the professional trader Charles Cressler.

We first meet Jadwin at an opera house, where *Romeo and Juliet* is playing. There Jadwin, an easygoing man about town, meets Laura, the sweetheart of artist Sheldon Corthell, and they fall in love. But after they marry, things change. While Jadwin becomes absorbed with making lots of money in steel and cotton at the pit, his wife finds herself lost and alone. She looks for salvation outside her marriage and makes plans to flee with her former lover, Sheldon.

But, wrote *Moving Picture World*, "there are no tempestuous love scenes" between the lovers. "It is done in cold blood — each with a full understanding of the gravity of the proposed step." However, at the last instant, financial ruin hits home as Jadwin's speculation turns to dust. His obsession, surprisingly, then abates and "the "threatened break is off"; Laura, true to her man, is last seen putting her arms "about the neck of her husband."

Moving Picture World called Tourneur's work a "big production — a good one. It is elaborately staged, well directed and finely played.... There are two interiors of uncommon and spectacular value even in these days of big productions. These are the scenes of the opera house and of the operators in the pit."

Motion Picture News praised Tourneur for something else: "In an exchange scene we have been accustomed to seeing shaky walls, men taking the parts of brokers who have spent most of their lives as truckmen or the like, and the whole spectacle has been grossly exaggerated. Here it is not; it is realistic; the men look like they might have come from State Street offices."

Alias Jimmy Valentine

(1915). Equitable–World Film Corp. and Peerless. Script: Tourneur. Photography: John van den Broek. With Robert Warwick (Lee Randall/Jimmy Valentine), Ruth Shepley (Rose), Robert Cummings (Doyle), Johnny Hines, Alec B. Francis (Bill), and Madge Evans.

Based on the play of the same name by Paul Armstrong (which Tourneur helped to bring to the stage in France), this tinted, five-reel thriller was one of the earliest crime dramas in American cinema, containing documentary footage of Sing Sing. The setting contributed to its being called a film with "good dramatic construction." Child actress Madge Evans made her debut in this film.

The film is the tale of a man who leads a double life — and of love between people of different backgrounds. By day, Lee Randall is a businessman; at night, he's the elusive Jimmy Valentine, a gentleman burglar. The lure of easy money makes Valentine feel good. But all good things come to an end. Eventually, Valentine is caught and sentenced to time behind bars. Valentine has years in front of him to reevaluate his life, and when he is finally freed, he emerges as a new man. Or so he imagines.

Lee tries to make a new life for himself. He meets and falls in love with Rose, whose father is none other than the Lieutenant Governor of New York. But Lee still has problems: Outside of prison, he is hounded by a single-minded policeman determined to send him back behind bars. That man makes it nearly impossible for Lee to prove that the life of crime is behind him. It is only when Lee sacrifices himself to save Rose's sister that it becomes evident to all — and especially to Rose — that he has changed for the better. He and Rose have earned the right to happiness.

"The quality of the story is the big thing in any picture," wrote *Moving Picture World*. "This picture is one of the kind of which there is no question or doubt; that it is a very good offering everyone, we think, will be quite agreed. The spectator who wants 'high brow' stuff and the one who wants 'low brow' stuff can generally get together on simple human stuff and that this picture, in both plot and detail, furnishes richly…. The quality of the story comes, in part, from the breadth of its emotional appeal." Extant.

Trilby

(1915). Equitable-World. Script: Tourneur. Photography: John van den Broek. Design: Ben Carré. With Clara Kimball Young (Trilby O'Ferrall), Wilton Lackaye

Clara Kimball Young, the highly acclaimed star of *Trilby* (1915).

(Svengali), Chester Barnett (Little Billy), and Paul McAllister (Gecko).

This drama was adapted from the 1894 novel by the Englishman with a French name, George L. du Maurier (1834–1896; author of *Peter Ibbetson*), and the subsequent dramatization by Paul M. Potter. Tourneur's five-reel (one-hour) adaptation was Equitable's first production and established Clara Kimball Young as a star. Its premiere in New York included a full orchestra led by Hugo Reisenfeld.

Tourneur's drama contains sets and scenes that gave du Maurier's hugely popular story a "new look," said Louis Delluc at the time. The film contains nudity on the part of Clara Kimball Young and focuses on the then novel, and mysterious, subject of hypnotism as well as its psychological underpinnings: the relationship between dependence and independence, submission and dominance.

Central to the emotional tale is the sweep of life in late 19th-century European theatrical circles, which is something Tourneur had experienced firsthand in France. The result is an early American example of the gusto with which Tourneur approached pictorialism, composition, narrative sequence, all in service to a story of artists and actors. Tourneur's style here is deliberately different from that of his earlier American masterpiece, *The Wishing Ring* (1914). In *Trilby* Tourneur made fewer cuts, had more long shots, and set a cooler, more confining tone to reflect the emotional and psychological dynamics of the story.

At the start of this tale of the rise to fame of a beautiful artist's model, Trilby is about to marry the English artist Little Billy. But on the night they intend to break the news to the world, the musician Svengali makes his appearance. He had met the model at Billy's Latin Quarter studio in Paris, where the joy of Bohemian life was in full swing. Now, in order to make Trilby his own, Svengali hypnotizes her, after which Trilby writes a good-bye letter to Billy.

Svengali begins Trilby's conditioning by persuading her to agree to a Mesmer-style induction by passes. He seats her on a divan, and, sitting opposite her, bids her look him well in the whites of the eyes. Then he makes little passes and counter-passes on her forehead and temples and down her cheek and neck. Soon Trilby's eyes close and her face grows placid.

In the tale, Trilby does not understand how a seemingly harmless first submission to hypnosis can develop into a terrible long-term dependence. Svengali gradually transforms her into an obedient subject. Conceited, derisive, and malicious, Svengali alternately bullies and fawns. Although Trilby is repelled at first by his greasy, dirty appearance, and regards him as a spidery demon, she nevertheless becomes his subject.

Unable to earn her love honestly, Svengali steals her away to England. There he uses his extraordinary powers to beguile and direct the life of this young woman in order to make her internationally famous—and to make himself rich. Svengali rehearses with an entranced Trilby and hypnotizes her before performances. Then Svengali directs Trilby during the great recitals. By turning her ordinary voice into a magnificent one—and curing Trilby's neuralgia along the way—Svengali creates one of the Continent's great singing sensations. But the strain of managing a magnificent star eventually takes a terrible toll on Svengali.

Tourneur's film was called a "masterpiece of atmospheric achievement.... Here was Paris! Not only the quiet banks of the Seine, and the majestic Church of Our Lady—actual views—but the Paris of the Quartier made in the World Film studio, the street taken in New York's MacDougal Alley, the Quartier ball, and the ateliers." *Moving Picture World* said that the

> result obtained by Tourneur and the cast under his direction place this motion picture among the finest examples of its kind. To start with, the scenario displays a keen appreciation of what is

The Cub (1915): John Hines, who made his screen debut in *The Man of the Hour*, is here shown portraying Steve Oldham, a man on the spot in search of a good story.

required.... The almost entire absence of "cutbacks" puts "Trilby" in the true drama class where the human will is shown in action and tells its own story.... The atmosphere of the Latin Quarter in Paris is reproduced most convincingly.... The beauty and originality of thought ... will not quickly be forgotten.

Variety noted that "the one thing that counts and means anything is that, taking it as a whole, the picture is ... worthy of being played in the best picture houses throughout the world." Extant.

The Cub

(1915). Equitable-World. Assistant Director: Clarence Brown. Script: Thompson Buchanan. Photography: John van den Broek. With Johnny Hines (Steve Oldham), Robert Cummings (Capt. White), Jessie Lewis (Becky King), and Martha Hedman (Alice Renlow).

The three-act 1910 play by Thompson Buchanan, who had once worked as a special correspondent in Kentucky, became the basis for Tourneur's adaptation, which is an extravagant early five-reel satire. It is also the first film that Clarence Brown assisted Tourneur in directing. Just as Emile Chautard had taken Maurice Tourneur under his wing in France, so Tourneur did the same with Brown in America.

After an introduction to the characters and the inhospitable and (as yet) uncivilized locale, the tale concerns Louisville *Courier-Journal* cub reporter Steve Oldham's naive attempt to cover a blood feud between the White and Renlow clans in the mountains of Kentucky. There, the newspapers reported, "Seventeen men killed in a feud over a sow valued at one dollar and eighty-seven cents; that makes each man of them worth just eleven cents."

Arriving by donkey in the town of Whitesburg, county of Breathill, the investigative reporter — he is no Rouletabille — immediately causes a stir because of his fashionable dress. Soon he's embroiled in the ongoing feud, a party to the combat. In this place, men shoot first and ask questions later. After the better part of valor tells Steve it's best to accept the invitation to join one of the mountain groups, he unwittingly becomes engaged to the daughter of a clan member. There is also another problem: he has fallen in love with the pretty schoolteacher Alice Renlow, who is allied with the opposing mountaineers.

Then the reporter finds himself in even bigger trouble, exclaiming "If only these people had a sense of humor, the whole thing could be settled in no time." "These people" include the likes of "Tombstone," so named because he never smiles, and Tilden McFields, a reputed killer who is himself a suitor for the schoolteacher's hand. Quite literally, the militia has to come to the cub reporter's rescue and put down the hard-drinking feudists before he can marry the mountain girl of his dreams.

Motion Picture News liked the natural realism: "Wild mountain land is the background for all the exteriors, while the settings, comprising mainly the interiors of the feudists' cabins are excellent.... The final fight, in which an entire house is completely wrecked, is truly thrilling." Martha Hedman was called a "valuable addition to the large gallery of photoplayers, for in addition to possessing all the natural charm and beauty that are the essentials of a screen actress she is also an actress of consummate ability." Extant

The Ivory Snuff Box

(1915). Equitable-World. Assistant Director: Clarence Brown. Script: Tourneur. Photography: John van den Broek. With Holbrook Blinn (Richard Duvall), Alma Belwin (Grace Ellicot), Robert Cummings (Prefect of Police), Norman Trevor (Dr. Hartmann), and Alec B. Francis.

In this timely five-reel mystery of international espionage from Frederic Arnold Kummer's novel, Tourneur brought his interest in Grand Guignol and the outlandish to America. He tells the tale of a Monsieur Lecoq–type American detective working for the French Secret Service in Paris during the war.

In the city of lights Richard Duvall falls in love with Grace, also an American. But on their wedding day, he is dispatched on a sensitive mission: to locate a secret French code hidden in a snuff box. Duvall heads for London to interview the owner of the box, the French ambassador to England. Duvall discovers that the ambassador's valet has been murdered and that the fate of a nation — France, it turns out — hinges on locating the missing code before it falls into the hands of the Germans.

The trail then takes Duvall to Brussels and to a sanitorium run by a "Dr. Hartmann." Hartmann is suspected of being a German agent. When Duvall shows up at the sanitorium, he is surprised to find that his wife, Grace, is there before him. She has gained entrance to the place by pretending to be in need of help because she is a sleepwalker. Inside the mysterious place, the two reunite and locate the missing box, make note of the secret codes within, and then replace the real codes with false information. Before they can make their getaway, however, they are taken prisoner by the diabolical head of the institution.

In order to find out what they know, Hartmann comes up with a scheme to make Grace talk. He throws her husband into a "torture chamber," subjecting him to deadly "ultraviolet rays." Nearly "crazed by watching his pain," Grace hands over the box. Released, Duvall and his wife head to Paris, where they give the secret codes to the authorities. Then Duvall and Grace head off on their honeymoon.

To give the five-reel film the appropriate atmosphere and suspense, Tourneur employed "ingenious" double exposures and flashbacks. "The photoplay is to be commended," wrote *Variety*. It "is a first-rate feature for any picture programme." The film, however, was banned in Chicago by the head of the police because it was imagined that it would be offensive to the city's German-born residents. (After America entered the war in 1917, anti–German propaganda swept the nation and people of German ancestry were accorded less respect.)

The Butterfly on the Wheel

(1915). Equitable-World. Assistant Director: Clarence Brown. Script: E. Magnus Ingleton. Photography: Lucien Andriot and Sol Polito. With Holbrook Blinn (Admaston), June Elvidge (Lady Attwill), Vivian Martin (Peggy Admaston), and George Ralph (Collingwood).

Working from the hit (1911) four-act British play by Edward G. Hemmerede, K.C., and Francis Nielson, M.P., Tourneur filmed a delicate five-reel psychological investigation of a marriage that suddenly faces dissolution — and offered an eye-opening look at divorce court proceedings of the day. It was the first of many films with photographer Lucien Andriot.

Admaston is single-minded when it comes to work; his marriage to Peggy, if he thinks about it at all, comes last. But when he receives an anonymous letter hinting at his wife's unfaithfulness — a ruse, of course — he leaps before looking. He sets her up to test her fidelity — and then files for divorce.

The "butterfly" whose wings Admaston sets out to clip is a young society wife, a woman too careless to keep out of dangerous waters but good and true in her nonchalant ways. A bit too innocent, she is blithely drawn into an apparently compromising position with her husband's friend Collingwood. When the circumstantial case is brought against her in court, strongly presented by a stern, cross-examining counsel, it has a good chance of ending her marriage.

The significant events take place when the young woman, who is part of a tour, finds herself alone in a Paris hotel with a rather handsome man who has been paying her a considerable amount of attention. Flattered that he seems to be speaking from the heart about his feelings for her, she allows him to remain in her room late into the night. She has a long, lingering cigarette and an amiable chat with him — and is then in trouble when, later, her husband hears about her trip to Paris. He refuses to believe her account of the innocent events that happened that night in the hotel room.

Almost immediately, her husband files for divorce. The turn of events allows the young woman to admit to herself that she might have been silly but that she has not sinned and is being made to suffer

Sol Polito, co-photographer of *The Butterfly on the Wheel* (1915), in the early 1920s.

a great deal. The tale ends on a happy note — the marriage is saved — when the identity of the letter writer is revealed: a Lady Attwill, who has designs on Admaston.

"The first three reels," wrote *Moving Picture World*, "have that double gift of making you interested in the dramatic action, making you want the story to keep going that you might see how it is turning out, and also of making you interested in the action for its own sake, so that you are willing to have the story delayed since the play is so pleasing by itself…. The staging of the picture … is worthy of high praise." The fact that filmgoers of the era were interested in seeing courtroom dramas also helped to make the film a popular one.

Human Driftwood

(1915, Tourneur and Emile Chautard). Equitable-World. Script: Emmett Campbell Hall. Photography: John van den Broek. With Robert Warwick (Robert Hendricks), Frances Nelson (Velma), Albert S. Hart (Lief Bergson), Alec B. Francis (Father Harrigan), and Leonore Harris (Myra).

The title of this five-reeler tells it all. It is about lost souls, the secrets that bind them, and the ruses of love they use to conceal the truth.

Human Driftwood (1915): In each other's arms at the end of a painful story of lost souls are Robert Warwick (as Robert Hendricks) and Frances Nelson (as Velma).

The Pawn of Fate (1915): Doris Kenyon (as Marcene) is the "pawn" of the tale George Beban (playing Pierre) is her gullible husband. John Davidson (as Lesar) watches on the couch.

Tourneur and Chautard's drama was the last film on which the two French-born filmmakers—the student and his mentor—collaborated. Their story, which is based on a work by Emmett Campbell Hall, begins in the shadowy New York underworld and shifts to the exotic and foreign landscape of a mining camp in Alaska, where the tale resolves itself.

At the root of the events is money, $20,000 in bonds in the hands of the young and aimless Robert Hendricks. His affair with Myra, a dancer of "loose morals" whom he meets at a "Bohemian resort," leads to an attempted robbery and the killing of another lover of Myra's. Myra flees the country.

Years later, Hendricks has become a new man. He has turned reformer, and is on a mission in Alaska to investigate vice conditions in a mining town. There he runs into Myra, though after so many years, he doesn't recognize her. But she has recognized him. She has opened up a dance hall in a mining town, and through her Hendricks meets Myra's beautiful "niece," Velma.

The things on most people's minds in this faraway place are money and lust. After a giant Swedish miner named Bergson has struck it rich, he tries to "buy"

Velma from Myra, and Myra agrees to the deal. But at a crucial moment, Hendricks arrives on the scene, and he and Velma fall in love. At that point, Myra tells Hendricks that Velma is his daughter. Then when Bergson tries to take Velma, he shoots Myra and kidnaps the beautiful young woman.

The tale includes Velma's rescue from an ice floe and closes with the death of Myra and the big miner. But before she dies, Myra reveals the truth: Velma is not their daughter. In the final scene, Hendricks and Velma are "in each other's arms."

"A story of the Alaskan dance hall is bound to contain much that is unpleasant," wrote *Moving Picture World*, "much that is unwholesome; but it has also the mystic charm of a life into which few of us have entered.... For a story of this kind the production will be found entertaining. The action ... does not flag."

The Pawn of Fate

(1915). Equitable-World. Assistant Director: Clarence Brown. Script: George Beban. Photography: John van den Broek. With George Beban (Pierre Dufrene), Doris Kenyon (Marcene Dufrene), John Davidson (André Lesar), Johnny Hines, and Alec B. Francis.

George Beban, the costar of *The Pawn of Fate* (1915).

Also called *The Genius — Pierre*, this early five-reel tinted American film by Tourneur is set in familiar territory for the director: Normandy and Paris. The plot centers around a deception at love and the fate of an innocent woman.

It begins on a farm where the Dufrenes play host to a visiting artist from the French capital. Taken with the pretty, young, and vivacious wife, who is the "pawn of fate" of the title, André Lesar invites the couple to his Paris studio under a pretext. He charms the naive Pierre into believing that he is a budding artistic genius waiting to be discovered. Pierre paints a huge canvas depicting life on his sheep farm and Lesar throws a party in honor of his "discovery," introducing Pierre to the glittering Paris art world.

While Pierre's work is being "evaluated" by the guests at the studio, Lesar gets down to business. He attempts to seduce Pierre's equally innocent young wife, Marcene. When it finally dawns on Pierre that he has been had by Lesar — many of the guests are laughing on the way out — he comes upon Lesar roughhousing with

The Hand of Peril (1916): In this production shot, Tourneur instructs the actors in the ingenious den-of-thieves set piece where the action shifts from room to room.

Marcene in another room. At this point Pierre concludes that his wife is in on the hoax. He throws her out of the room and threatens to kill Lesar.

Moving Picture World noted that the film, which contains nudity, "keeps one's interest by the art of its rural scenes, by the situations which are often human and simple and at times tense, and by a sense of light-heartedness that the actors give to much of the early part of the story."

"It all ends happily for Pierre and Marcine," wrote *Variety*, "but there are troublous times before it comes out right." The trade journal also pointed out that "it is unpardonable for a French director to permit a police commissionaire to visit the scene of a melee in an ordinary bowler. Everybody knows it can't be done without a silk hat."

The Hand of Peril

(1916). Paragon-World. Assistant Director: Clarence Brown. Script: Tourneur. Photography: John van den Broek. Design: Ben Carré. With House Peters (James Kestner), June Elvidge (Maura Lambert), Doris Sawyer ("Bull's Eye" Cherry), Ralph Delmore (Frank Lambert), and Ray Plicer.

This tale of the attempt by another

Rouletabille-type sleuth, Secret Service agent Kestner's effort to uncover and bring to justice the Lambert gang of counterfeiters, is unusual for two reasons. The brains behind the criminal activity — the "hand of peril" of the story — turns out to be a young woman named Maura who is known for her skill with engraver's tools. In addition, director Tourneur's innovative re-creation of the gang's nine-room hideaway — all shown in a single scene — was made possible by the use of a cross-section of a house, which allowed viewers to follow the action in different locations as it was happening. The film also contains a subplot whose theme intrigued Tourneur throughout his career: the waif (Maura) — snatched from her surroundings and brought up illegitimately — who searches for love.

Filmed in New Jersey's Palisades Park and adapted from the 1915 novel by Arthur Stringer, the five-reel melodrama unfolds "with the speed of a racehorse. The suspense is constant," commented *Variety*, with action shifting from one room to another. *Moving Picture World* agreed. This film "is a pleasant surprise. It is a story utilizing familiar material ... in an unfamiliar way.... First attention goes to director Tourneur for his revival of the method of staging used in early French pictures but new to American productions and conspicuously serviceable in presenting a story of this description."

In many parts of the film, the trade journal noted that Tourneur made use of the element of surprise. He "was careful to provide something a bit out of the ordinary in settings." At the end of the thriller, Kester, the detective, and Delmore, the gang's ringleader, "meet in the ominous surroundings of a dingy deserted wharf, just the location for the settlement of an uncompromising conflict."

The Closed Road

(1916). Paragon-World. Script: Tourneur. Photography: John van den Broek. Design: Ben Carré. With House Peters (Frank Sargeant), Barbara Tennant (Julia Annersley), Lionel Adams (Dr. Hugh Annersley), Leslie Stowe (Dr. Appledan), and George Cowl (Griswold).

Upon the release of this five-reeler, which argues against capital punishment (called "the closed road") that is based on circumstantial evidence, *Variety* wrote: "If the World Film had one or two additional directors of the calibre of Maurice Tourneur, that releasing corporation would be enabled to establish a standard of picture releases that would be hard for any other program to touch. But why wish for the impossible — there is only one Maurice Tourneur."

A cleverly crafted murder mystery, Tourneur's drama (which he produced) centers on Hugh and Julia Annersley, brother and sister living together. He is a cancer researcher. When he finds himself short of cash, he decides it is time to collect on a debt from his musician-friend Griswold. But then Griswold is found dead — and the young doctor is accused of his murder. In her efforts to save her brother from the electric chair, Julia convinces a would-be suicide — apparently he has only a few months to live anyway — to take the rap for the murder. Why waste your death? she asks. He agrees, and the doctor is set free. Just as suddenly, the real killer, a Dr. Appledan, gives himself up, and the would-be suicide is released from jail.

The film contains hints of the Grand Guignol that Tourneur favored from his beginnings in France: Griswold, for instance, had been a patient of the "mild maniac" Dr. Appledan, who is Hugh's uncle; and there are striking scenes of the

Barbara Tennant, the Eclair star and lead of Tourneur's *The Closed Road* (1916).

The Velvet Paw (1916): Avarice and intrigue are among the corrosive elements of the game in Tourneur's film, which was one of the earliest films to depict politics in Washington, D.C.

Tombs, Sing Sing, and the death house. At the same time, there are instances in the tale in which "another director would have gone into the harrowing details," as *Variety* put it, and which Tourneur "graciously spared us."

Film Daily pointed out that the "Detail of the scenes leading up to the electrocution was also quite impressive because it was different, and it was chiefly because things were offered from new angles that this production holds so remarkably through all the scenes.... The element of mystery which runs through the story helps to a marked degree in maintaining the suspense." Extant (reels 2-3).

The Velvet Paw

(1916). Paragon-World. Assistant Director: Clarence Brown. Script: Gardner Hunting. Photography: John van den Broek. Design: Ben Carré. With Ned Burton (Sen. Barring), Frank Goldsmith (Congressman Drake), Gail Kane (Mary Dexter), and House Peters (Robert Moorhead).

This is a five-reel story of graft, political corruption, and influence-peddling in high places, which was adapted from a story by Paul West. *Variety* characterized it as a "classy drama without any unnecessary attempt at sensationalism, well acted with some exceptionally fine studio reproductions of scenes in and around the Capitol."

The trouble in the story begins when Mary Dexter, an attractive young woman, and her husband arrive in Washington, D.C., to try to stimulate interest in an invention of his. Her husband has created a device that might prove of value to the U.S. Navy. She tries to sell the idea to Washington's power brokers. Right from the start, the case for honesty in high places seems almost hopeless. The inventor refuses to play the shady games demanded by people in power; his wife is quickly over her head when she gets involved in the intrigue; and then her husband, despairing over the course of events, commits suicide.

Attracted to her, a political boss befriends her in her hour of need. By playing on her desire for revenge — the ruse of the tale — he gets her to become a lobbyist under his influence. In the halls of Congress, Mary uses her wiles to get the powerful and egotistical to do her bidding. She becomes known as the "velvet paw." But after Mary falls in love with a politician of integrity, and is nearly murdered by an unscrupulous congressman, she sees the light and changes course. She begins to fight for the rights of the underprivileged and exploited children.

"In all of its physical aspects," wrote *Moving Picture World*, the "photoplay is unfailingly true to its subject ... the Washington of avaricious senators and congressman, of unscrupulous lobbyists, of beautiful women and a few young idealists.... Streets and buildings made famous the country over ... are used as a background for most of the action; there is a detailed depiction of congress in session; in fact, there are no shortcomings in suggesting the atmosphere demanded by the story."

Film Daily concurred when it said, "Any audience will consider this splendid entertainment although some may take exception to the ... assertions made in some of the titles in reference to Congress being ruled by lobbyists and grafters. It all works out with a hurrah finish, however."

The Rail Rider

(1916). Paragon-World. Assistant Director: Clarence Brown. Script: Gardner Hunting. Photography: John van den Broek. Design: Ben Carré. With Zena Keefe (Mildred Barker), Bertram Marburgh ("B"), House Peters (Jim Lewis), A. Harrington (Theodore C. Barker), and Henry West.

The lighting is the main attraction in this five-reel mystery, adapted from a story by Edgar Franklin, about the men of the "D & O" railroad who take matters into their own hands to right the injustices meted out by an exploitive company. In the course of events, the protagonist uncovers a million-dollar theft and finds love in the most unlikely of places.

For ten years, the men of the D & O, a short line, have been at the mercy of an executive known only as "B," supposedly the company's president, named Barker, whom the men have never laid eyes on. Although the line is run from faraway offices in New York, any infraction by an employee is immediately met with a severe reprimand or worse. The climax comes when train number 48, driven by engineer Jim Lewis, goes off the rails on a soft spot, tying up the whole system for a day. Facing punishment, Lewis, supported by his coworkers, heads to New York to settle matters with "B." What Lewis discovers is that an incompetent general manager has been the cause of it all, and that he has disappeared into the night with a suitcase full of securities.

Produced around New York, Tourneur's film, which contains night photography, ends with the protagonist

A Girl's Folly (1916): Josef von Sternberg is the cameraman and Emile Chautard is the director in Tourneur's humorous depiction of how films are made.

marrying the boss's daughter, while, wrote *Moving Picture World*, "the boys of the road have gained more than they hoped when they sent him to see 'B.'" Extant (reels 1-2).

A Girl's Folly/ A Movie Romance

(1916). Paragon-World Films. Assistant Director: Clarence Brown. Script: Frances Marion and Tourneur. Photography: John van den Broek. Design: Ben Carré. With Doris Kenyon (Mary Baker), Robert Warwick (Kenneth Driscoll), Chester Barnett (Johnny Applebloom), Jane Adair (Mrs. Baker), June Elvidge (Vivian Carleton), Johnny Hines (Hank), Leatrice Joy, Emile Chautard, Maurice Tourneur, and Josef von Sternberg.

This five-reel allegorical comedy gives a sense of Tourneur's opinions about actors while exploring the nature of love. While the tale centers on a country girl trying to make it in films, it is also an inside look at the workings of a movie studio where life and love, not surprisingly, do not imitate art.

The hero of the tale is the movie star Kenneth Driscoll and the beautiful heroine, Mary Baker, is an innocent young

Doris Kenyon (second from left) is the girl dreaming of love and a future in films, in *A Girl's Folly* (1916).

country girl bored with her boyfriend Johnny Applebloom but filled with romantic notions about making it the big city. She falls for a visiting screen actor — the lure of love — and runs away to New York to be in pictures. She manages to gain a small part in a film. While the actors in the film within a film are making a romantic Western in which all's well that ends well, life outside of make-believe is a bit more complex, involving flirting, courtship, fights, and reconciliation.

Tourneur's old colleague, Emile Chautard, makes a cameo appearance as a film director, while a newcomer to filmmaking, named Josef von Sternberg, plays the cameraman shooting the movie-within-the-movie.

"This plot," wrote *Moving Picture World*, "which does not reflect too much credit upon the moving picture actor, is assisted materially by the comedy situations and by the care given the production. The cast is of unusual strength."

"The story is worked out very cleverly," concluded *Variety*, and is full to overflowing with comedy. The public should be greatly interested in seeing how moving pictures are made — It is all here." Extant.

Josef von Sternberg in the early 1920s.

Emile Chautard in the 1920s.

The Whip

(1917). Paragon Films. Assistant Director: Philip W. Masi. Script: Charles E. Whittaker. Photography: John van den Broek. With Alma Hanlon (Diana Beverley), June Elvidge (Mrs. D'Aquilia), Irving Cummings (Herbert Brancaster), Warren Cook (Judge Beverley), Paul McAllister (Baron Sartoris), Alfred Hemming (Joe Kelly), Dion Titheradge (Harry Anson), and Jean Dumas (Myrtle Anson).

The play by Cecil Raleigh and Henry Hamilton on which Tourneur's film is based had long and well-received runs in England and the United States (1912). It was called "ripping good stuff, full of thrills, full of laughs, full of surprises and not without considerable ingenuity expended to advantage." The play, the critics said, "is as good as a half a dozen moving picture shows rolled into one."

The eight-reel film that Tourneur made was apparently as successful as the stage work and far more atmospheric. It centers on a racehorse called the Whip, but it is really a story of true love triumphant against the odds and of villainy baffled and humiliated. The racehorse, which is owned by a judge, is the central element in a plot hatched by a bookie, Joe Kelly, and his cohort, Baron Sartoris, to fix a race at glittering Saratoga, in upstate New York.

The tale opens in Britain, then quickly switches to America. The characters come together aboard ship where the drift of the plot is foreshadowed. With the landing of the ship in New York, "the big sensations of the story are pictured with a degree of realism that far surpasses the canvas sets of the spoken stage," wrote *Moving Picture World*. They include a car crash, a train wreck in which the horse is nearly killed, and the thrilling race with Diana, rather than the jockey, riding the horse. Also included is a favorite macabre touch of Tourneur's: scenes of Madame Tussaud's Chamber of Horrors at the Eden Museum, where the horse's unlucky jockey finds himself imprisoned with only wax murderers for company.

It's a heady blend of laughs and plot. Needless to say, the Whip wins its race and virtue is properly rewarded, and vice gets it, as the popular song used to say, where the collar ought to be. "If the present generation hasn't had all the primitive emotions refined out of it by sex plays, pathologic dramas and other intellectual oddities, the red blood in its veins will respond to the sensations of a thriller whose highest aim is to entertain," said *Moving Picture World*. This "great picture stuff," noted the trade journal, turned out to be "one of the most phenomenal successes of the ... season."

Variety pointed that "lovers of straightaway melodrama of the old school will revel" in Tourneur's film. "It is refreshing," continued the trade journal, "to see the scheming machinations of the conventional villain, the wily bookmaker to have the horserace thrown ... the heroine who rides the horse to victory — the whole thing so marvellously worked out that at times it fairly lifts you out of your seat." *Film Daily* made note of the "classy, distinctive sets, some truly beautiful exteriors, and a general atmosphere of distinction" that "helped to make this offering unusual."

The terrible and somber news about the course of the war in Europe kept the lighthearted British-based film off the market for a year until its release in 1917. Extant (reels 4-8).

The Undying Flame

(1917). Lasky-Paramount. Assistant Director: Philip W. Masi. Script: Charles E. Whittaker. Photography: John van den Broek. Design: Ben Carré. With Olga Petrova (Princess Zania/Grace Leslie), Mahlon Hamilton (shepherd/Capt. Harry Paget), Edward Mordant (the king), Violet Reed (Mrs. Harvey), Warren Cook (General Leslie), and Charles Martin (Colonel Harvey).

Adapting this atmospheric film from a story by Emma Bell, Tourneur made a two-part, five-reel fantasy about the power of love that also marked Olga Petrova's debut with Lasky's studio.

The often unbelievable story is told in the leisurely pace of the novel. Beginning in ancient Egypt, the prologue (shot in Florida) focuses on a princess who would rather be turned to stone than marry against her will. When her shepherd lover is entombed and faces an awful end — in a bit of Grand Guignol — the princess prays that someday her soul and that of her lover will be united. The tale

Maurice Tourneur in a publicity shot used to promote *The Whip* (1917).

then jumps two thousand years into the future. Once more in Egypt, we meet Grace Leslie, who is the spitting image of the princess, and daughter of a British officer. She meets Capt. Paget. He, not surprisingly, is the reincarnation of the long-dead shepherd. A scabbard, which was a lovers' token of the princess and the shepherd, plays an important part in the development and dénouement of the story: The modern-day lovers, holding pieces of the scabbard, come to the startling realization of who they once were. They overcome a jealous woman's attempt to gain the affections of the captain and are joined at the end.

The action in Tourneur's film, wrote *Exhibitor's Trade Review*, "while at no time rapid, holds the attention by reason of the unusual settings in which it takes place.... The direction of the piece was in the capable hands of Maurice Tourneur and he has made the most of the script. The settings are novel and often fantastic."

Exile

(1917). Lasky-Paramount. Assistant Director: Clarence Brown. Script: Charles E. Whittaker. Photography: John van den Broek. Design: Ben Carré. With Olga Petrova (Claudia Perez), Wyndham Standing (Vincente Perez), Mahlon Hamilton (Richmond Harvey), Warren Cook, and Charles Martin.

Tourneur drew upon his knowledge of North Africa and his experience in filming mass movements to make this exotic five-reel film (shot in Florida) based on a tale by the British writer Dolf Wyllard.

This film is set on an island called Exile, a Portuguese colony populated by Arabs. Richard Harvey, an American engineer, has helped to vastly improve living conditions on the island—for whites. So while new systems of lighting and water supply have made the place much more physically habitable for a select few, trouble is brewing below the surface.

Harvey works for a government run by one man. He is called the Lord Chief Justice, and he is the brutal, exploitative, and hated Vincente Perez, who holds the power of life and death over thousands of Arabs. Using his office, Perez has oppressed the native population. He has even bigger plans; he wants to gain control of the profitable silk trade, and will do that by forcing the local merchants out of business.

Perez's plans go awry, however, when, in a letter, he lets Harvey know of his scheme because Perez has assumed Harvey is just as unscrupulous as he. When Harvey threatens to expose Perez's underhandedness, Perez sends his wife Claudia on a delicate mission: recover the letter from Harvey by seducing him. The ruse, of course, is transparently clear to the American. But then comes the surprise. She falls in love with him, and he with her.

Harvey gives Claudia the letter. Claudia than hands it over to Perez—and tells him she is leaving him. The following day, everything comes to a head when the Arabs riot—and hang Perez. The mob very nearly gets its hands on Claudia before she is saved by the American.

"The last scene," wrote *Moving Picture World*, "shows them listening together to the diminishing sounds of the Arabs as the angry mob disperses, safe in the knowledge of their further inseparable happiness." Petrova, wrote *Variety*, "has the advantage of an interesting story, a capable supporting cast and excellent direction." But the actual "star is Maurice Tourneur," wrote a critic, thanks to his pictorialism and his handling of the violent mob scenes.

Olga Petrova, the renowned star, in *The Undying Flame* (1917).

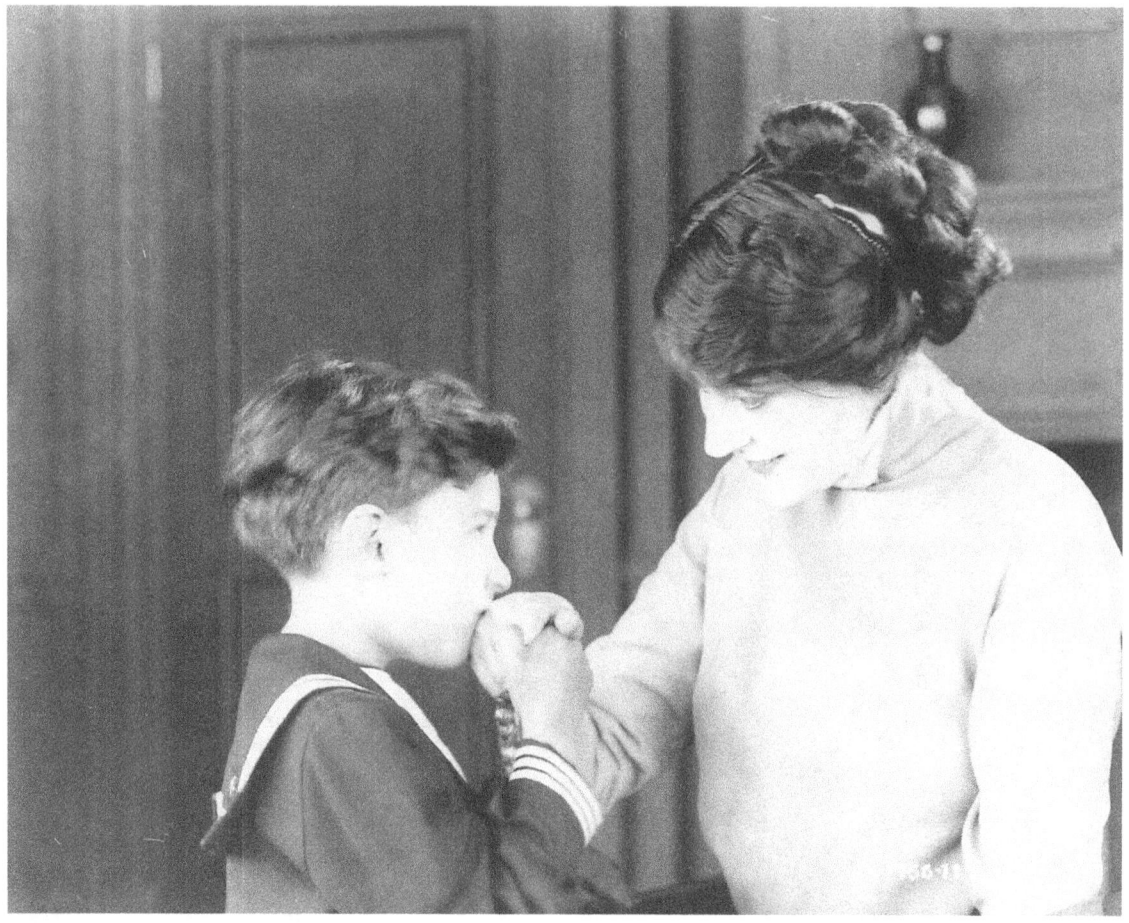

The Law of the Land (1917): Olga Petrova (as Margaret Harding) takes matters into her own hands when she kills her brutal husband to save her son.

The Law of the Land

(1917). Lasky-Paramount. Assistant Director: Clarence Brown. Script: Charles E. Whittaker and Tourneur. Photography: John van den Broek. With Olga Petrova (Margaret Harding), Wyndham Standing (Richard Harding), Mahlon Hamilton (Geoffrey Morton), J. D. Haragan (Brockland), Robert Vivian (Chetwood), Riley Hatch (Inspector Cochrane), and William Conklin (Bennie).

Adapting the story from a 1914 four-act play by the British-born George Broadhurst (1866–1952), who managed to write a play a year between 1896 and 1916, Tourneur created a disturbing film of laughter and horror, love and hate, set on the French Riviera (but shot in Florida).

In this grim drama that contains incongruous moments of drollery, a woman murders her vicious husband. The story's appeal to Tourneur, and to audiences of the day, was in the shocking sight of a knife suddenly thrust in, turned, and then slowly drawn out. The film experience, it seems, was rendered endurable, even pleasurable, by a sense that things would turn out all right. And they do.

The film centers on Margaret Harding, a mother who goes against convention: She does not sacrifice herself for the honor of the family. She does not allow her abusive husband to browbeat her into submission, or accept pieties about a woman serving her husband.

She is in love with another man, Geoffrey Morton, and her husband knows it. Richard Harding, however, also knows something else: that Bennie, the boy they're raising, is not his. Driven frantic by her brutal husband, Margaret shoots him dead when he begins whipping the boy. The investigating doctor concludes it was suicide. A police investigation, however, leads to a charge of murder. Her lover at one point tries to throw the blame onto himself.

Margaret is saved by a stroke a good fortune: a soft-hearted Inspector of Police who has just become the father of two. Realizing that Margaret had more than sufficient cause to do what she did, he destroys the evidence against her, which leads the jury to believe that Richard Harding's death was an accident. After the trial, the delightful inspector calls home to find out how his twins are doing.

"Old Simon Legree, with his hat tilted, black tie askew and whip poised, was never the villain of the Richard Harding type," noted *Variety*. "This Harding fellow surpasses him. He is a scalamonger incomparable." The director, wrote the trade journal, "has presented a gripping picture that holds one's interest to the end."

Moving Picture World noted that the five-reel film's "artistry of directing and interpretation may be called complete," and that Petrova portrayed a "character rarely seen as yet, that of a modern women of high intelligence, of as an acute sensibility as the traditional stage heroine, yet with a high-strung nervous temperament under the control of a sound, normal and well-trained mind."

The Pride of the Clan

(1917). Artcraft-Paramount Pictures. Script: Ralph Spence. Photography: John van den Broek and Lucien Andriot. Design: Ben Carré. With Mary Pickford (Marget MacTavish), Matt Moore (Jamie Campbell), Warren Cook, Kathryn Browne-Decker (Countess of Dunstable), Edward Roseman, and Joel Day.

This tender, exceptional five-reel (eighty-minute) drama of betrothal, renunciation, and reunion, based on a tale by Elaine Sterne, put Tourneur in the big leagues, directing the superstar Pickford in one of her most restrained performances. The film focuses on the harsh life of a clan on an island off the western coast of Scotland. Its leader is a woman of character who at a moment of great personal happiness is persuaded to give up her lover for what she is told is *his* own good.

The tale opens with one of the tragedies of the sea with which fishing communities of the time were familiar. A small craft is beaten about by the waves offshore. Its mast falls. The loss of the crew implies tragedy: MacTavish, the head of the clan, has died. The heir to leadership is his daughter, Marget. When Marget becomes engaged to a local fisherman named Jamie Campbell, a crisis brews. Jamie's mother writes to the Countess of Dunstable with a terrible confession. Years earlier, she, as Jamie's nurse in service to the Countess, lied about Jamie's death so that she could have a child of her own. The Countess heads for the village to claim Jamie as her long-lost son. She confronts Marget and asks her to give Jamie up "for his own good."

Marget is thunderstruck. She orders the aristocratic-born Jamie never to come near her again. Heartbroken, she then takes to the open sea where her rickety vessel begins to sink. At the last moment,

though, the young woman is saved by Jamie, who carries her to his mother's yacht. The lovers unite when the mother signals her approval.

Tourneur and Carré's carefully arranged interiors and natural landscapes created a special, stylized world whose composition is nearly perfect. John van den Broek's photography reminded some of the genre works of the 17th-century Dutch masters Frans Hals and Jan Steen, and of the landscape artists Caspar David Friedrich, John Martin, and J.W.M. Turner. Tourneur's carefully crafted sea scenes, said Richard Koszarski, represent "the real editorial set pieces ... orchestrated out of only three or four separate takes." Tourneur's "eye for composition is flawless, equalling or surpasing Griffith's work of the same period," noted Koszarski when the AFI screened the film in 1970. "Clearly this film was 10 years ahead of its time," he said.

In its day, *Moving Picture World* called the picture "well staged; and it is worth noting that in its entire length there is no trace of a villain." *Variety* wrote that under the director, the film is "marked by many incidental details which ... enrich the picture and go to the building of atmosphere.... It has the strength of simplicity in the telling and picturesqueness of locale and character types." *Exhibitor's Trade Review* made note of the clever outlining

The Pride of the Clan (1917, opposite and above): Mary Pickford is the leader of the clan in this tale of sacrifice and reconciliation.

of the "quaint betrothal ceremonies by the light of torches and bonfires.... The plot is remarkable for its simplicity, and a judicious blending of the lights and shadows of comedy and pathos effectually banishes the curse of one groove of sentimentality which so frequently handicaps the appeal of many otherwise commendable screen attractions." Extant.

The Poor Little Rich Girl

(1917). Artcraft-Paramount Pictures. Assistant Director: M. N. Litson. Script: Frances Marion and Ralph Spence. Photography: John van den Broek and Lucien Andriot. Design: Ben Carré. With Mary Pickford (Gwendolyn), Frank McGlynn, Charles Graig, Madeleine Traverse, Gladys Fairbanks (Jane), Emile Lacroix, Charles Wellesley, and Herbert Prior.

Mary Pickford made scores of films between 1909 and 1917, during which time audiences embraced the beautiful girl with the golden curls. At the age of 24 — in this second feature for Tourneur — Pickford went against the grain: She made her first appearance as an adult playing a child. It would remain her definitive, typecast character. It was also the type of character, the loveless waif, that Tourneur often favored.

Poor Little Rich Girl (1917): Mary Pickford plays the mistreated child who nearly dies for lack of love.

The production's elaborate set design, consisting of oversized furniture, made the diminutive star appear even smaller. Tourneur's esthetic techniques, visual values, settings, composition of scenes, and photography — in word, his imaginative direction — made believable the dream and fantasy sequences. Pickford, with the assistance of her scriptwriter Frances Marion, was responsible for the humor and warmth of her character. The actress would suddenly come up with surprise comedy pieces, and Tourneur, taken aback, would stop the camera. "Mlle. Pickford," he would ask, "where in the script does it say you are to do that?" But whatever Pickford did, it stayed in the picture.

The poor little rich girl of the six-reel (99-minute) story, based on Eleanor Gates' well-received 1913 play (which starred Viola Dana), is Gwendolyn, a neglected eleven-year-old daughter of preoccupied parents (played by Madeline Traverse and Charles Wellesley). This girl has everything — and nothing. Her father is too busy making money to make time for her, while her mother is the social bee who buzzes so busily elsewhere that the girl has to pretend to be sung to and said goodnight to. She is kept at home after school with a horrid lot of teachers, tutors, nurses, and governesses. When her nanny, Jane, seeks a night off, she carelessly gives the girl an overdose of a sleeping potion. The girl becomes delirious, wanders in search of her mother, and is found at the bottom of the stairs.

The innocent child finds herself in the "land of happy children" with a succession of incidents and a procession of characters part and parcel of the real, yet distorted enough to bring it into the realm of the fantastic: the Tell-tale Forest, where there is no deception; and Robin Hood's barn, where the people closest to her are stripped of pretention. So the governess is seen for what she is: a snake; the father is strapped to a money-making machine; and the mother has an encounter with a bee. In the "Land of Light," the dark angel offers her eternal sleep.

After these fantastical encounters, it's not clear whether the girl will — or wants to — return to life, or whether she can be saved. At the climax, in the girl's nursery, the real battle is on to save her life. When she recovers, her father notes, "We have been fighting death itself ... and we have learned what is truly precious. There is enough left for the life we are going to lead."

Variety pointed out that "The most effective role ... given Mary Pickford in years—if not in her entire picture career — is that of Gwen ... in the screen version of Eleanor Gates' wonderful play." *The New Republic* said: "In the audience ... were at least seven maidens wearing the Mary Pickford curls that mix up eight and sixteen. Girls wear them to the age of twenty-two. They wear them to the university classes.... Walk three blocks and note how, though no fashion magazines have endorsed it, Mary Pickford is imitated as was Queen Victoria in her youth." *Moving Picture World* said, "A separate paragraph is due the star for her portrayal of this ... girl.... Her Gwendolyn will rank as one of the best screen creations."

As for the director, *Exhibitor's Trade Review* noted, "That Maurice Tourneur has excelled all his previous efforts as a director in his staging of the feature will be admitted by the numerous admirers of the French craftsman. For him, as well as for the leading lady, the picture marks an epoch in the history of film production." The film was added to the AFI's National Film Registry in 1991. Extant.

Barbary Sheep

(1917). Artcraft-Paramount. Script: Charles Maigne. Photography: John van den Broek and Lucien Andriot. Design: Ben Carré. With Elsie Ferguson (Lady Katherine "Kitty" Wyverne), Lumsden Hare (Sir Claude Wyverne), Pedro de Córdoba (Benchaalal), Macey Harlam (Archmed), Alex Shannon (Marabout), and Maude Ford (innkeeper).

Tourneur's composition, lighting, design, knowledge of an exotic setting, and his psychological acuity helped assure that stage performer Elsie Ferguson's screen debut would be a success. This was one of the films that led the critics to call Elsie Ferguson an "aristocrat of the screen."

In this suspenseful and rich six-reel tale, she plays a neglected and lonely Englishwoman of noble birth in search of renewal and love in Algiers. Here, exotic North Africa contains a lure to love. Accompanying her is her self-absorbed husband, who is more interested in hunting the rare, mountainous Barbary sheep.

Under the spell of the seductive Arabian chief Benchaalal, Kitty herself imagines

Barbary Sheep (1917): Elsie Ferguson (as Lady Katherine "Kitty" Wyverne) seeks love and adventure in an exotic locale.

what might be. It helps that there is a glorious moon and soft music in the night air. The mere fact that she allows herself to dream of an unimagined other life and of an impossible love, while sensing trouble, leads to the clearing up of a mystery — and to a renewed life with her husband.

Based on the popular 1907 novel of the same name by the British author Robert Hichens, the film garnered acclaim for star and director. *Dramatic Mirror* noted that "all the romance and sensuousness of the East were portrayed with remarkable realism." *Photoplay* wrote that "here is poetry, here is mystery, here almost hypnotic handling of light and shade."

"It is difficult to determine between Elsie Ferguson's beauty and talent or Maurice Tourneur's artistry and sublety as being responsible for the superiority" of the production, said the *Motion Picture News*. "The descriptive beauty of Mr. Hitchen's book has by no means been lost in its migration to the screen.... Mr. Tourneur ... has proven before that he is an artist. If he wasn't he couldn't have staged a scene between an Englishwoman in evening dress and an Arab in picturesque robes on the Sahara desert and make it appear convincing."

The film "ranks up there with the best of modern releases," wrote *Variety*. The

The Rise of Jennie Cushing (1917): Elsie Ferguson is Jennie, the woman who seeks to rise above her beginnings, in her finest film role for Tourneur.

locale was one Tourneur was well familiar with from his earliest days as a filmmaker, notably his Algerian work *Jean de Poudre* (1914). "The exteriors are particularly good and look far from the stereotyped studio village scenes," wrote the trade journal. "The direction ... calls for commendation, the general work being especially good, while the selection of locations showed excellent judgment."

Finally, *Moving Picture World* singled out the film for "some fascinating psychology ... especially where it reveals the effect of primitive passions on the refined mentality of a modern society woman. This ... feature of the story is largely responsible for the suspense and it is handled with skill by the director."

Tourneur made all this possible because of his gentle and persuasive manner with the lead actress. "I soon found my audience in the director," said Ferguson. "But if he cannot feel with me, react to my emotions, then I am lost. That is why, it seems to me, a great director must be a man of infinite, delicately strung feelings."

The Rise of Jennie Cushing

(1917). Artcraft-Paramount. Script: Charles Maigne. Photography: John van den Broek and Lucien Andriot. Design: Ben Carré. With Elsie Ferguson (Jennie), Elliott

Fania Marinoff, costar of *The Rise of Jennie Cushing* (1917).

Dexter (Donelson Meigs), Fania Marinoff (Marie), Frank Goldsmith (Mr. Harrish), Edith Mcalpin, Mae Bates, Isabel Vernon, and Sallie Delatore.

Tourneur's and Ferguson's greatest work is this eye-opening film, based on a 1914 novel about a resourceful young waif who struggles to free herself from poverty and marry the man she loves, who loves her in return. The real subject is woman in search of happiness.

Of particular note is the moment when Jennie Cushing, having become a lady's maid, meets her fate. Rather than drag the artist Meigs whom she loves down to her level, she says, "No, I won't marry you, but I'll live with you." She remains with him for several years and then flees from him when her past becomes known. Two years later they are reunited, and they marry.

Moving Picture World was unstinting in its praise. It waxed poetic:

> The Artcraft production, "The Rise of Jennie Cushing," is a pictured story of symmetrical design and definite contours, from the novel by Mary S. Watts. The two principal characters, and even those of minor importance, have distinct individual attributes—they do not simply move through a series of incidents—they live in an environment of actuality, and they have souls to rouse audience sympathy and absorbed interest. It is not a case of unreal people placed in unnatural situations—we watch the career of a girl engaged in the deathless struggle of the human being against environment—the very essence of high drama—and surroundings of immediate realism.
>
> While the story is that of a profoundly affecting human experience admirably told, it depends for interest heavily upon a vital and entirely modern realization that woman is a human being with individual characteristics as broad and deep as those of man, and should be accorded rights as sweeping and sacred as those to which he has laid claim in all the ages, a very timely theme, though far from being obtrusive—it is felt rather than being perceived. Jennie Cushing's nature is apparently a very simple one, but it unfolds from the ugly bud into a flower of great beauty. She is a product of the world's unfortunates who are warped of character by insistent poverty, and her combativeness, nothing worse, lands her in a reformatory. She manages to rise a little above that deadening monotony during three years, and she improves when farmed out to a kindly old couple; but her progress comes from a great and aspiring heart in her bosom and a fine selective taste which is native. As a lady's maid she reaches the attention of an artist who is painting the portrait of her mistress. The artist is a man of wealth and social station, but he falls violently in love and a situation ensues which has the powerful appeal of "Camille" more delicately set forth and more happy in its conclusion.
>
> In these love scenes Miss Ferguson, admirably supported by Elliot Dexter, rises to the exceptional opportunities offered her and shines forth as never before in screen impersonation. Whatever has been transmuted from the poetic consciousness of the author is not only preserved but intensified and beautified by the attractive personality and intelligent interpretation of the actress. She joins hands with the author in delineating intense and true-hearted womanhood as minutely observed in real life, an analysis and penetrating conception of remarkable dramatic effect. This characterization, resulting from a harmony of spirit between author and interpreter, whether direct or insensible, raises the entire product to a very high plane, and it was probably the result of the scenario by Charles Maigne.
>
> In addition to these exceptional elements, the direction of Maurice Tourneur is that of a man who made more than a sincere effort to interpret faithfully. His exquisite effects, both interior and exterior, have accurately affirmed all

that the author and actor have contributed — there is nothing to warp the spectator's mind — but he has caught the whole spirit of this imaginative art, at one moment spreading the illusion of reality over imagined experiences, at another illustrating and enforcing the universal truth in the theme and characterization, indelibly stamping the whole mood of the play.

This union of artistic and dramatic elements is so perfect and so rare, that I would unhesitatingly choose "The Rise of Jennie Cushing" as one of those rare examples to be shown the incredulous, the skeptical and the ignorant, who deny that there is a high art in motion-picture production. Taken altogether, in its nice harmony of relations considered with discerning taste, "The Rise of Jennie Cushing" is one of the best releases of the year. It held a large audience at the Rialto spellbound and aroused favorable comment all around.

Rose of the World

(1917). Artcraft-Paramount. Script: Charles Maigne. Photography: John van den Broek and Lucien Andriot. Design: Ben Carré. With Elsie Ferguson (Rosamond English), Wyndham Standing (Capt. Harry English), Percy Marmont (Lt. Bethune), Ethel Martin (Lady Cunningham), and Clarence Handysides (Sir Gerardine).

Based on the exotic novel by Agnes Castle and Edgerton Castle, this Tourneur-Ferguson vehicle hoped to match the artistic and commercial success of their superb emotional tale *The Rise of Jennie Cushing*. Containing beautifully tinted landscapes, the film is set in India and England, and concerns a young woman who early in life faces the loss of love.

Rosamond is the young bride of British soldier Harry English, in India. Just as their love begins to grow, Capt. English is called forth on a dangerous assignment. Then comes terrible news: Capt. English has been killed in battle. Numb, lifeless, Rosamond weds the middle-aged and prosaic Sir Arthur Gerardine, the governor-general of the province, but her emotional life is none the better. Distraught to the point of despair, she hopes that by helping to write the biography of her first husband, she will feel alive again.

But the soul-searching activity only increases her anguish and her sense of loss. She falls ill, and returns to England. Soon after, Sir Arthur joins her in England. Strangely, the governor-general is accompanied by a mysterious Indian servant. One evening, in a state of acute anxiety, and with a storm raging outside, Rosamond asks the mysterious man from the East to pray for Capt. English's return. What follows then is both shocking and a revelation.

The five-reel film, which includes a thrilling battle, wrote *Variety*, contains "many little touches that bespeak" Tourneur's "handiwork." *Moving Picture World* predicted that the film "may go on file with those exceptional products which can be shown year after year, the theme immortal, 'the only heart that truly loves is that of woman.'"

Exhibitor's Trade Review went further: "Staged with infinite care and artistic skill by that most artistic of directors," Tourneur's motion picture "promises to live in film annals as an exquisitely developed and dainty production, breathing an atmosphere of suspense and romance, vibrant with thrills…. Many of the leading lady's myriad admirers will be inclined to consider this her greatest triumph in the silent drama…. It would be a wonder if this picture failed to awaken a high degree of appreciation."

A Doll's House

(1917). Artcraft-Paramount. Script: Charles Maigne and Tourneur. Photography:

Elsie Ferguson, who made her best films with Tourneur, in the highly regarded *A Doll's House* (1918).

John van den Broek and Lucien Andriot. Design: Ben Carré. With Elsie Ferguson (Nora Helmar), Holmes E. Herbert (Thorvald Helmar), Ethel Terry (Mrs. Linden), Alex K. Shannon (Krogstadt), Warren Cook, and Tula Belle.

Based on Ibsen's 1879 classic play called *Et Dukkehjem*, Tourneur's splendid five-reel (one-hour) adaptation, containing quotations for captions, "held most consistently to Ibsen's theme" of woman's ignominious position in marriage, said a critic. Tourneur's historical tale "took no licenses.... The picture holds far more tension than first imagined." It is a drama that condemns the societal stands by which women are sheltered in life and shackled in marriage.

In the Scandinavian drama, Nora Helmar is the self-conscious wife of the striving, shallow young lawyer, Thorvald. Having been taken care of by her father when she was a girl, Nora is now taken care of by a husband. Although she and Thorvald seem content at the beginning of the tale, Nora soon finds that they do not have a true marriage of equals, a *real* wedlock. The two of them have never even had a serious discussion. When Nora, for instance, expresses an interest in something outside of the home, Thorvald exclaims, "Come now — little Nora talking about scientific research!" "There are some people one loves most," Nora confides to a friend, "and other people one would almost prefer being with."

Nora is "at sea as to what is right and wrong under man-made laws." However, when her husband falls ill and is need of a period of rest abroad to restore his health, Nora takes a bold step during this moment of crisis: she comes to the rescue. She obtains the necessary money from the banker Krogstadt by forging her dead father's name to a bank note. By this action, she saves her husband's life but has opened herself up to censure — or worse — in a male-dominated society. She knows that she cannot confide her secret to her husband. "Thorvald — with all his masculine pride — how painfully humiliating for him if he ever found out he was in debt to me. That would just ruin our relationship."

Years later, when Thorvald has risen to become head of Krogstadt's bank, he fires his longtime colleague Krogstadt for irregular financial dealings. The latter retaliates, revealing Nora's long-secret financial activity in a letter to Thorvald. The self-important Thorvald is shocked that his wife had done such a thing without his knowledge. With his "honor" at stake, for he is indebted to his wife, Thorvald reacts with fury against her. At that moment, Nora realizes that her husband is primarily concerned with one thing: keeping up appearances.

Although she is terror-stricken, Nora sits her husband down and tells him how she feels about their eight-year marriage and about her life in a "doll's house." She is leaving him, at least for a while if not permanently. Nora rejects Thorvald's offer to write to her and to give her financial assistance if she needs it. Then she returns her wedding ring to him and walks out into the world to pursue her own growth. She abandons three children and leaves in bitterness, resentment, and revolt against the humiliating position of the Northern European wife of the late 19th and early 20th centuries.

"Among all versions of the Ibsen drama which have appeared on the screen," wrote *Moving Picture World*, "none seem to approach more nearly the Ibsen theme than that of the Artcraft." However, the film "depicts a social condition which no longer exists," said the trade

The children and the fairy leader in search of elusive love, in Tourneur's exceptional *The Blue Bird* (1918).

journal. "Thus, because of the close adherence to the Ibsen idea the play is not likely to find favor as a screen product except to the limited extent that it depicts two kinds of conscience, one for each sex, still a live theme." *Film Daily*, however, came to a different conclusion. It wrote: "Don't let the fact that Ibsen plays are supposed to be high brow worry you. This has been done humanly. It's real, it's convincing, it rings true!"

In addition to admirable sets and scenes filmed in Maine, the film was singled out for its acting. The beautiful star gave ample evidence of her intelligence, emotional power, and poise. Ferguson called upon her famed histrionic ability "to send the screen characterization over with realism and naturalness.... She is at home ... before the camera," wrote a critic.

The Blue Bird

(1918). Tourneur-Paramount. Script: Charles Maigne. Photography: John van den Broek and Lucien Andriot. Design: Ben Carré and André Ibels. With Tula Belle (Mytyl), Robin Macdougall (Tyltyl), Edwin E. Reed (Daddy Tyl), Emma Lowry (Mummy Tyl), William J. Gross (Grandpa Gaffer Tyl), Florence Anderson (Granny

The Blue Bird (1918): In this production shot, Tourneur instructs the child leads of the fantasy tale.

Tyl), Edward Elkas (Widow Berlingot), Lillian Cook (Berylune), and Rosa Rolanda.

From the 1890 allegory *L'Oiseau bleu*, by the Belgian poet Maurice Maeterlinck (staged in Paris in 1909), Tourneur created a classic: a marvelous, tinted, six-reel fantasy, a deliciously stylized, humorous, and imaginative work, gloriously designed and lighted, that deals with the fear of death and its transcendence through love.

In this sensitive and sympathetic film, similar in theme to his *Poor Little Rich Girl* (1917) and featuring the dancer Rosa Rolanda, Tourneur said he "tried to sound the note of fragile phantasy."

Tourneur, who was familiar with the latest theatrical approaches of Reinhardt, Gordon Craig, Stanislavsky, and Jacques Coupeau, employed André Ibels, a collaborator of André Antoine in France, to help design the sets. The painted-set fantasy they created predated Wiene's expressionistic *The Cabinet of Dr. Caligari* and Lang's *Der Mude Tod*. Tourneur's maturing method of lighting included placing people around a central source of light.

Don't be lured, the film says, by romantic stories that maintain that love is to be found in faraway places. Many times it can be found right under your nose.

It starts during Christmas, when two unhappy peasant youngsters, Mytyl and Tyltyl, are led by the fairy Berylune in search of the elusive "Blue Bird of Happiness." Berylune gives Tyltyl a cap with a diamond setting, and when Tyltyl rotates the diamond, the children become aware of the souls of things, animate and inanimate, around them: a dog and cat, as well as fire, water, bread, and light. In the most moving and tender of moments, they meet their dead grandparents Granny and Gaffer Tyl at the graveyard at midnight; enter the enchanting Palace of the Night and Palace of Luxuries, the Cathedral of Happiness, and the Azure Palace; and survive the loss of companions.

What they, and viewers, discover is that the object of their search—the Blue Bird—dwells right where they stand. At the end, Tyltyl makes a direct appeal to the audience: "Please, all of you, look for our Blue Bird with all your hearts. Be sure to look first in your own homes, WHERE HE IS MOST APT TO BE FOUND."

"Here's to a flock of 'Blue Birds'!" wrote *Moving Picture World*. "Famous Players–Lasky ... should be repaid by achieving financial success equal to the artistic merits of its production…. The scenario ... the direction ... and the acting ... all have a share in shaping" the film "into a screen poem of rare beauty…. To sit under its spell is to receive an impulse for good that will never be affected. It is a potent argument in favor of the screen." The trade journal also called the film a "master work of photographic interpretation of life's deepest values."

Photoplay reminded viewers that "There is no director of moving pictures with a keener sense of the beautiful" than Tourneur, and that "his genius for creating scenes of exquisite loveliness comes to its full fruition" in this production. "It is so beautiful ... that it fairly stings the senses, awakening in the spectator esthetic emotions so long dormant, so seldom exercised, that the flashing light of the awakening is almost a surfeit of joy." Its simple yet profound message had the magazine calling the work "one of the most important photodramas ever made. It blazes a new trail in production…. It defies the hypercritical. For the vision to see the possibilities, the Artcraft executives deserve praise, scarcely second to that which must be accorded the genius of the play himself—Tourneur." Extant.

Prunella

(1918). Tourneur-Paramount. Script: Charles Maigne. Photography: John van den Broek and Lucien Andriot. Design: Ben Carré and André Ibels. Script: Charles Maigne. With Isabel Berwin (Prim), Nora Cecil (Privacy), Marguerite Clark (Prunella), William J. Gross (the gardener), Marcia Harris (Prude), Charles Hartley, Arthur Kennedy, Henry Leone, and Jules Raucourt (Pierrot).

Tourneur's exquisite fantasy of rhapsodic love, based on the early 20th-century ballet-like play *Prunella; or Love in a Dutch Garden*, by British dramatists Harley Granville-Barker and Lawrence Houseman, is another classic. It is about the kind of protagonist Tourneur favored his entire career: the intrepid waif in search of love. Tourneur said that in this film he tried to "catch the gossamer of whimsical romance." But when the story is stripped of its poetry, it is a tale of unhallowed passion and the desire for love. Here the protagonist gives in to a ruse of love, and it is for the better.

Prunella (1918): Marguerite Clark (Prunella) and the strolling players' caravan in Tourneur's whimsical tale of passion.

The heroine is Prunella (played by Marguerite Clark, who had the role on the New York stage in 1913), reared by her watchful aunts, Prim, Prude, and Privacy. She lives near a rigid, formal garden, where the yew trees, "all elbows and knees, perk themselves as they please," and the gardeners must forever be giving nature a lesson in behavior. In that garden, seventeen years ago, a French landscaper has come and gone, leaving two signs of his visit: a statue of Love, bearing a viol, which is voiceless and mute — and the child Prunella.

Now that she's grown, the rigor of Prunella's training is apparent in the lines that prepare her for her daily tasks: "Not to allow my thoughts to stray / Beyond the duties of each day; / Thus only can I hope to be / A type of maidenly modesty." Between needlework and lessons and the good, uncomprehending aunts who close the house's ears to the revelry in the streets, Prunella, "the pretty Dutch doll," yet has a very cheerful time of it. She reads of fables and life, and one day meets the mummer Pierrot and his troupe.

Suddenly, there is magic in the air, and Prunella is stirred. The charming Pierrot serenades her and carries her down in the moonlight. For a moment she hesitates, thinking of "those who might miss me, those whom I might miss." Then, standing before the statue of Love, Prunella takes a chance on a new life: she allows herself to be wooed, and carried into the world, by Pierrot.

Delicate, quaint, fantastic as a dream, the film achieves a dainty and elusive mood perfectly supported by the acting and setting. The costumes of Pierrot's associates are suggestive of the Hôtel de Bourgogne in the time of Molière. Critics lauded the French-born Tourneur for his

Sporting Life (1918): Dashing Ralph Graves is the center of attention in Tourneur's atmospheric tale of action and living well.

pictorialism and sensitivity, which, they said, advanced the art of motion pictures to the point where it "can stand on the same high plane as the other fine arts."

In this five-reel work, Tourneur "has utilized the new impressionistic stage art throughout," wrote *Motion Picture Classic*. "He has achieved a splendidly sustained atmosphere of fantasy and some screen pictures of rare imagination and suggestion.... One scene, a striking study in black and white, shows the lonely Pierrot at a table, while an endless chain of shadows pass the curtained windows in the background.... The strolling players' caravan, the wanderings of the troupe through strange lands and the scenes in Prunella's garden are handled with the feeling of a painter." Extant.

Sporting Life

(1918). Tourneur-Paramount. Script: Winthrop Kelley. Photography: John van den Broek and Lucien Andriot. Design: Ben Carré and André Ibels. With Ralph Graves (Earl of Woodstock), Warner Richmond, Charles Eldridge, and Henry West.

Based on Cecil Raleigh and Seymour Hicks' long-forgotten play about upper-crust Britishers and villains being foiled at the eleventh hour, this action-filled, suspenseful comedy-drama was Tourneur's first independent production. Its theme is similar to that of *The Whip* (1917).

One of his not-so-rare comedies, and also known as *Lady Love*, this film is significant for its lack of stars—signaling once again Tourneur's reservations about Hollywood's "star system"—and for "the London night street scenes with the fine effect of dense fog," said *Motion Picture Classic*. "The dim depths of real night in the exteriors have never been equaled," wrote Julian Johnson in *Photoplay*. The tale culminates in the running of the English Derby.

Winthrop, Lord Woodstock, a sporting man in financial straits, hopes to see his horse, Lady Love, win the classic race. But there's a plot afoot to keep the horse, if not Winthrop, out of competition. Thieves steal the horse, and then Winthrop is himself kidnapped. Escaping and recovering his prize possession, he has to make a last-minute dash to the Derby to enter the horse in the race.

Thanks to Tourneur's highly regarded sense of effect and lighting, "the [seven-reel] film will make an attractive special release and ... give satisfaction to any audience," wrote a critic. *Moving Picture World* noted that the old story "turns out to be excellent entertainment for the general public." That's because of the fundamental appeal of its red-blooded hero, and the "fact that all the veneer of culture and advanced thought in the world cannot curb the primitive passions when we see a man battling his way to right and justice by brute force."

Filmgoers were told that they would follow the unfolding of the story "with interest, and find it vastly more entertaining than some of the original scenarios that have neither the vitality nor the varied incident of this survivor of the old English racing drama." Tourneur's direction was called "masterly" by the trade journal. "It is difficult to recall any detail of production that could have been bettered. The English atmosphere, the night effects and the care shown in every scene are admirable. The interiors of the National Sporting Club and the running of the race are among the best of the episodes."

Georges Sadoul observed that Tourneur's use of atmosphere and lighting in this film influenced D. W. Griffith when he made *Broken Blossoms* (1919). Tourneur remade *Sporting Life* in 1925 for Universal, and in that version he stuck closer to the original source—and used a more well known cast.

Woman

(1918). Tourneur-Paramount. Script: Charles E. Whittaker. Photography: John van den Broek and René Guissart. Design: Ben Carré and André Ibels. With Florence Billings (the woman), Warren Cook (the man), Ethel Hallor (Eve), Henry West (Adam), Flore Revalles (Messalina), Paul Clerget (Claudius), Diana Allen (Heloise), Escamillo Fernandez (Abelard), Gloria Goodwin (Cyrene), Chester Barnett (the fisherman), Faire Binney (the girl), Warner Richmond (the officer), Lyn Donaldson, and Rose Rolanda.

Tourneur's well-received allegory was suggested by a quotation from George Moore: "The legitimate occupation of man's mind is woman."

The extravagant production begins when an angry wife storms out of the house, leaving her husband in a state of bewilderment. To calm himself, he reviews stories of the lives of several notable women, concentrating on the trials and tribulations that their men faced.

In this series of five stories, plus an

epilogue and prologue, all of which encompass seven reels, the film covers the mythical tales of Eve and Adam, Messalina and Claudius, Héloïse and Abelard, and Cyrene and the Fisherman, as well as that of a young woman who betrays her lover during the turbulent period of the American Civil War. In the early episodes, Tourneur paints a picture of woman as seductress and siren. Then Tourneur reverses himself. He points out the underappreciated roles and influences of women during times of peace and of conflict, notably the period during the First World War when women worked as Red Cross volunteers and labored in American industry.

At its release, the film, which contains remarkable bits of photography, including double exposures and other tricks, was hailed as Tourneur's contribution to the Great War because of its call for Americans to recognize the many valid contributions that women make to the life and the culture of the nation. But the film is also a summing up of what Tourneur had been expressing in his many films about the complex, mysterious, and often painful nature of love.

The film was instantly acclaimed for its artistry. On its release, the New York Times wrote that in telling the disparate stories, Tourneur "found full expression for his genius and created a succession of ballads in pictures, each of which was a

Tourneur in a late-1918 publicity photograph. The accompanying copy identifies him as a "famous French director who took up motion pictures after a brilliant career as a painter and actor at the Theatre Antoine. He directed Elsie Ferguson in all her pictures, including *Barbary Sheep*; directed Clara Kimball Young in her greatest success, *Trilby*; and directed Maeterlink's *The Blue Bird* and Lawrence Houseman's *Prunella* to name a few of his many celebrated high art productions for the screen. He is one of the few directors who can register atmosphere and phantasy and high imaginative creation on the film when the script demands it."

thing of beauty by itself with the convincing power of a good story exceptionally well told."

Exhibitor's Trade Review wrote, "Hats off to Maurice Tourneur! Once again he has produced a picture that, for downright artistic value, has never been equalled." Exquisite scene follows upon exquisite scene.

As a parallel to Griffith's *Intolerance* (1917), the production "is a thing of rare screen beauty: once or twice it reaches genuine heights," said *Motion Picture Classic*, while *Photoplay* ranked it "one of the most beautiful things physically that has ever been made, with the most superb lighting and photography, and further evidences of Mr. Tourneur's positive genius in grouping and general composition."

But there was also an element of tragedy in the making of this production. Dutch-born photographer van den Broek, Tourneur's colleague for the last four years, who was only 23 at the time, drowned during the shooting in Bar Harbor, Maine. He was filming giant waves slamming against the cliffs when he was suddenly swept out to sea by a ferocious series of waves. His body was never recovered.

Tourneur noted that van den Broek, who studied and lived in America for seven years, was "responsible for all the splendid photography" of *Barbary Sheep*, *The Blue Bird*, *Prunella*, "and all the others. He was more than a cameraman; he was a lovely, sensitive, delicate artist. My intention was to surprise him by making him a director … and he would have been among the best." Extant.

My Lady's Garter

(1919). Tourneur-Paramount. Script: Lloyd Lonergan. Photography: René Guissart. With Sylvia Breamer (Helen Hamilton), Wyndham Standing (Bruce Calhoun), Holmes Herbert (Henry Van Derp/the Hawk), Warner P. Richmond, Paul Clerget, Charles Craig (Keats Gaunt), and Warren Cook (Brokaw Hamilton).

This thriller is based on the 1912 novel of the same name by Jacques Futrelle, the American journalist, theatrical manager, and mystery writer who died on the Titanic at the age of 37. His wife, May, who survived the disaster at sea, published the novel after her husband's death. The novel opens with a full-page, formal photograph of Jacques Futrelle and an inscription: "To the heroes of the Titanic I dedicate this my husband's book." Tourneur's film was written by Lloyd Longergan, the chief scenarist from the old Thanhouser Film Corporation of New Rochelle, New York.

Tourneur filmed a mystery-comedy, not so rare an undertaking for him as many have imagined, since Tourneur had often demonstrated an instinct and talent for directing comedy. The film allowed him to indulge in a bit of historical fantasy. The English tale begins in the period of Henry III and presents the engrossing incident from which emanated the famous Order of the Garter. The lovely Countess of Salisbury, a favorite of the king, drops her diamond-studded garter onto the floor of the ballroom. On the following day, she is given a jeweled substitute; the king, it seems, has decided to keep the original as a souvenir. Eventually, the garter becomes part of the collection in the British Museum.

The five-reel (sixty-minute) film then plunges ahead to contemporary times, and concerns itself with the loss and pursuit of the garter, which has been stolen from the famous museum. The prime suspect is an international jewel thief known only as the Hawk. Scotland Yard detective Bruce Calhoun — another Rouletabille-type investigator — is on his trail. However, Calhoun

My Lady's Garter (1919): Sylvia Breamer (as Helen Hamilton) becomes the object of attention of Wyndham Standing (as Bruce Calhoun), a Scotland Yard agent who is seeking the international jewel thief known as "The Hawk."

is acting under cover. Calhoun's search for the thief leads him to the country estate of the railroad baron Brokaw Hamilton — and to Hamilton's beautiful daughter, Helen, a free-spirited young woman who intends to elope with a poet named Keats Gaunt.

Calhoun has made his home on a yacht in the harbor, and meets Helen when he saves her from drowning. But his presence arouses the suspicions of one Henry Van Derp, another suitor for Helen's hand. Before the dénouement, in which Van Derp is revealed as the Hawk, the film features such Tourneur staples as a bank robbery, a yacht explosion, and a near train wreck. After the dust has settled, it is Calhoun who will marry Helen. "The hero's secret is splendidly concealed," wrote *Moving Picture World*, "affording a pleasant diversion of mental exercise not always supplied in film productions. Adventure, mystery and suspense characterize the picture."

The *New York Times* noted that the film, which was released in March, 1920, was held up for a year before being shown commercially. "Certainly its proprietor could not have feared that it would fail, for it is an unusually interesting picture.... Mr. Tourneur is a skillful cinematician."

The White Heather (1919): The crush of people at the dramatic court trial that sets the stage for the thrilling search for a missing document under the sea.

The White Heather

(1919). Tourneur-Paramount. Script: Charles E. Whittaker. Photography: René Guissart and Harold Sintzenich. Design: Ben Carré. With Ralph Graves (Alec McClintock), John Gilbert (Dick Beach), Spottiswoode Aitken (James Hume), Ben Alexander (Donald Cameron), Mabel Ballin (Marion Hume), and Holmes Herbert (Lord Angus Cameron).

From the play by Cecil Raleigh and Henry Hamilton — a (London) Drury Lane melodrama — Tourneur made this, his debut production in California. To complete the film, he donned a diving suit developed by J. Ernest Williamson, the pioneer of undersea photography. Wearing the diving gear, Tourneur directed critical underwater scenes.

Tourneur came up with a little-known gem, a swift-moving, six-reel (seventy-minute), tinted thriller about a family secret. Opening in the banquet hall of a Scottish manor, the tale switches to the haunts of the underworld and the hectic London Stock Exchange, and from there to the courtroom and then to the ocean floor.

It begins when the unscrupulous Lord Cameron wants to marry a woman of nobility. But there is a problem: he is

Spottiswoode Aitken, who was featured in *The White Heather* (1919) and *The White Circle* (1920), and daughter.

already married to Marion Hume, the housekeeper of his castle. Having charmed Marion into wedlock, Cameron now wants out. Repudiating his wife and child, Cameron imagines that there is no obstacle in his way because the only evidence of his union is a signed contract of marriage in the log of the "White Heather," a yacht that has been lost at sea, and two eyewitnesses, the ship's skipper and mate, who have vanished.

Marion, however, has other ideas. She searches the London underworld for the missing witnesses and then takes the case to court, but comes up empty because she has no evidence to back up her claim of marriage. So, having failed to prove in court that she is the wife of Cameron, Marion and her lover, Alec McClintock, head to the open sea to locate the sunken yacht and secure the proof. That will not only prove that Cameron is a liar and a rascal but will also ensure the rights of her son by Cameron. But Cameron is headed out to open water, too, to make sure that nothing is recovered.

The fact that the direction was in the hands of Tourneur "is sufficient testimonial to the excellence of the filming," wrote *Exhibitor's Trade Review*. "The scenes which have their locale at the castle of the Camerons in Scotland have unusual beauty as to landscape and settings. A series of hunting scenes were particularly good."

Mabel Ballin, who starred in *The White Heather* (1919).

Variety labeled the film, which contains a sensational fight to the death under water, an "absolute masterpiece of motion picture direction." With novel and authentic undersea photography, "there is nothing better that could be asked for," said the trade journal.

Film Daily hailed Tourneur's "truly artistic production ... its variety in locale and characterization," while The *New York Times* noted that the scenes "shaded by fog and night are masterpieces of their kind." The newspaper named Tourneur's film, which contained at the time no big-name stars, one of the best of the year.

Jack Holt, the handsome star of three Tourneur films: *The Life Line* (1919), **Victory** (1919), and *The Broken Butterfly* (1919).

The Life Line

(1919). Tourneur-Paramount. Script: Charles E. Whittaker. Photography: René Guissart. Design: Ben Carré. With Jack Holt (Jack Hearne/Romany Rye), Wallace Beery (Bos), Tully Marshall (Joe Heckett), Seena Owen (Laura), Lewis J. Cody (Phillip Royston), and Pauline Starke (Ruth Heckett).

From the startling and intricate 1882 drama called *The Romany Rye*, by George

R. Sims (1847–1922), who was a leading reform advocate, Tourneur created a five-reel Dickensian tale of the "vulgar and criminal classes" of London. It centers on two outcasts of society: the half-gypsy artist Jack Hearne, who is also a vagabond hero called the Romany Rye, and Ruth Heckett, a girl of the slums. The protagonists are in search of love. There are numerous obstacles to their finding it.

The complex story goes like this: Phillip Royston is a young aristocrat, the owner of Cragsnest, a magnificent old English house in Hampton, England. In early life, his father dallies with a gypsy girl, the tents of whose people had, for generations, been erected upon the grounds of the estate. In a moment of passion, he strikes her. The mark on her face becomes the seal of a settled hatred between the Roystons and the Romanies. The girl flees from her protector; a son is born; the mother dies; the child also, according to rumor; the father marries, and has a son, Philip.

Like his father, Phillip has found a pretty face in the tents of the gypsies, named Laura. Suspected of betrayal by her people, she flees to the estate. Her father follows her, carrying a gun. He is prevented from shooting Philip by the sudden appearance of the Romany Rye. A fight breaks out between the gypsies and Royston's people. At the height of the brawl, when the Romany Rye is about to be arrested, horsewhipped or shot, or something to that effect, he makes a surprising statement. He says he is the master of Cragsnest and brother of Phillip.

It turns out that the elder Royston had married the gypsy girl—and that their child lived. There exists a marriage certificate to prove it. From that moment, Phillip Royston vows to destroy the evidence—and to kill the Romany Rye. There is also something between them: the additional bitterness of a divided love in the shape of Ruth, a bird-fancier's pretty London daughter—a flower born of the gutter of Seven Dials. The Romany Rye falls in love with her. But Phillip, who wants to get his hands on a certain London property, to which he discovers she is the heiress, is determined to marry her first.

A Bible, which contains the sought-after marriage certificate, has been stolen by Ruth's father—who, it turns out, is illiterate. In addition, witnesses to the marriage are known to live in America. The Romany Rye sets out to find them. He marries Ruth and buys tickets on the steamer *Saratoga* from London to New York. Ruth's father is also aboard, heading to America to start a new life.

At this point, Royston and his scheming lawyer plan to kill the Romany Rye with the help of Laura. She tells the Romany Rye, two hours before his ship embarks, that Black Nathan, a gypsy, has the documents he seeks. He can be found in Blackcroft, an unsavory district of the East End.

There Royston's thugs surprise and garrote him and carry him to an old cellar by the Thames. While tied up there, the Romany Rye becomes aware that, upstairs, Royston is offering 500 pounds for the return of his body. But he frees himself so that when the thugs come for his body, the Romany Rye only feigns unconsciousness. Carried aboard a boat, he suddenly jumps into the river and swims to safety.

The *Saratoga* is now three days out from London, at Southampton. There Royston plans to take the place of his half-brother. Royston has found the document in the Bible. The Romany Rye, however, arrives just as a violent storm breaks out. The steamer goes ashore and the Romany Rye saves his wife from drowning—and gains possession of the vital documents—while Royston and Laura perish in the waters.

The story becomes a tale about righting a wrong — and discovering love in the process. Tourneur's film is as complex as any he ever filmed, a look at the sunshine reflected in the dirty pool of the times, dealing with tramps and thieves, hustlers, guttersnipes, burglars, body-snatchers, and the dead that float up and down the Thames.

Exhibitor's Trade Review noted that "the good old stage thriller gets its thrill across in truly spectacular fashion, vibrates with suspense and hair-raising adventure and love interest, and in point of vivid detail stands head and shoulders above the average program offering.... Tourneur never does things by halves. His whole soul is 'bound up in his heart.'" *The Life Line*, it continued, "indicates in every reel the guiding influence of his master hand.... The effects obtained in the filming of the wrecked ocean liner and the burning theater are simply immense and register in the very acme of realism. Nor must the fox hunt be forgotten in reckoning up the list of good things, with its gaily accoutred riders, following the scent over vale, river and hill, brown Reynard fleeing swiftly before the pursuing hounds and over all the indefinable charm and beauty of a quiet English landscape."

"Those who go to see" this film, wrote the *New York Times*, "will expect big, thrilling scenes, little amusing bits, beautiful vistas, something of originality and subtlety, and realism in all things except plot. They will not be disappointed." The film is "up to the standard of the best."

The tale's storm and shipwreck were said to be the equal of anything of their kind, while another effective scene is that of a stage melodrama as reflected in the audience. "Nothing of what takes place on the stage is shown, said the *Times*, "but the whole course of the thriller is followed through the expressions and actions of those ... watching it." The paper named the stirring film one of the best of the year. It was longtime colleague Ben Carré's last major film with Tourneur.

Victory

(1919). Tourneur-Paramount. Script: Jules Furthman. Photography: René Guissart. Design: Ben Carré and Floyd Mueller. With Jack Holt (Axel Heyst), Seena Owen (Alma), Lon Chaney (Ricardo), Wallace Beery (August Schomberg), Ben Deely (Mr. Jones), Bull Montana (Pedro), Laura Winston (Mrs. Schomberg), and George Nichols (Capt. Davidson).

Very loosely based on the 1915 novel by Joseph Conrad, Tourneur's five-reel (4735-ft) drama is the earliest screen adaptation of this often filmed story of lovers on the run in the middle of nowhere.

It is a harsh and brutally realistic story set on the island of Samburen, in the Dutch East Indies. There Alma, a violinist on tour in a women's orchestra, meets Axel Heyst, a recluse who has pacifist views of love and war. His protective instincts are aroused by threats posed to Alma. He also secretly falls in love with her.

When his island is visited by three of the worst desperadoes in that part of the world, Axel finds himself involved in a terrific conflict, illuminated by a suddenly active volcano. Separated by a series of malevolent intrigues, the lovers triumph — unlike the unhappy ending in the novel — after hair-raising adventures against the unscrupulous bunch of characters named Jones, Ricardo, and Pedro.

A taut, forbidding drama that grows in malevolence, the film contains changes

Lon Chaney (as Ricardo, hat in hand) is one of the desperados after the young musician Alma in *Victory* (1919).

in camera angles by Tourneur, shocking dialogue by Lon Chaney's character Ricardo, and a particularly grisly murder by burning. The intertitles stress the foreboding atmosphere, for example: "Night came with heavy stealth, bringing a dreaded murk, broken now and then by the infernal glare of the pit."

At one point Ricardo says to Alma, "Come, I want you to see me kill…. Their blood will give our love a touch of color." And later on, Ricardo says that his accomplice Pedro is able to snap a man's back as if it were a twig.

The film remains noteworthy for Tourneur's skillful direction and its lighting and shading. *Moving Picture World* called Tourneur's film "An original and interesting picture, picturesque in detail, splendidly typed, a refreshing change from the conventional in nearly all respects."

Variety said, "Probably the eagle eye of the censor is responsible for cutting the fight between Alma and Ricardo, but it is well cut. Of the latter character Lon Chaney gave a visualization that was very effective."

The *New York Times* noted that Tourneur's film "demands special mention … a triumphant motion picture. In it are

Victory (1919): Jack Holt (as Axel Heyst) helps Seena Owen (as violinist Alma) out of a terrible jam in the Far East.

scenes surpassingly beautiful, picturesque, dramatic, and horrible…. The most compelling characters in *Victory* are three roving birds of prey — Mr. Jones, the leader, Ricardo, his secretary, and Pedro, his strong man. The most diabolically conspicuous of the three is Ricardo…. No screen actor whose name comes to mind can equal Mr. Chaney in the impersonation of intense, strongly marked types. He does with consummate skill and fine finish the kind of acting that many attempt with lumbering ponderosity and … exaggeration." Again, it named this adventure one of the best of the year. Extant.

The Broken Butterfly

(1919). Robertson-Cole. Script: Tourneur and Margaret Turnbull. Design: Ben Carré. With Lew Cody (Darrell Thorne), Seena Owen, Pauline Starke (Marcene Elliot), Jack Holt, and Mary Alden (Aunt Zabie).

Adapting the heartrending tale of Penelope Knapp's story "Marcene," Tourneur made the most of the slender material at hand, that of the life of an innocent waif and an ambitious lover. Tourneur developed it into a five-reeler of "exceptional artistic merit." Throughout his career, Tourneur examined the theme of a naive young girl falling in love with a man

The Broken Butterfly (1919): Pauline Starke (as Marcene Elliott) is the waif in search of salvation.

of the world. Sometimes the affair would end well, but more often it did not.

The action here is set in French-speaking Canada, where Marcene, a barefoot young woman "who don't know nothin'," lives with her aunt. She meets and falls in love with the composer Darrell Thorne. He is inspired to write a symphony in her honor and in her name. They have a daughter out of wedlock.

Eager to make a name for himself, Darrell leaves Marcene — and that leads to trouble. Anxious that she will never see him again and feeling that differences in social standing preclude their ever marrying, Marcene apparently commits suicide. But the composer's feelings for her have been, and are, true.

He does return, only to hear the awful news of her terrible fate and that of their daughter. He also learns that Marcene was the offspring of a lord, stolen from her family at birth. Thorne flees to the Riviera. Yet this story of love found and lost is not quite over, to Thorne's — and filmgoers' — surprise.

Thorne meets Marcene's younger sister, and the two fall in love. After they marry, Thorne takes his new bride to Canada, to the locale where Thorne and Marcene first met. To their great surprise they discover that Marcene and her daughter are alive, although Marcene is gravely ill. Marcene and the child had been saved from death by a faithful collie, but Marcene still felt the shame of abandonment and kept to herself. Now Thorne spares her any further anguish by keeping the news of his own marriage a secret from her. Not long after, Marcene dies. Thorne and his wife adopt the young girl, and cherish the memory of Marcene in her.

"From the point of view of production as well as heart appeal," wrote *Harrison's Reports*, the film "is the best picture Maurice Tourneur has ever produced. A deep feeling of sympathy and tender pathos is awakened for the principal characters. The spectator feels their joys and sorrows intensely." The film has "a wonderful atmospheric setting," noted *Film Daily*.

The County Fair

(1920, Edward J. Mortimer). Groswell Smith. Supervisor: Tourneur. Script: S. Grubb Alexander. Photography: René Guissart and Charles van Enger. With Wesley Barry, Charles Barton (Tim Vail), David Butler (Joel Bartlett), Edythe Chapman, Helen Jerome Eddy (Sally Greenway), Maxine Elliott Hicks, Arthur Housman (Bruce Hammerhead), William V. Mong (Solon Hammerhead), Hector Sarno, and John Steppling (Otis Tucker).

In this comprehensive five-reel (5,000-ft) adaptation of the long-forgotten 1889 rural classic of the American stage by Neil Burgess, Tourneur and his colleagues had "taken hold of ... one of the very popular plays of the last generation," wrote *Film Daily*. They "transferred it to the screen with the same spirit in which it must originally have been written, and with keen insight into the manners, customs, and peculiarities of New England village life." It is a tale that hinges on a race horse, like *The Whip* (1917) and *Sporting Life* (1918).

The film is the love story of two ordinary people, Sally and Joel, that begins slowly, then gathers tension and momentum. Sally, an orphan, lives on a farm with the woman who has adopted her, Abigail. But their tranquil lives are threatened with foreclosure by the man who owns the mortgage, the banker Solon Hammerhead. The only way out is a loathsome choice they've been given: either Sally marries Hammerhead's son, Bruce, or Abigail, who is being wooed by the shy Otis Tucker, marries Solon Hammerhead himself. Sally, of course, loves the hired hand, Joel, but she's willing to go through with the loathsome deal to save the farm.

When the down-at-the-heels jockey Tim Vail lets Sally and Abigail know that Abigail's horse, called Cold Molasses, is a real racing animal and that the big race at the upcoming county fair has a purse of $3,000, the conditions are right to turn the tables on the villains. But first the Hammerheads employ one more trick to insure that their own horse, Lightning, takes the prize. Though the villains' horse "wins" the big prize, it is disqualified when it is discovered that they used illegal means to get their horse to run faster. Tourneur's novel ending and the efforts of the entire cast have "made real entertainment of this," wrote *Film Daily*.

Moving Picture World made mention of the fact that "it is refreshing to note the absence of a 'wronged woman,' which so often forms a prominent part of pictures of this type." Extant.

The Great Redeemer (1920): House Peters (as the cowboy Dan Malloy) finds salvation in prison. Peters' performance was called the best of his screen career.

The Great Redeemer

(1920, Clarence Brown). Metro. Supervisor: Tourneur. Script: Jules Furthman and John Gilbert. Photography: Charles van Enger. Design: Floyd Mueller. With John Gilbert, Marjorie Daw, Joseph Singleton (murderer), Jack McDonald (sheriff), and House Peters (Dan Malloy).

From the story by H. H. Van Loan, this Western represents the directorial debut of Tourneur's longtime assistant, Clarence Brown. He worked under Tourneur's supervision, and their film was an artistic and commercial success, becoming the first Metro film ever to play on Broadway.

The central moment in this six-reel tale about redemption comes in prison. Dan Malloy, who is a cowboy with a wild and artistic bent, has been framed for a holdup by a ruthless sheriff in love with Dan's girlfriend. Dan is sentenced to prison for ten years. Languishing in jail, he draws a figure on the cell wall of another man once unjustly punished—Jesus—and the figure comes to life. Along with Dan, the brutal prison guards, a murderer about to be executed, and a priest are witnesses to the miracle. The whole order of the prisoners' lives is then changed.

The condemned man calmly walks to the scaffold. The jail becomes a site of pilgrimage. A petition to the governor by Dan's girlfriend frees the cowboy. And in the end, when Dan is about to exact vengeance on the man who framed him, a terrific storm rages. The heavens open up, and lightning strikes the sheriff dead.

That a man can enter prison to serve a long sentence and then be pardoned has rarely been shown more effectively, observed the *New York Times*. "In some respects it is an exceptional picture," wrote the *Times*. Several "scenes come near to being inspired. For the things in it that are good, chief credit must go to Mr. Tourneur. His skill is in making moving pictures tell his story." Brown, the players, and the cameraman were praised for their work on the critical scene of the miracle, making it "almost faultless, as it must be to save the scene from banality." An insert read, "Is it true, or not? What does it matter?" which reportedly moved audiences.

Variety found that "the story is told so simply, directly, and with such economy of means as to draw the more discriminating applause.... The prison life is depicted with a faithful realism that makes you shudder." *Harrison's Reports*, however, differed in its appraisal: "Blasphemy against God and Christ and miracles commingle with sex."

While Paris Sleeps

(1920). Hodkinson. Script: Wyndham Gittens. Photography: René Guissart. With Lon Chaney (Henri Santados), Mildred

House Peters, the leading man in Tourneur's *The Hand of Peril* (1916), *The Closed Road* (1916), *The Velvet Paw* (1916), and *The Rail Rider* (1916), is shown here in a publicity shot that identified him as "The virile hero" of *The Great Redeemer*, directed by Clarence Brown under Tourneur's supervision.

Manning (Bebe Larvache), John Gilbert (Dennis O'Keefe), and Jack McDonald (Father Marionette).

Adapted from Basil Woon's disturbing story "The Glory of Love," Tourneur's atmospheric, suggestive, one-hour (five-reel) film harkens back (but with less shock) to his formative time in Paris and to the kind of Grand-Guignol tale he relished bringing to the screen at the start of his career. But unlike his earlier silent and later sound work in France, it is more in the mood than in explicit action that the

While Paris Sleeps (1920): In this Grand-Guignol tale released two years after its completion, Lon Chaney (as the sculptor Henri Santados) is in love with the indifferent model Mildred Manning (as Bebe Larvache).

suggestion of unwholesomeness lies. This slight, atmospheric story ends happily for American audiences.

It's the tale of Henri Santados, a sculptor living in the Latin Quarter of Paris. He harbors undeclared love for his beautiful model, Bebe, but she cares nothing for him. She falls for Dennis O'Keefe, a wealthy young American on tour. Santados becomes insanely jealous, and to get his way, he makes a deal with the half-demented "Father Marionette," owner of a wax museum called "The Chamber of Horrors." They agree to a plot: In order for Santados to be rid of the rival American so that he can get the girl, Marionette will take the American off his hands by subjecting him to his "chamber."

The unsuspecting American is lured into the "Cave of Death"—half of the action takes place there—which contains "diabolical torture contrivances." He is about to be electrocuted when Santados is overcome with remorse at his participation in such a scheme. He saves the American, who then marries the girl he loves.

The film, which contains scenes of the Mardi Gras, "is an unusually attractive production," wrote *Moving Picture World*. Tourneur "has invested it with distinctive settings and skillful photography. The streets of Paris have been produced with fascinating effect, showing picturesque architectural designs and an appreciation of perspective." This appealing investiture, however, it was predicted by the trade publication, "is more certain to please than is the theme. The story is ... gruesome and exaggerated, although similar ideas have been used before in successful dramas. There are no doubt a considerable number of patrons who are fascinated by a strain of morbidity. For this class, the picture will provide thrilling entertainment."

Harrison's Reports, too, observed that the "settings, whose reproductions of the French Quarter are correct to the smallest detail, are worthy of note.... The French atmosphere ... may appeal to a certain type of picturegoer."

Though not released until January 1923, the film was a hit for Chaney. "He is better in this picture," wrote *Variety*, "than he has been in some of his more recent efforts." And for those who were familiar with New York, the film's "wax museum" brought to mind the Eden Museum with its famous chamber of horrors.

Treasure Island

(1920). Tourneur-Paramount. Script: Jules Furthman. Photography: René Guissart. Art Director: Floyd Mueller. With Shirley Mason (Jim Hawkins), Lon Chaney (Pew/Merry), Charles Ogle (Long John Silver), Sydney Dean (Squire Trelawney), Charles Hill Mailes (Dr. Livesey), Josie Melville (Mrs. Hawkins), Al Filson (Bill Bones), Wilton Taylor (Black Dog), Joseph Singleton (Israel Hands), Bull Montana (Morgan), and Harry Holden (Capt. Smollett).

Maurice Tourneur, in a mysterious guise.

This film was apparently the first pirate film, a whimsical rendition of Stevenson's classic. Despite opposition, Tourneur followed the approach in the stage adaptation by casting a female in the role of the protagonist Jim Hawkins. Tourneur's film turned out to be one of the most successful films in his career in America, coming in as one of the top box-office productions of the year.

The story begins when Bill Bones shows up at the Admiral Benbow Inn, on England's west coast, which is run by poor Mrs. Hawkins. The wealthy Bones, a man with plenty of gold to spend — in fact, he's the only paying customer in the place — begins to spin some blood-curdling yarns about desperate deeds on the Spanish Main. "A Tale Untold of This Pirate Bold. He Held Them Under His Spell," says the caption. After Bones alludes to "Fifteen men on a dead man's chest," Mrs. Hawkins suspects that this man has sailed under a pirate's flag. When the pirate Black Dog, one of Bones' old shipmates, arrives, Jim finds out the real identity of Bill Bones, who has stolen a map to a buried treasure. Bones drives away Black Dog, but it's another matter when the notorious, blind pirate Pew sets foot in the inn. "I never saw in my life a more dreadful figure," says Jim Hawkins. Pew seals Bill Bones' fate. Stabbed to death by Pew, Bones dies, however, without revealing the secret of the map.

Further, the old pirate has not paid his bill. When Jim and his mother go through his chest, they come across the priceless map, which details the whereabouts of the buried treasure of the notorious Capt. Flint, now fortunately dead. Jim gives the map to Squire Trelawney and Dr. Livesey, who secure a ship and hire a crew to find the lost loot. Jim, however, not to be left behind, stows away on the ship, the Jolly Roger, whose cook is the much admired, one-legged pirate, Long John Silver.

The night before reaching the island, Jim Hawkins overhears something terrible: the crew is planning to mutiny and kill the squire and the doctor. Jim then realizes that the hired crew, including Long John Silver, had sailed with none other than the infamous Capt. Flint. Jim warns his friends, who manage to fend off the pirates until they reach the island and find shelter.

Even safely ashore, however, things continue to go badly: Jim, his companions, and a few of the loyal crewmembers have to fight a number of battles against the vicious mutineers. They even lose the map. Jim meets Ben Gunn, a former pirate, now reformed, who helps them in their quest. In the course of the fighting, Long John Silver changes allegiance and Ben Gunn appears to have been killed. When the survivors locate the purported site of the treasure, they dig up an empty chest.

Then Ben Gunn reappears, and reveals a secret: He had dug up the treasure and hidden it elsewhere on the island. The party of four recovers it, takes it to the ship, and sets sail. Of all the crew that sailed with them, only a few now remain alive, and they are left on the island. The following morning Long John Silver disappears — along with some of the treasure. He is never heard of again. Ben Gunn becomes a respectable citizen, and Jim Hawkins, who had found the map and been the catalyst of the frightful expedition, vows never to go hunting treasure again. But he has made sure his mother will never be in need of anything for as long as she lives.

"The story is improbable — but who cares," wrote *Exhibitor's Trade Review*. "It has action and it has thrills but above all it represents characters that are fictionally historical. The scenes are laid out in the atmosphere of the book itself. The water scenes are especially worthy of every praise. The fight scenes, the old boat 'Hispaniola,' and last but not least the type of selections, have all been combined with a capital filmization."

"No director has outclassed Maurice Tourneur as a producer of seafaring adventures and his sailor men and their

Treasure Island (1920): Shirley Mason (as Jim Hawkins) is in the clutches of a pirate in Tourneur's early adaptation of Stevenson's classic.

goodly ships would pass inspection before the briniest old salt that ever helped man the main brace," said *Moving Picture World*. This "wonderfully photographed and effectively acted" screen adaptation of Stevenson's classic adventure contains swift movement and sharp action right from the first scene. "There's always something doing," wrote another critic, while "the choice of locations, lighting effects and attention to detail are so expertly attended to as to leave all but those on the lookout unable to guess just what it is they miss." In addition, if the "sons of hell" who roamed the Spanish Main as pirates aboard the "Hispaniola" resembled the cast, "let us be duly grateful they caught Captain Kidd and his crew and hanged them," pointed out the reviewers.

Vivid, disturbing scenes in the six-reeler include "Two pirates in a death struggle with the thumb of one slowly gouging out the eyeball of his mate," wrote the critics, "two gentlemen of fortune killing a third before a deep blue background, and racing down to the sea waving their blood-stained cutlasses. And last a whole ship's company dangling in the

The White Circle (1920): John Gilbert (as Frank Cassilis), Janice Wilson (as Clara Huddlestone), Harry Northrup (as Northmour) in the tale of vengeance and rediscovered love.

wind from the yards of their vessel — black bundles against a vivid blue sky.... A buccaneer is pinned to the cabin door by a knife through his chest, and there he hangs stiff and dead with the blood spot widening on the door behind him."

"In order to visualize the outstanding details," wrote *Motion Picture News*, the scenarist has taken liberties with Stevenson and he may be excused upon the ground that even the screen has its limitations.... Charles Ogle is immense as the peg-legged John Silver and Lon Chaney gives another of his vivid character studies as one of the pirate cutthroats or two."

The White Circle

(1920). Tourneur-Paramount. Script: Jules Furthman and John Gilbert. Photography: Alfred Ortlieb and Charles Rosher. Design: Floyd Mueller. With John Gilbert (Frank Cassilis), Spottiswoode Aitken (Bernard Huddlestone), Janice Wilson (Clara Huddlestone), Harry Northrup (Northmour), Violet Rose, and Jack McDonald.

Turning again to a story from the pen of Robert Louis Stevenson, the evocative and descriptive "The Pavilion on the Links," written in 1879, Tourneur made a fascinating five-reel (4,000-ft) thriller that contains hints of a ghost story.

As a film that cried out for atmosphere, it had the *New York Times* noting that the director "has a special liking ... for the mechanics of picture making. He uses the tricks of the camera and the mechanism of photoplay to produce startling results, momentary thrills, and sudden spurts of interest." That included scenes that could be tinted or toned through a bit of creative lighting: a central area of light often illuminates everything except the outside edges of frames, which remain much darker.

Co-scriptwriter John Gilbert, a favorite of Tourneur's, "had never been so happy," he said. "Working eighteen hours a day — writing, codirecting, titling, cutting, and, least of all, acting. Glorious work! ... I had become, in Tourneur's own words, his right hand."

The story Gilbert scripted is set in 1860, in England and on the harsh coast of Scotland. On the surface the plot deals with the vengeance of the Carbonari, or the White Circle, a secret Italian society fighting for Garibaldi and the liberation of Italy. They are after the frightened old London banker Bernard Huddlestone. As treasurer of the White Circle, he has embezzled its funds. The old man is now on the run, accompanied by his daughter, Clara, and a longtime friend and accomplice, the adventure-seeker Northmour. Northmour is quick-tempered, handsome, and repulsive.

John Gilbert, Tourneur's longtime assistant and cast member, shown in the early 1920s.

Then the plot deepens. On the move and just ahead of their pursuers, Huddlestone and his beautiful daughter Clara (played by the expressive Janice Wilson) seek shelter in Northmour's home in Graden-Easter, in Scotland. There, in the northern part of the estate, in a wilderness of links and blowing sandhills, and between a plantation and the sea, stands a small pavilion or belvedere, of modern Italian design, which suits their needs. In this hermitage they find shelter.

Deep Waters (1920): Left to right: John Gilbert (as Bill Lacey), Broerken Christians (as Caleb West), and Barbara Bedford (as Caleb's young wife, Betty West) in a lovers' triangle

No thoroughfare passes within three miles of the place; the nearest town, and that is but a fishing village, is six or seven miles away. For ten miles and a width varying from three miles to half a mile, this belt of barren country lies along the sea. The beach, the natural approach, is full of quicksand. Indeed, notes Huddlestone, there is hardly a better place of concealment in the United Kingdom.

But there is one condition that Northmour imposes on his guests: Clara must agree to marry him. Father and daughter are in no position to refuse this bargain which offers salvation for the frightened old man, if also despair for Clara. Then matters become more complicated when Northmour encounters an old adversary, Cassilis. He, too, is in love with Clara.

Bernard Huddlestone, though physically safe for the moment, has already died a thousand deaths, through terrifying and ghostlike visions. These imaginings are shown coming to life. Finally, Huddlestone gets up the courage to face his stalkers, who have tracked the party down. Huddlestone is shot to death by the killers. At that moment Northmour has the chance to shoot Cassilis, but he hesitates. He sees himself married—according to the bargain he demanded that Clara accept—and suddenly senses that his spirit for adventure would be diminished if not suppressed completely. He departs, leaving Clara and Cassilis in each other's arms.

Stevenson, the paper noted, "is melodramatic enough and Mr. Tourneur has never been moderate in this respect; therefore, when Mr. Tourneur translates a work of Stevenson into moving pictures, the public may expect swift melodrama."

Deep Waters

(1920). Tourneur-Paramount. Script: John Gilbert. Photography: Alfred Ortlieb and Homer Scott. Design: Floyd Mueller. With Broerken Christians (Caleb West), John Gilbert (Bill Lacey), Barbara Bedford (Betty West), Henry Woodward (Henry Sanford), Florence Deshon (Kate Leroy), and Jack McDonald (Morgan Leroy).

From the 1899 novel (and later stage play) about harsh seaport life, called *Caleb West, Master Diver*, by Hopkinson Smith, Tourneur directed a five-reel (5,000-ft), "double narrative" love story about the emotional conflicts faced by two married women. Each is in love with another man and each must make difficult choices.

Elderly Caleb West, a master diver at the lighthouse in Keyport, in New England, has a pretty young wife. She becomes attracted to, and runs away with, Bill Lacey, a handsome young crewmember of her husband's team, who professes his love for her. But Betty West soon realizes

Director Tourneur getting ready to descend under the sea to select locations for his tale of lovers in conflict, *Deep Waters* (1920).

her rash mistake—it was all a ruse—and returns to the husband she knows she loves. When tragedy strikes, Caleb West, though heartbroken at the turn of events, puts pride aside to try to save the life of the man who nearly destroyed his marriage. Caleb manages to bring Lacey's body up after a shipwreck and learns that his wife worked the air pumps that insured his own survival.

"The screen version," wrote *Moving Picture World*, "permits the showing of the master diver's splendid character when he goes down to the sunken ship and brings

Hope Hampton, the star of Tourneur's tale of entrapment, *The Bait* (1920).

to the surface the young man without whom he thinks his wife can never be happy."

The other woman in the tale is the wealthy and attractive Kate Leroy, who has caught the attention of Henry Sanford, a contractor of a lighthouse. She profits by her friend's experience: to save her marriage, she breaks with her lover. At the end, she and her husband "come to an understanding."

Tourneur "is noted for the skills with which he produces marine scenes," wrote the trade journal, "and he has not let any of the opportunities ... for realistic atmosphere escape him. The dramatic tone of the story is held down to conform with the nature of the New England character, but is nonetheless real. The men and women of the seaport behold the soul of a strong man rent and torn by love and pride and see his just reward when he puts his wife's happiness before his own grief and pain."

Exhibitor's Trade Review noted that Tourneur's film "is not a great picture, but does not lack emotional interest or sympathetic appeal, and like all Tourneur productions possesses considerable value from an artistic standpoint." His directorial skill at continuity "avoided any break in the action and its interest holds to the finish."

The Bait

(1920). Tourneur-Paramount. Script: John Gilbert. Photography: Alfred Ortlieb. With Hope Hampton (Joan Granger), Harry Woodward (John Warren), Jack McDonald (Bennett Barton), James Gordon (John Garson), Rae Ebberly (Dolly), Joseph Singleton (Simpson), Poupée Andriot (Madeline), and Dan Crimmins (Jimmy).

Adapted from the intricate play *The Tiger Lady*, by Sidney Toler, this is a five-reel (5300-ft) underworld drama of intrigue that is told entirely in flashback. The story begins when a beautiful saleswoman must explain why she was found at the scene of a murder. Further, if she isn't the killer, who is? Her tale hinges on the fact that she has been used as bait by a devious gang leader.

Beginning at the beginning, Joan Granger relates how she came to be a member of a gang whose leader, named Barton, has used her for his own purposes. First he frames her for theft. Then, after she is tried and convicted, she is abducted by the man who set her up. Barton sends her out of the country, to Paris, where Joan imagines things will be different. But she quickly discovers that her apparent protector has other plans.

He is a blackmailer who wants to use her in a devious scheme to make a fortune by having her marry a wealthy American, John Warren. Joan meets the American when he saves her from a runaway tiger at the Folies Bergère. But Joan refuses to go along with the duplicitous plan, even though she is in love with John Warren. Fleeing to America, she seeks the help of a gambler named Simpson to extricate herself from the gang—and this leads to the mysterious murder of the crime boss.

In the end, after it is revealed that it was Simpson who killed Barton, "Warren is willing to have Joan despite all and they are happy," wrote *Film Daily*. "The picture arrests your attention the moment it starts," wrote *Variety*. "The direction is painstaking and artistic, the photography is exceptionally clear, and Miss Hampton's support competent to the point of brilliancy."

"Tourneur's artistic judgment," wrote *Exhibitor's Trade Review*," is made manifest by the abundance of colorful atmosphere, rapid action and well-sustained continuity."

The Last of the Mohicans (1920): Harry Lorraine (as Hawkeye) and Alan Roscoe (as Uncas) protect Barbara Bedford (as Cora Munro) and Lillian Hall (as Alice Munro) from a fierce-looking Wallace Beery (as Magua), in Tourneur's greatest silent film.

The Last of the Mohicans

(1920, Tourneur and Clarence Brown). Associated-First National. Script: Robert A. Dillon. Design: Floyd Mueller. Photography: Philip R. Dubois and Charles van Enger. With Boris Karloff (Indian), Theodore Lorch (Chingachgook), Harry Lorraine (Hawkeye), Alan Roscoe (Uncas), Jack McDonald (Tamenund), Nelson McDowell (David Gamut), Henry Woodward (Major Heyward), Barbara Bedford (Cora Munro), Wallace Beery (Magua), Lillian Hall (Alice Munro), Sydney Deane (General Webb), and George Hackathorne (Captain Randolph).

Tourneur and Brown's acclaimed six-reel rendition of James Fenimore Cooper's famous tale is probably the best known and greatest film of Tourneur's American career. A nonstop thriller with the number of titles kept to a minimum, the film, which is set during the French and Indian War, is also one of the most brutal of the period.

"It was a feature peculiar to the colonial wars of North America," begins the tale, "that the toils and dangers of the wilderness were to be encountered before the adverse hosts could meet." Dark-haired Cora Munro and her blonde sister Alice are on their way to Fort William Henry, which is under the command of their father. Their attempt to reach their father leads to disaster.

They are being guided by the renegade Huron Indian Magua, who is in league with the French. The women are taken prisoner by the Indians. Chingachgook and his son Uncas, the last of the Mohican tribe, and their ally, the frontiersman Natty Bumppo, known as Hawkeye, make strenuous efforts to rescue them. The heart of the story is the unfolding and tragic love affair between Uncas and Cora Munro, another example of Tourneur's sense of the ultimate impossibility of love between people of different cultures.

Just as the party, which has eluded the French and the Indians, comes within sight of the fort, Colonel Munro surrenders the fort to the French and their Indian allies. A terrible massacre ensues, during which Magua once more captures Cora and Alice. Uncas' attempt to rescue Cora leads to his death as well as Cora's.

Barbara Bedford, the star of Tourneur's most acclaimed American film, *The Last of the Mohicans* (1920).

The excellently photographed tale, which includes shots of people in silhouette, came from the efforts of assistant director Brown, who shot the great, natural outdoor scenes according to Tourneur's instructions. But they made a disturbing thriller, one of the bloodiest of the era. Rather than live with the death of Uncas and the depredations that await her, Cora Munro, the young heroine, kills herself. She slashes her wrists before jumping off a cliff into the churning waters below.

For the Fort William Henry massacre scene, Tourneur and Brown filled the screen with blood, showing mothers murdered and infants tomahawked. And for Magua's death scenes, they had him stabbed, thrown from a cliff into the rapids, and sent over a waterfall "more than a thousand feet high." In the book, Hawkeye merely shoots him.

"We knew Tourneur would not fail with this production — that every detail would be complete — that the expert photography and tinting and suggestive backgrounds would be evident throughout," wrote *Motion Picture Herald*. "There are moments that are simply breathtaking and the suspense of the book becomes overwhelmingly acute.... The action moves against marvelous backgrounds — backgrounds which are rather awe-inspiring, and give one an eery feeling.... There is not a false touch in the picture.... The camera work is exceptionally good. It's the greatest Indian picture ever shown."

The *National Board of Review* noted that the film's

> composition ... is superb. It ranges in almost exact impression from that of the color sketches of Remington to that of the drawings of Doré. Here are color, tone, line, sky, cliff, forest and human figures at their most impressive in motion-photography. It is the forerunner of that impressionism which the future of the motion picture holds perhaps beyond that of all other arts.... Mr Tourneur's shots ... are dramatic in themselves, his lights and shadows strike back on the nerves and make pictures beyond the picture on the screen, create moods and bring the onlooker into understanding with the feeling of the actors in the given situation of which the composition of the picture is an analysis in terms of line, light and shadow.

Robert E. Sherwood, writing for *Life*, pointed out that the loose adaptation "had little effect upon our enjoyment of the picture. We could not help feeling, a trifle timidly, perhaps, that the mauling process had rather tended to improve the original; but of course we wouldn't want to say that out loud." The drama was added to the American Film Institute's National Film Registry in 1995. Extant.

Foolish Matrons

(1921, Tourneur and Clarence Brown). Associated–First National. Script: Wyndham Gittens. Photography: Charles van Enger. With Kathleen Kirkham (Annis Grand), Hobart Bosworth (Dr. Ian Fraser), Mildred Manning (Sheila Hopkins), Wallace MacDonald (Anthony Sheridan), Doris May (Georgia Wayne), Charles Meredith (Lafayette Wayne), Betty Schade (mystery woman), Margaret McWade (Mrs. Eugenia Sheridan), Michael Dark (Chester King), and Frankie Lee (Bobby).

Based on the best seller of the same name by Brian Donn Byrne, Tourneur directed an overt message film about the destructive powers of ambition and the redemptive powers of love, which can be read as partly autobiographical.

In the eighty-minute (six-reel) film that deals with the need to create a nurturing home life (for husbands), Tourneur developed the theme into three stories that run parallel. For the most part, the locale for the stories is fast-paced Broadway, an area with which he became familiar in his earliest years in America.

The first episode of the trilogy deals with the successful actress Annis Grand, who meets and then marries a physician. In order, as she has told others, to "make some man happy," she unhesitatingly forsakes her ambition and her career to become a devoted wife. Showing her man a great deal of love and self-effacement, she rejuvenates the world-weary doctor and turns their home life into something approaching contentment.

The second tale deals with a different kind of woman. Young Georgia Wayne, who holds no job, induces her husband, a lawyer, to leave their southern home for the more thrilling possibilities in New York. There he obtains a well-paid position. Georgia then begins spending their money, and soon her extravagance leads her into trouble — other men. She has an affair. When her husband finds out, he leaves her in New York and returns to the South. The young woman gains a reputation as a "man's plaything." This episode, wrote *Variety*, "is so handled as to hold interest."

In the final episode, New York newspaperwoman Sheila Hopkins is very anxious over the fact that she hasn't married. When she meets the unassuming Anthony Sheridan — he is a poet by nature who has grown up in small-town America — she quickly marries him — but under one condition: that she will continue her career. Lonely most of the time, her sensitive husband is uncomfortable with the pace of life in the city. He turns to drink and then returns to his family in the country. A beautifully filmed montage signals his death from a broken heart.

The film's exceptional cinematography, wrote the *National Board of Review*

> has been used with masterly skill to tell a story that needed masterly treatment to save it from being merely an illustrated novel.... The weaving together of the three strands is remarkably well managed, as a matter both of continuity and writing and direction. The whole thing is in the nature of a tour de force for Mr. Tourneur, for it is not at all the kind of thing his fame as a director has been built on.... It is what might be called a problem picture, and the problem is no less a one than marriage: why is it a success or a failure — the sort of thing one would expect, done in a different way, from von Stroheim or DeMille.

"Seldom has a film translation of a novel adhered so faithfully to the original," wrote *Moving Picture World*. The disintegration of the two young couples whose unions involve ambition and living the good life is the more vividly portrayed, wrote the trade publication.

During this period of his career, Tourneur's own marriage to an actress was on the ropes. He had married in 1904, and would separate from his wife — and leave Hollywood — in 1926. The seeds of his marital difficulties were apparent by the early 1920s when he was also struggling, despite earlier success, to keep his head above water in Hollywood. Extant.

Lorna Doone

(1922, Tourneur and Robert Thornby). Ince-First National. Script: Wyndham Gittens, Katherine Reed, and Cecil Mumford. Photography: Henry Sharp. Design: Milton Menasco. With Madge Bellamy (Lorna Doone), John Bowers (John Ridd), May Giracci, Charles Hatton, Norris Johnson (Ruth), Frank Keenan (Sir Charles Ensor Doone), Donald MacDonald (Carver Doone), and Jack McDonald (Counsellor Doone).

This eight-reel (seventy-two-minute) historical romantic drama is based on the vivid, classic, and sweeping (75 chapters long) 1869 novel by Scotsman Richard Doddridge Blackmore (1825–1900). The film had the critics saying, "Maurice Tourneur again comes to the front as a maker of motion pictures." It's a wonderful tale of a waif coming to adulthood and finding love in an unlikely setting, in late Restoration England.

In the beginning, in the rough times of James II in 1673, the carriage in which the young Lorna, a child of noble birth and the King's ward, and her mother, a countess, are riding is traveling on a lonely road in Exmoor, in England's West Country. The carriage is suddenly set upon by raiders, led by the infamous Sir Charles

Lorna Doone (1922): Madge Bellamy (as Lorna Doone) is the waif, Donald MacDonald (as Carver Doone) her nemesis, and Frank Keenan (Ensor Doone) in Tourneur's historical thriller.

Ensor Doone. The young girl is seized and kidnapped by the outlaws. Her mother is thrown to the ground stretching out her arms helplessly, reaching for her child, her partly raised figure reflected brokenly in the glistening wet sand on which she lies. Then there is a flash of the carriage, abandoned by horses and men, sitting hub-deep in water, the waves licking the decorated sides and soaking the soft cushions.

With a keen eye for effect, crisp shots in soft tones, intricate and elaborate set designs, and striking contrasts—all linked by a tight-knit story—Tourneur brought the romantic, sentimental tale to life, while also sticking closely to the details of one of the most famous stories of its day.

Years pass during which Sir Ensor, the leader of the outlaw family and its estates—he is a man obeyed and feared by those around him—comes to feel affection for the girl. Lorna, now a beautiful 18-year-old maiden, has been made a part of Sir Ensor's family. One of his men, however, is intent on marrying Lorna Doone, and that is her eldest cousin, Carver Doone, who is Ensor's nephew and the son of the Counsellor to the family. Carver is described as "being very hot and savage, and quite free from argument" with a smile that is "truly a frightful thing."

Both he and his crafty father are for forcing the marriage, but Sir Ensor will not hear of it. They hold off extreme measures until Sir Ensor is past knowing or, at least, beyond preventing them. Lorna is watched, spied upon, and followed, her liberty lost. Ensor Doone dies after ruling his band for more than forty years, leaving Lorna to her fate. As the wife of the 35-year-old Carver Doone, it would be a fate which the girl knows is worse than death. Lorna is not taken in by the vile man's professions of love.

She is eventually saved from the clutches of the new leader of Doones by the handsome young yeoman John Ridd, whose own family has suffered at the hands of the bandits: Ridd's father was murdered by Carver Doone. Lorna's rescuer, who kills Carver Doone in a valiant struggle in a bog, is the kind of man heroines dream of: a man of strength, force, and vigor (like his own father) who has a gift for picturesque attitudes and for uttering irreproachable sentiments largely in blank verse.

Here is how John Ridd describes their first meeting:

> Here was I, a yeoman's boy, a yeoman every inch of me, even where I was naked; and there was she, a lady born, and thoroughly aware of it, and dressed by people of rank and taste, who took pride in her beauty and set it to advantage. For though her hair was fallen down by reason of her wildness, and some of her frock was touched with wet where she had tended me so, behold her dress was pretty enough for the queen of all the angels. The colors were bright and rich indeed, and the substance very sumptuous, yet simple and free from tinsel stuff, and matching most harmoniously. All from her waist to her neck was white, plaited in close like a curtain, and the dark soft weeping of her hair, and the shadowy light of her eyes (like a wood rayed through with sunset), made it seem yet whiter, as if it were done on purpose. As for the rest, she knew what it was a great deal better than I did, for I never could look far away from her eyes when they were opened upon me.

The revelation of her birth into one of the oldest families in Northern Europe takes Lorna back to the court. But near the end, Lorna's great and growing love for John Ridd leads the heroine to do the only thing she can: to renounce her title and follow the dictates of her heart. Ridd and Lorna marry. John Ridd can only thank his lucky stars for his good fortune:

> Of Lorna, of my lifelong darling, of my more and more loved wife, I will not talk; for it is not seemly that a man should exalt his pride. Year by year her beauty grows, with the growth of goodness, kindness, and true happiness—above all with loving. For change, she makes a joke of this, and plays with it, and laughs at it; and then, when my slow nature marvels, back she comes to the earnest thing. And if I wish to pay her out for something very dreadful—as may happen once or twice, when we become too gladsome—I bring her to forgotten sadness, and to me for cure of it, by the two words "Lorna Doone."

Exhibitor's Trade Review called the love story "a tender and graceful idyl," and the film an "intensely realistic production, vibrating with action, pulsating with colorful atmosphere." Containing picturesque exteriors, including a wild, rugged moor, the Bagworthy Valley, and the cave where the Doones have their lair, the stirring tale "catches the popular fancy by its spectacular lure.... The hero's rescue of Lorna from the Doones ... is an affray so full of whirling action that it dazzles one's eyes.... Exquisite lighting effects govern the entire production."

Tourneur's picture, concluded *Harri-*

The Christian (1923): Richard Dix (as John Storm) and Mae Busch (as Glory Quayle) in the tale of obsession, passion, and death.

son's Reports, "should give far better satisfaction than pictures made of similar quality that are based on an original scenario; people become fascinated in seeing the characters of a book they love take flesh and blood, and in going over situations they have visualized." Extant.

The Christian

(1923). A.P.R.-Goldwyn. Script: Paul Bern and Wyndham Gittens. Photography: Charles van Enger. Design: Hugo Ballin. With Richard Dix (John Storm), Mae Busch (Glory Quayle), Gareth Hughes (Brother Paul), Phyllis Haver (Polly Love), Cyril Chadwick (Lord Robert Ure), Mahlon Hamilton (Horatio Drake), Joseph J. Dowling (Father Lampleigh), Claude Gillingwater (Lord Storm), John Herdman (Parson Quayle), Beryl Mercer (Liza), Robert Bolder (Reverend Golightly), Milla Davenport, Alice Hesse, Aileen Pringle, and Harry Northrup.

After making the British-based *Lorna Doone*, Tourneur took off for Britain itself for his next film. Based on the popular late-19th-century novel and play by Thomas Henry Hall Caine (1853–1931), Tourneur's 120-minute (8,333-ft) powerful, sweeping drama wowed the critics.

"Here is a picture!" raved *Variety*. "A real picture with a corking story, a great cast and finely produced." The *New York Times* noted that "every one who has followed Mr. Tourneur's work knows that he can make moving pictures that make you open your eyes and look at them. He has done it in this film. Some of the scenes are beautiful. Others are so sharply significant, or so teeming with headlong action, that they break down all resistances."

The intensely emotional story was shot where it takes place in the novel, on the Isle of Man in the Irish Sea, in London, and at Epsom Downs, where the Derby provides a thrilling background for the dramatic action. It is a tale of over-the-top passionate love. The Episcopal minister John Storm is in love with the worldly actress Glory Quayle. Renouncing his vows of celibacy and abandoning his monastery on the Isle of Man, he founds a mission for the homeless and downtrodden in London and goes in search of the woman who was his sweetheart in childhood. Accused of predicting the end of the world, John Storm is stoned and beaten by a nighttime mob at Trafalgar Square. Glory takes him to the mission, and he dies after they wed.

The conflicted minister makes every effort to reject the world, the flesh, and the devil, but is drawn back by his passion for a woman of the world. Glory initially rejects his offer of marriage and a life of poverty and preaching. Instead she works as a nurse, and then becomes a music hall singer in London. Later, however, after John, in an outburst of jealousy, tries to kill her, she throws away her champagne and flowers to join him in his missionary work. She has fallen prey to guilt.

The "meaning" of the story is perfectly clear: The world of the flesh is sinful; the spirit triumphs over all; those who seek pleasure in this life are doomed.

Despite the critical commentary that, in matters of religion and morals, it is a safe world within this conservative, orthodox, Hollywood-backed film, reviewers hailed Tourneur's realistic effort as an unusually stirring melodrama and great entertainment that need not be approved, applied in life, or make viewers uncomfortable. Tourneur's film, wrote *Exhibitor's Trade Review*, "is one of the few great pictures of the screen.... It will prove one of the biggest box-office attractions in the history of the industry ... acclaimed as a masterpiece.... Dix gives a performance which lands him in the actor's hall of fame."

After completing the smash film, Tourneur concluded that "it is no more expensive to take a company abroad than it is to keep it at home and build extravagant sets that are mere imitations of the European originals." But the next time he went to Europe, it would be for good.

The Isle of Lost Ships

(1923). Levee-First National. Script: Charles Maigne and Wyndham Gittens. Photography: Arthur Todd. Design: Milton Menasco. With Anna Q. Nilsson (Dorothy Fairfax), Milton Sills (Frank Howard), Frank Campeau (Detective Jackson), Herschel Mayall (Capt. Clark), Walter Long, and Bert Woodruff.

A stirring and thought-provoking drama of seafarers trapped in an inhospitable sea — the Sargasso Sea, in fact — representing life's pushes and pulls, this eight-reeler is based on the little known novel by Crittenden Marriott. *Harrison's Reports* called Tourneur's tale "different ... realistic in the extreme."

It begins on the coast of Mexico, where Detective Jackson — a Rouletabille-type — apprehends Frank Howard, a fugitive from justice who has been convicted of a crime he didn't commit. The detective

The Isle of Lost Ships (1923): Anna Q. Nilsson (as Dorothy Fairfax) comforts Milton Sills (as Frank Howard) in a melodrama of lost souls at sea.

puts him aboard the ship *Queen*, bound for New York. Also on board is the beautiful and wealthy Dorothy Fairfax. They set sail into disaster.

According to legend, there is a mysterious place where derelict vessels are taken by ocean currents to become trapped in a sort of island of ships. A storm sends their ship into this very location: a "maw of islands of seaweed" in which their ship becomes clamped alongside other wrecks. There Howard and Fairfax meet the brutal Capt. Clark, who presides over the trapped colony — and who has been trapped long enough. He has gotten a good look at Miss Fairfax, is more than ready to do anything to get out, and now sees his chance. The only escape for Howard and Fairfax is by submarine.

From the opening scene, which carries the promise of action and adventure, to the final embrace of the lovers, Tourneur's film is a lavish example of his directorial ability. When Tourneur, wrote *Exhibitor's Trade Review*, "determines upon equal accents for the pictorial, the action, the characters, and the plot ... the public is sure to receive an entertainment that is rich with all the elements making up photoplay diversion.... Tourneur gives the spectator scenes which fairly reek with the tang of the sea. Nothing finer has ever been

The Brass Bottle (1923): A stylish mixture of magic, the exotic, romance, comedy, and a genie (right, played by Ernest Torrence) comprises Tourneur's fantasy.

done with the motion picture camera than these scenes of a voyage over heaving waters." His scenes in the isle of lost ships were called "equally brilliant in their settings and atmospheric content."

The film "possesses a highly imaginative plot," wrote the *New York Times*, and "has all the earmarks of good direction and considerable attention to detail.... The production holds one from the opening scene to the last few feet" of footage. "Tourneur's spark is obvious throughout the photoplay and ... scenes of the storm at sea are as good as any if not better than have been put in other pictures."

The *Times* concluded, "It is a picture that is a glorious relief after some of the recent [May 1923] displays on Broadway."

The Brass Bottle

(1923). Levee–First National. Script: Fred Myton. Photography: Arthur Todd. Design: Milton Menasco. With Harry Myers (Horace Ventimore), Ernest Torrence (Fakresh-el-Aamash), Charlotte Merriam (Marjorie Hamilton), Tully Marshall (Prof. Hamilton), Clarissa Selwynne (Mrs. Hamilton), Ford Sterling (Rapkin), Aggie Herring (Mrs. Rapkin), Edward Jobson (Samuel Wackerbath), Barbara

Harry Myers (as Horace Ventimore) and Charlotte Merriam (as Marjorie Hamilton) face a mob after rumors of a genie spread, in *The Brass Bottle* (1923).

La Marr (the Queen), Otis Harlan, and Julianne Johnston.

Tourneur's original, fantastic tale, akin to *Aladdin's Lamp*, is a stylish mix of magic, romance, and fun, and is perhaps the best comedy of his career in silents. The script is based on a 1909 four-act play by the British dramatist F. M. Anstey that was called "the best farce seen in London for many a day." The owner of the transatlantic rights, wrote an observer, "will have gained ... a gold mine."

The same could be said for the film adaptation. It is, said the *New York Times*, "a film which one can anticipate seeing with a great deal of pleasure." It stars the wacky Harry Myers, who had the lead in the hit *A Connecticut Yankee in King Arthur's Court* (1922). In Tourneur's comedy he has a similarly offbeat role: He plays a hopeful but serious young London architect, who, in love with Marjorie Hamilton, is suddenly the owner of a marvelous but uncontrollable genie. With it, the architect may be able to win — through a series of ruses — the girl of his dreams.

The tale begins with a beautifully filmed prologue: More than 6,000 years ago, in the reign of King Solomon, a brigand plots to murder his royal master and carry away his wife, who is in love with him. The man is betrayed, caught, and condemned by King Solomon to be imprisoned forever in a brass bottle. The brass bottle is hurled into the sea.

Jump to contemporary England, where the struggling architect buys a seemingly innocent brass bottle as a gift for Prof. Hamilton, an antiques dealer whose daughter the young architect wishes to marry. But the professor is not a fan of the architect and declares the bottle spurious. When Horace throws it away in disgust, the bottle explodes — and out pops a genie. Horace's life changes forever — and not necessarily for the better. In fact, the hero's dealings with the genie, who insists upon showering him with gifts and benefits, bring only trouble in their wake.

Before the inevitable happy ending when Horace wins the girl of his dreams, the genie turns Horace's future father-in-law into a jackass. This happens after the wildest example of the genie's largess plays itself out. The genie (played by Ernest Torrence, one of the greatest "heavies" of the screen) turns the architect's humble home into an enormous Arabian palace — complete with Nubian slaves and dancing girls. This final, grand act of munificence forces Horace to demand that the genie get out of his life — actually, disappear — forever.

Tourneur "has done wonders in the way of diffusing the mystic spirit of the mysterious East through the picture and contrasting the land of shadows and demons with the practical, prosaic life of modern London," wrote *Exhibitor's Trade Review*. "The London night scenes are sterling examples of camera technique and the illusion of Fakresh emerging from the bottle in cloudy grandeur ranks as a rare bit of film trickery." The gleeful production, concurred the *Times*, "is entertainment with plenty of fun, calculated to make one forget the hot weather [July 1923] and business bothers."

Jealous Husbands

(1923). Levee–First National. Script: Fred Myton. Photography: Scott Beal. With Earle Williams (Ramón Martinez), Jane Novak (Alice Martinez), Ben Alexander (Bobbie), Don Marion (Sliver), George Siegmann ("Red" Lynch), Emily Fitzroy (Amaryllis), Bull Montana (the Portland Kid), J. Gunnis Davis (Charlie), Carl Miller (Harvey Clegg), Wedgwood Nowell (George Conrad), and Carmelita Geraghty (Carmen Inez).

A dramatic series of complications about an unwanted boy — a waif in effect — and subsequent events to reunite him with his parents make up the heart of this 6,500-ft (85-minute) psychological tale, which represents a change from Tourneur's earlier whimsical and imaginative themes. It is a painful film based on a story by Fred Myton about jealousy, the green-eyed monster whose mildest whiff can wreak havoc.

The tale begins on a desperate note: Alice makes an unplanned visit to help her sister-in-law, who is having marital problems. It seems that her sister-in-law and a former lover have had a child. Alice has gone to plead with the man to keep the fact of the birth a secret from the husband.

When Alice returns home, she arrives just as her husband, Ramón, returns from a trip to Europe. When Alice hesitates to explain where she's been, Ramón becomes suspicious of his wife. Then he comes across what he thinks is an even more incriminating piece of evidence: a letter that hints at his wife's unfaithfulness and something even more shocking. The letter he has read is, in fact, an anonymous letter to his own sister.

Jealous Husbands (1923): Earle Williams (as Ramón Martinez), Jane Novak (as Alice Martinez), and, far right, Ben Alexander (as Bobbie), in Tourneur's drama of a troubled family.

Ramón immediately imagines the worst about his wife. Further, he comes to a conclusion that, in the light of what he has read, makes some sense: that their young boy Bobbie is not really his. Ramón then does something extraordinarily rash. He hands his boy over to a complete stranger, a gypsy. When his wife discovers what he has done, she leaves him, and heads out in a panic to find her lost boy.

As in many of his films, Tourneur indicts the male head of household and shows great sympathy for mother and child, who in this case struggle to locate each other over a period of five years. Tourneur has, said *Film Daily*, an "evident delight in long drawn close-ups and occasional overdone detail." There is "much human interest," wrote *Harrison's Reports*. "The mother's finding of the boy, for example, is a powerfully moving situation ... the action ... is fast all the way through." The tale ends happily when the boy reappears with several letters that prove his mother's innocence.

Despite the fact that Tourneur didn't have a meaty plot to film, and that the tale's "construction is of rather slender variety," wrote *Exhibitor's Trade Review*, "the director's craft and keen sense of dramatic values, combined with the high quality of the cast, score over the somewhat inadequate material.... There is colorful atmosphere in generous abundance, a sure bet in every Tourneur production."

Torment

(1924). Levee–First National. Script: Fred Myton and Marion Fairfax. Photography: Arthur Todd. With Bessie Love (Marie), Owen Moore (Jimmy Hansen), Jean Hersholt (Boris) Josie Sedgwick, Barbara La Marr, George Cooper, Maude George, Joseph Kilgour, and Morgan Wallace.

Based on a story by William D. Pelley about an attempted heist of valuable jewels, Tourneur's film takes place against the background of an earthquake. Ostensibly an international caper that goes from Russia to San Francisco to Japan, it is really about the redeeming powers of love.

The tale begins on a high note: A man named Boris plans to sell Russia's crown jewels to the highest bidder in order to help relieve the suffering of the masses in his country. A trio of thieves, including Jimmy Hansen, has other plans: to steal the money before it can be used for its intended purposes. All hands journey to Yokohama, and while they are in the vaults where the deal is to be put over, a devastating earthquake strikes the city. (Tourneur's film includes actual footage of the destructive earthquake hitting Yokohama).

Then, having gotten hold of the precious jewels, which were smuggled out of Russia, Jimmy Hansen finds himself trapped, along with his cohorts and an innocent American maid named Marie, in the vault. As the days go by and they begin to lose all hope of a rescue, the weary pris-

Bessie Love, in *Torment* (1924).

oners begin to speak openly to each other, and Jimmy becomes a changed person within the confines of his imprisonment.

Film Daily noted that the picture "affords action, suspense, thrills, and a general atmosphere of audience appeal." At the turbulent climax of the six-reel (5,400-ft) drama, "There is a general confessing and regeneration while all are entombed. They are freed and all mend their ways, with Jimmy happy in his love for Marie."

The White Moth

(1924). Levee–First National. Script: A. Shelby Le Vino. Photography: Arthur Todd. Design: Jack Okey. With Barbara La Marr

Charles De Roche in a publicity shot promoting his appearance in Tourneur's *The White Moth* (1924).

(Mary Reid), Conway Tearle (Robert Vantine), Charles De Roche (Gonzalo Montrez), Ben Lyon (Douglas Vantine), Edna Murphy (Gwen), Josie Sedgwick (Ninon), Kathleen Kirkham (Mrs. Delancey), and William H. Orlamond.

From the novel by Izola M. Forrester, director and executive producer Tourneur filmed a broad, sweeping, passionate melodrama of the lifestyles of a millionaire colony and the theatrical people in Paris, centering on one young woman referred to as "The White Moth." Alive with the spirit of the Jazz Age, emotional stress, and ablaze with colorful atmosphere, Tourneur's film echoes his later sound film about another desperate woman and a host of would-be lovers, *Maison de dances* (1931).

The protagonist here is Mary Reid, from the nowhere town of Batavia, Kansas. At the start of the drama, she is set to kill herself. About to jump into the Seine, she is dissuaded from this irrational act by Gonzalo Martinez (played by the handsome French expatriate Charles De Roche). He helps her get back on her feet, and within two years she has made a name for herself as an alluring dancer on the stage. Although Gonzalo has fallen in love with her, Mary does not return his feelings.

Later on, a number of men fall victim to her allure, but Mary shows little real emotion for any but Robert Vantine. Robert sets out to prove to his younger brother, Douglas, that Mary is not in love with Douglas. He does this by marrying Mary himself! After Robert succeeds in his mission, he leaves Mary, though he makes generous financial arrangements for her future. But a bit later he realizes that he — and by implication all the other men — may have misjudged his wife. He returns to her and begs forgiveness.

Money was no object in making this

The White Moth (1924): Barbara La Marr (as Mary Reid) and Conway Tearle (as Robert Vantine) in a sizzling story of unfulfilled desire.

picture, its settings and scenic effects were "marvelously elaborate, a regular debauch of color and artistic glow," raved *Exhibitor's Trade Review*. The interior of the theater, the big costume ball, the galaxy of radiantly clad, beautiful women, and an atmosphere of abandon "are a lasting delight to the eye," wrote the trade publication. Indeed, the picture's charm was certainly its strongest drawing card, a close second being the sexual suggestiveness that "comes close to crossing the risqué border" and the subtitles "that will probably have to be revised before presentation in certain houses."

While the production was praised by some for its exoticism, its collection of beautiful scenes, notably those of the Bal des Artistes, in which scores of participants are in masquerade attire and confetti bursts over the beautiful women, and the wonderful dance numbers, could not carry the film. Tourneur's "latest celluloid effort," wrote the *New York Times*, "reflects the business mood of that director rather than his artistic inclination.... The story ... is filled with exaggerated situations, which would never have been accepted if Mr. Tourneur had been intent on fashioning a masterpiece." Extant.

Sporting Life

(1925). Universal-Jewel. Script: Curtis Benton. Photography: Arthur Todd. Design: Léo E. Kuter. With Bert Lytell (Lord Woodstock), Marion Nixon (Norah Cavanaugh), Cyril Chadwick (Phillips), George Siegman, Paulette Duval (Olive), Charles Delanay (Joe Lee), Arthur Lake, and Myrna Loy.

Tourneur's crowded, incident-filled seven-reel remake of his 1918 drama, based on the 1898 play by Cecil Raleigh and Seymour Hicks, is about a young British nobleman, Lord Woodstock, the impoverished and desperate gambler, horse-racer, and prize-fighter who is also an excessively virtuous hero. The subject matter runs from forgery, murder, and seduction to suicide and abduction—spicy material for the roaring '20s—along with smart dialogue.

At the same time, the film idealizes a peer of the realm who finds his pleasure in the most democratic ways and marries the trainer's daughter. There are no ruses to prevent him from finding real love.

The young man who scorns pride of birth and breaks bread with jockeys and postboys clings to the hope that bets on a boxing match and then on a racehorse in which he holds an interest can restore his fortune. At the key moment in a boxing match, he takes the place of the boxer he has backed—because the fighter has been drugged—and wins the match.

The complete story, which is very faithful to the play, goes like this: When Lord Woodstock loses money in a musical revue in London, he plans to recoup it by betting on Joe Lee, a boxer and protégé of his, and by winning the Derby with his

Marion Nixon, the star of Tourneur's roaring *Sporting Life* (1925).

horse, Lady Love. He incurs the enmity of Olive Carteret, an actress, by falling in love with Norah Cavanaugh, daughter of his trainer. Phillips, a gambler, and Olive then conspire against him.

The boxer is drugged on the night of the fight, and Woodstock takes his place. He wins the fight, but Phillips kidnaps Norah. Woodstock and the boxer are then locked up when they try to rescue her. An hour before the race, they escape, but the boxer is killed. Lady Love wins the race; Phillips is arrested for murder; and Woodstock and Norah are free to marry.

Tourneur's 1918 "version was a good one," wrote *Harrison's Reports*, "but this one is still better; he has made his sequences more logical, and has kept up the suspense tenser throughout the entire length.... The suspense, thrills and human appeal in it ought to satisfy the most exacting melodrama-loving picture-goer." Tourneur's film succeeded because of its pictorial variety and excellence, along with its bustling rendition of the surface of life. As a film in touch with the times, it was what 1920s America demanded.

Never the Twain Shall Meet

(1925). MGM. Script: Eugène Mullin. Photography: Ira Morgan. Design: Joseph Urban. With Anita Stewart (Tamea), Bert Lytell (Dan Pritchard), Huntley Gordon (Mellenger), Justine Johnston (Maisie), Boris Karloff, George Siegman, Lionel Belmore (Capt. Gaston Larrieau), Florence Turner, and Marie de Bourbon.

Bert Lytell, the costar of *Sporting Life* (1925) and *Never the Twain Shall Meet* (1925).

Working at the newly created MGM studios, Tourneur was said to have had differences with Irving Thalberg over the making of this exotic tale, which was filmed in the South Pacific. It signaled future trouble for the director in Hollywood.

The story is based on the 1923 novel by Peter B. Kyne, who was given responsibility for "editorial direction." The theme is one Tourneur explored throughout his entire career: how difficult, if not impossible, it is to create lasting relationships, if not love, between people of different cultures and backgrounds. One could almost apply its theme to the business relationship between the French-born Tourneur and his Hollywood superiors.

"Joy and sorrow always meet around the corner," reads the introductory title to this story of a white man marrying a native girl of the South Seas. The eight-reel (100-minute) tale, a great deal of whose action is told by subtitles, was one of the studio's most lavish in a year of lavish productions. It begins on a disturbing note in San Francisco where Tamea, daughter of the queen of the island kingdom of Riva, arrives with

Never the Twain Shall Meet **(1925): The exotic Anita Stewart (as Tamea) is comforted by Huntley Gordon (as Mellenger) in the drama of impossible love.**

her father, Larrieau, a bearded French sea captain. The well-traveled seaman is diagnosed with leprosy. Putting his daughter in the care of his friend and business partner Pritchard, the captain commits suicide.

Though Pritchard is engaged to Maisie and enlists the help of a reporter named Mellenger to help him take care of the young woman, he can't help falling in love with the island maiden. When his business fails, Pritchard abandons his life in America and follows her to the South Seas. They marry, but his stay in the South Pacific leads to the bitter realization that he won't be able adapt to the culture, the heat, and the lassitude of the South Pacific. His shocking deterioration becomes manifest when the once ambitious, handsome businessman turns into an unshaven, unkempt embarrassment to those around him.

Mellenger and Maisie travel to the South Seas to try to help Pritchard cope, but it's no use. Pritchard, at Tamea's urging, returns to the United States, accompanied by Maisie, while Tamea becomes fast friends with the more malleable and dependable Mellenger. The two become lovers in the end.

"There is romance galore, the thrill of physical combat, a spice of humor, and a

Clothes Make the Pirate (1925): Leon Errol (as Tremble-at-Evil Tidd) and Dorothy Gish (as Betsy Tidd) in Tourneur's comedy of how clothes remake the man.

bit of pathos," wrote *Exhibitor's Trade Review*. Some of the most affecting scenes of the film are of native wedding customs. They "are extremely beautiful and full of exquisite symbolism," wrote the trade publication.

"There are constant touches of apt characterization and enlivening incident," wrote the *New York Times*. The heroine's introduction to such technological marvels of the era as the elevator, telephone, and pushbuttons and her "suspicion of the butler who tries to seat her at a table are most entertainingly set forth," wrote the newspaper.

Clothes Make the Pirate

(1925). Rork–First National. Script: Marion Fairfax. Photography: Henry Cronjager. Design: Charles Sessell. With Leon Errol (Tremble-at-Evil Tidd), Dorothy Gish (Betsy Tidd), Nita Naldi (Madame De La Tour), George F. Marion (Jennison), Tully Marshall (Scute), Frank Lawlor (Crabb), Edna Murphy (Nancy Downs), James Rennie (Lt. Cavendish), Walter Law (Dixie Bull), and Reginald Barlow (Captain Montague).

From the novel by Francis Holman Day, Tourneur filmed a highly diverting nine-reel (8,000-ft) farce about buccaneer—and home—life. It's a one-man

Nita Naldi, who costarred in *Clothes Make the Pirate* (1925).

comic-opera picture in which the lead, played by Leon Errol, is almost never sober. He sets the pace for the fun by falling down hatchways, tripping over ropes, hiding when the fighting is heaviest, and melting to the floor when completely drunk. The tale's humor derives from the very idea of a timid, spindle-legged misfit commanding a pirate expedition.

The hero is an unusual one for Tourneur: a 17th-century henpecked tailor who, after putting on pirate's clothing, is mistaken by everyone for "Dixie Bull," a fearsome and loathesome pirate, a scourge of the Spanish Main. He is quickly taken and carted off to a pirate craft by a band of cutthroat mariners. In his new persona, Tidd manages to even the score with his enemies back home, especially his shrewish wife. Of course, the real "Dixie Bull" soon shows up, but Tidd gets the better of him, too. He is acclaimed a hero by his townsfolk — and even by his officious wife.

The lead character embraces his dearly beloved role as a swashbuckling pirate, and his garb awakens "laughter in the most morose bosom," wrote *the New York Times*. "There are a number of ludicrous situations in which Tidd, through sheer good luck comes out with flying colors, but in the end he is glad to enter his home and bring the firewood his wife had ordered before he went a-pirating."

But there is a surprise at the end of the comedy: When he looks at his wife, Tidd's pirate self returns and he ends up "wearing the trousers in his own home." The film's titles are a nice touch: they are in old English.

Tourneur also included scenes that could be tinted or toned. He did that by using a lighting method that stressed a central area of light and that left the outside edges of frames much darker. "All in all, you have here," concluded *Exhibitor's Trade Review*, "palatable entertainment."

Old Loves and New (1926): Lewis Stone (as Lord Carew), **right**, is the man who loses his wife, Katherine McDonald (as Lady Elinor), to Walter Pidgeon (as Lord Geradine), but who finds redemption and love in North Africa.

Old Loves and New

(1926). Rork–First National. Script: Marion Fairfax. Photography: Henry Cronjager. Design: Jack Okey. With Lewis Stone (Lord Carew), Barbara Bedford (Marny), Tully Marshall, Walter Pidgeon (Lord Geradine), Katherine McDonald (Lady Elinor), Albert Conti, Arthur Rankin, and Ann Rork.

Based on Edith M. Hull's 1923 novel *The Desert Healer*, this is Tourneur's homage to the men who lost their lives in the Great War and a powerful, emotional tale of the redeeming power of love — if it can be found. In this case, it is to be found in North Africa. Tourneur was familiar with North Africa, having filmed there when he began his career in France. Walter Pidgeon appears here in one of his first major roles.

The exotic tale centers on an English aristocrat who becomes known as "The Desert Healer." Lord Carew, a devoted husband and father, returns home wounded from the front. He discovers that his wife Elinor has left him (for the alcoholic Lord Geradine) and that their child is dying. Shocked, embittered, disillusioned, and with no reason to remain in

Lewis Stone and Barbara Bedford (as Marny), the woman whose love saves him, in *Old Loves and New* (1926).

Britain, he heads for Algeria. In his new surroundings he makes a new life for himself as El Hakim, a man who "lives like a saint and rides like the devil." He becomes a kind of patriarch to the locals.

Carew eventually learns to love again — thus healing himself — when he saves Marny from horse thieves. There is also an element of justice in the film: the man who ran away with his wife is killed in a hunting accident.

"There is decided sincerity in this eight-reel production," wrote the *New York Times*. "One strong scene is where the ambulance train glides into Charing Cross station, in London. Here one perceives on the platform the anxious relatives awaiting the wounded fighters. Marny O'Meara greets her brother ... who has lost both his legs. This is a truly stirring chapter, for it brings back to mind the heroism of the brave and the bowed hearts that in those days were to be found in so many countries."

Aloma of the South Seas

(1926). Paramount. Script: James A. Creelman. Photography: Harry Fischbeck. Design: Charles M. Kirk. With Gilda Gray (Aloma), Percy Marmont (Bob Holden),

Aloma of the South Seas (1926): Gilda Gray (as Aloma) comforts Percy Marmont (as Bob Holden), a man who eventually loses his lover because he is unable to adapt to life in the South Seas.

Warner Baxter (Nuitane), William Powell (Van Templeton), Harry T. Morey (Red Malloy), Julanne Johnston (Sylvia), Joseph W. Smiley (Andrew Taylor), Frank Montgomery (Hongi), and Michelette Burani (Hina).

From the play by John B. Hymer and LeRoy Clemens about the curative powers of love, Tourneur directed one of his longest American films, an exotic nine-reel (2100-m) effort, shot in Puerto Rico, that tried to emulate the success of *Moana of the South Seas*, released earlier that same year by his studio.

Tourneur's is a lush tale in which the lives of the characters are passed in the midst of swimming, exotic fruits, seaweed, and sea shells. The islands off the Australasian shores are plainly magical in their naive sexual allusions and love-hate relationships. The people speak a brand of South Sea English, and when the occasion demands, they exhibit the most exotic reactions. They invent singular, disconcerting images from the love life of animals, their remarks managing to turn into delicious defeats of conventional propriety. The people, both brown-skinned and white, are shown to be musical, loving, and bare-bodied.

The sympathetic tale begins when

Gilda Gray as she appeared in her first starring picture, *Aloma of the South Seas* (1926), a Maurice Tourneur production for Paramount, adapted from the New York stage success.

Bob Holden returns from the war to find that his fiancée, Sylvia (played by the beautiful Julanne Johnston, who gained distinction in *The Thief of Baghdad*), has been lured away and has married someone else. He takes to the South Seas, where he runs a business for his uncle — and begins to drink. He also meets the beautiful Aloma, who tries to lift him from the depths of despair.

She succeeds in bringing hope, and perhaps the possibility of more, back into his life. At the same time, a young native named Nuitane schemes to prevent the white man from marrying the maiden. He has cause to feel this way, because he has seen too many white men like Holden take advantage of native women. He's going to feed this white man, as he has done others, to the sharks.

The outstanding feature in the film, wrote *Harrison's Reports*, "is, aside from the personality of Gilda Gray, the beautiful tropical scenery. There are shown angry waves breaking upon the shore which, for beauty, have never been surpassed in pictures."

The film's storm — a favorite element in any Tourneur tale of loss and upheaval — and the disruptive tropical weather are significant ingredients that help set things right in the end: native marries native; American marries American.

Mysterious Island

(1926–1929, Tourneur, Benjamin Christensen, and Lucien Hubbard.) MGM. Script: Tourneur. Photography: Percy Hilburn, Howard Green, and J. Ernest Williamson. With Lionel Barrymore (Count André Dakkar), Jacqueline Gadsdon (Sonia Dakkar),

Mysterious Island (1926–29): Mysterious being and undersea adventure form the bases for Tourneur's last American effort.

Lloyd Hughes (Nicolai Roget), Montague Love (Falon), Harry Gribbon (Mikhail), Snitz Edwards (Anton), Gibson Gowland (Dmitry), Dolores Brinkman (Teresa), Karl Dane, Pauline Starke, and Jane Daly.

This film was to have been one of the big films of 1926, a three-hour color adventure having the benefit of major stars and a million-dollar budget. Tourneur had used J. Ernest Williamson's undersea equipment to shoot the well-received *The White Heather* (1919). Here, Tourneur was to direct the studio portions in Hollywood, while Williamson himself would shoot the underwater scenes in the Bahamas.

The film turned out to be Tourneur's last American effort. A 95-minute Technicolor work containing ten minutes of sound in the first reel, it was based on Jules Verne's classic science-fiction novel. Tourneur dropped out of the film for what were said to be professional differences with the studio, complicated by production difficulties.

From the outset, the work was hampered by studio attempts to update Verne's appeal with a new story, which delayed the start of filming. When Williamson was eventually dispatched to Nassau in July 1926, the best weather had

Two of Tourneur's cast members, Milton Sills and his wife, the lead actress Doris Kenyon, in the late 1920s. Kenyon appeared in *Pawn of Fire* (1915) and *A Girl's Folly* (1916); Sills, in *The Pit* (1914) and *The Isle of Lost Ships* (1923).

come and gone. Williamson, however, managed to overcame difficulties caused by three hurricanes. Then after several weeks of shooting, another script arrived from Hollywood. After Williamson re-shot those scenes, yet another rewrite was dispatched to the team in the Caribbean.

Tourneur's longtime colleague, Clarence Brown, was asked to direct the Hollywood portions after Tourneur departed. He rejected the offer out of consideration for his mentor. "Tourneur," he said, "taught me all I know. He's like a god to me." Danish director Benjamin Christensen, in Hollywood since the mid–1920s, accepted the assignment, but soon bailed out, too. He returned to Europe shortly thereafter.

Lucien Hubbard completed the film. "A lot of footage had been shot but there was no script," he recalled. "I wrote one around the footage." The film turned out fairly well, although complicated by the transition to sound. Hubbard shot the sound sequences to add allure to the mys-

Director Clarence Brown, whose career was influenced by Tourneur, shown here in the late 1930s.

William A. Brady, Tourneur's old studio boss, in the late 1920s.

Maurice Tourneur in later years. Tourneur's screen vision, said the critics, needed clarity in his last days in Hollywood.

terious, offbeat tale that contains Tourneur's favorite themes.

It is set on a volcanic island where Count Dakkar, a man with a scientific bent, rules over a classless people. He, his daughter, Sonia, and her fiancé, engineer Nicolai Roget, have designed a submarine, which Roget pilots on its maiden voyage just before the island is taken over by a Baron Falon. Falon sets out after them in a second submarine and the two subs, diving to the ocean floor, discover what Count Dakkar had predicted would be there: a strange arena populated by dragons, giant squids, and humanoids.

When the film was released in December 1929, *Film Daily* noted, "Political treachery, warfare on sea and on land, the romance of a commoner and a royal lady, all are woven into an adventurous spectacle that is intensely engrossing.... And there is a new face, Jane Daly, who shapes up as great dramatic material."

Variety, however, had this to say: "There is a steep production cost to overcome ... with a wealth of special sets, costumes, mechanical devices, and elaborate miniatures. Picture is reported to have been two years in the making, probably on the shelf most of that time." Extant (in black and white).

Tourneur in Europe, 1927–1961

What happened to Tourneur after he left Hollywood in 1926 was this: He landed initially in France — and ran into trouble. Veterans of the Great War were incensed that Maurice Tourneur had avoided service during the awful war years. Never mind the facts that when the war began, Tourneur was already 38 and had served in the French military in the first years of the 20th century; he was accused on his return of cowardice and "desertion." To make matters worse, Tourneur had turned his back on France by becoming an American citizen.

But Tourneur was indomitable. He quickly departed France to make a film in the country that was France's enemy in the Great War — Germany. Instead of adapting to the new demands of cinema audiences during the transition to sound, Tourneur poured effort and money into another silent film. He asked his son Jacques to join him as editor in Berlin's Staaken film studios. Jacques, tired of scraping by on small acting stints and ushering assignments at the Hollywood Bowl, jumped at the chance to rejoin his father.

In Berlin and Hamburg, Maurice Tourneur wrote, directed, produced, and spent heavily on *The Ship of Lost Souls* (released in 1929). A reminder of his 1923 American hit *The Isle of Lost Ships*, the film claimed an international cast: Robin Irvine from England, Vladimir Sokoloff from Russia, Fritz Kortner from Germany, Gaston Modot from France, and the not-yet discovered Marlene Dietrich, playing an American aviatrix trapped aboard a ship with an unsavory crew.

The eighty-minute extravaganza on which Maurice Tourneur claimed, perhaps surprisingly, to have applied "Hollywood principles," failed to arouse the kind of interest he had anticipated. Maurice

Tourneur and Jacques quietly slipped backed into Paris for their next film—their last silent.

L'Equipage is an emotional tale reminiscent of William A. Wellman's *Wings* and *The Legion of the Condemned*—the heroic tale of two war pilots in love with the same woman. Unfortunately for Tourneur, the film, which was released in a shortened version in New York, competed for attention against early sound films. They had just become the rage, and Tourneur's touching tale about lovers during the Great War was ignored. Only later was the film recognized by veterans and others in France as a significant statement about France and World War I.

Undeterred, the quick-working Tourneur and his son signed with Pathé-Natan, the largest producer-distributor in France. Tourneur would make ten films for the studio in the next five years. He began with a subject that had been a trademark from his time in America: a murder-mystery in which a woman is accused of homicide. During filming, Tourneur discarded the original scenario written by a Frenchman and used the scenario, continuity, and dialogue written by the 17-year Hollywood pro, Mary Murillo. In his next offering Tourneur emphasized camera angles and lighting to highlight his drama starring Gaby Morlay, *Accusée, levez-vous!* (*Accused, Stand up*). Released in September 1930, it was hailed as the best French sound film to date. This first of his sound films was polished and effective, but it never made it to the United States.

Tourneur followed this effort with an exotic Spanish-locale drama of intense love, *Maison de dances* (1931), from a story by Paul Reboux, which again starred Gaby Morlay as the hot-blooded dancer who attracts rogue males; and then with a romantic crime-thriller, *Partir* (August 1931), about a man on the run who finds love on a ship bound for the Far East.

Tourneur's next two films helped to re-establish his reputation in European film circles. *Au nom de la loi* (1932) is a thriller about a woman accused of murdering one detective and getting another to fall in love with her. In this work, Tourneur brought his American experience to the fore. Going against the filmmaking custom in France, the master director wasted little footage in exposing police methods, and brought the climactic scene—the protagonist's suicide when faced with capture and the truth about her lover—to an abrupt, unsentimental close. The film was shown at the Venice Film Festival of 1932. It was one of France's earliest entries in that festival.

Later that year, Tourneur completed the smash comedy *Les Gaîtés de l'escadron* (1932), a remake of his 1913 silent based on the work by Georges Courteline. Here the director used color to invoke prewar life, highlighting soldiers in their distinctive red pants. This sly, sentimental tribute to French fighting men marked a departure for the filmmaker; in only one other film in his career had he used a full color palette: the ill-fated *Mysterious Island* (1926–29).

The French film, starring the excellent cast of Raimu, Fernandel, and Jean Gabin, is about a subject dear to the hearts of the French—their army. Tourneur knew the institution firsthand, though his critics in French circles were apparently unaware of the fact that Tourneur had served in the French artillery for three years at the beginning of the century. Showing uncharacteristic extravagance, Tourneur spent $100,000 on the film—more than twice the going rate for top productions at the time—but his producer recouped the investment quickly.

In early 1933, Tourneur filmed a stage adaptation that briefly returned his name to American attention. His *Les Deux orphélines* (1933), from d'Ennery, became the first of his sound films to reach New York. This was perhaps apt, for the film was a remake of D. W. Griffith's *Orphans of the Storm* (1922) without the spectacle but with as much tenderness and gripping drama.

It is a period drama of the early 19th century that centers on the fate of two young lost girls. The film was shot in a way that made audiences forget the period and see only living human beings, said the critics of the period. It starred several beautiful women, noted a reviewer for *Variety*. "That's something new for a French picture, and it's probably the Maurice Tourneur influence."

Tourneur then filmed three shorts: the twenty-minute military comedy *Lidoire* (1933), starring Fernandel; the sixty-minute theatrically based drama *Le Voleur* (1933), about a woman unsure of her husband's love; and a bit of Grand Guignol reminiscent of his start in films — about an insane, jealous man on the loose — called *Obsession* (1934).

Tourneur's last work for Pathé-Natan was the highly regarded and well received *Justin de Marseille* (March 1935), a story of love found amid gang rivalry, calculated to meet the new French and American appetite for crime films. It was the only film during this period on which Jacques Tourneur was neither editor nor assistant to his father.

The younger Tourneur had lost patience with his subordinate role. He'd gained considerable experience at his father's side in France, where, unlike Hollywood, most film work was done without a schedule — this particularly suited the elder Tourneur — and so the son had decided to become a director himself. When, years later, Jacques Tourneur had established himself as a director in America, he recalled his early experience with his father:

> In those days I was my father's assistant and editor. But I wanted to become a director, and whenever I met Natan in a corridor, I stopped him and said: "When do I start shooting?" After several weeks of this, he got fed up and shouted: "Get this idiot off my back ... give him something, anything, only I don't want to see him any more!"

So between 1931 and 1934, while still working for his father, the younger Tourneur took whatever film assignments he could get — in this case, four comedies, the most interesting of which was *Les Filles de la concierge / The Concierge's Daughters*, (1934). The young director described it as a "little unanimistic comedy ... realistic, giving a fairly accurate portrait of a social milieu." Of his other efforts at direction he said, "They weren't very good, as least as far as I remember."

But the younger Tourneur was developing a facility for lighting and an interest in the macabre — interests kindled at his father's side — and he shortly thereafter returned to Hollywood to make his name with *Cat People*, *I Walked with a Zombie*, and *Leopard Man* (all 1943), eerie, grotesque works that his father would have favored.

Maurice Tourneur, who remained in France, said of his son after the war: "I am awfully pleased to see that my son Jack ... is doing very well, and at last has got big pictures assigned to him. He is a very capable fellow, and I always knew he had it in him."

Jacques Tourneur may very well have had it in him, because in Hollywood the younger Tourneur — unlike his father —

made little fuss about scripts that were offered to him. "Indeed," he once said, "how is one to know what can be done with a script? It is very easy to … think that you are incapable of doing a good job with such and such a story or, alternatively, that you will be successful with some other type of story. Do you really know your own sensibilities that accurately?"

Evidently during the period before the Second World War, Maurice Tourneur had a change of heart, and was willing to take what was offered, because until 1941 and his work under the Occupation with Continental A.C.E., Tourneur was again a director for hire. He was about to reach his peak—culminating with *Volpone* (1941)—in the era of sound.

December 1935 saw the premiere of Maurice Tourneur's *Koenigsmark*, adapted from the novel by Pierre Benôit. The first of several historical romances that he would shoot over the next few years, it is about an aristocratic woman's tragic love affair. Completed in a scant six weeks, it was notable for the fact that leading actors spoke their lines in both the French and English versions. The film was praised as a remarkable linguistic demonstration by the director and the cast. Tourneur had not forgotten the strong market outside France, where the film was released by Paramount as *Crimson Dynasty*.

A half-year later came *Samson*, the intense and heartbreaking story about a love triangle, starring Gaby Morlay and Harry Baur, which represented another stage adaptation by Tourneur. Then in December 1936, *Avec le sourire* (it premiered in the U.S. in 1939) became an instant French comedy classic. It recounts a tale in which the main character's dishonesty is instrumental in his success in finding love — and in his upward mobility. Starring the ever-charming Maurice Chevalier in his first French role since leaving Hollywood in 1934, *With a Smile* contains a satiric bite about how best to make it in a rigid and hypocritical society.

As political and social tensions mounted in Europe, Tourneur mirrored them in his films. *Le Patriot* (1938, released as *The Mad Emperor* in the United States in 1941) portrays the crazy, overbearing, pathetic, and uncontrollable Czar Paul I who reigned in 1800 Russia. It stars Harry Baur in one of his best roles. The czar is brought down by the man who cares for him the most. In the same vein, the historical tragedy, *Katia* (1938), concerns the doomed love affair between Alexander II of Russia and a youthful and attractive princess, played by Danielle Darrieux in her first role since leaving Hollywood.

Then for more than a year Tourneur worked on the theatrical classic *Volpone*, based on Ben Jonson's respected but rarely performed 1606 comedy. The director remained faithful to the ribald text but spruced it up with wit, and moved the film along at breathtaking speed. Among a stellar cast, it stars Tourneur's old colleague Harry Baur in the tale of a rogue who, wishing to find out which of his friends really cares for him, pretends that he is dying. When the film arrived in the U.S. after the war, it was hailed as a film full of that Tourneur trademark: surprises. It now stands as the one Maurice Tourneur sound film generally available for viewing in the United States.

In March 1940, Tourneur was preparing to direct a story of Chopin's life, called *La Valse de l'adieu*, starring Pierre Blanchar, from a script by his old colleague, Henri Roussell. The Nazi invasion of Western Europe two months later put an end not only to that project but to nearly all film work in France. But during the next four years, even though film stock, equipment, and money were in short supply for film production, Tourneur managed to continue filmmaking.

Tourneur directed five films— more than most directors in France managed to make — during this troubling period. He worked on a steady schedule. The 65-year-old was married to the actress Louise Lagrange (1898–1979) during these years. He was stoic about wartime conditions: "Outside of having my beautiful Packard stolen by German soldiers, our little house near Paris totally wrecked by bombs, our place near Toulon riddled like a sieve by various projectiles, and a little boat I had on the Marne sunk without a trace, we have no complaints."

Péchés de jeunesse (1941) was his first wartime sound film — a somber tale of youthful sins and forgiveness recalled by an old man, played by Harry Baur. The role was Tourneur's old colleague Baur's last film with Tourneur before he was killed by the Nazis in 1943. The film premiered in Paris in November 1941, six months after Tourneur began filming under the eyes of the German occupiers.

In January 1942, in Normandy, Tourneur's *Mam'zelle Bonaparte* opened, and it turned out to be one of the most popular films of this anxious period. The historical romance is about a high-ranking aristocrat who uses a ruse to make sure a commoner doesn't discover her identity, which permits him to fall in love with her. The film was a big hit. One reason for its success is that it belongs to a genre that became enormously popular in France during these years: the costume drama. The favored setting for such films was the 19th century. Set during the Second Empire, this biography of a love-starved woman is highlighted by a sword fight between its female stars, Edwige Feuillère and Monique Joyce.

A little more than a year later, Tourneur returned to a theme that could not lend itself better to his sensibilities or to film adaptation. Taken from a novel by Gérard de Nerval, the remarkable *La Main du diable* brings in the macabre, the devil, the fantastic, and the search for love via another kind of ruse. It seems that a frustrated painter buys a hand that mysteriously confers upon him fantastical powers. The one proviso in his using it is that he must sell it within a year, and when he does, it must be for less than he paid for it — or face eternal damnation. This presents a problem, since he paid only a penny.

In this Faustian film, a fatal atmosphere surrounds the last owner of the hand. Released in the U.S. after the war as *Carnival of Sinners*, this effort left the impression that it was the final work of Tourneur's long career, if anyone cared to remember that career. But Tourneur had continued to direct under wartime conditions, even though none of his films after this one made it to the American market.

In the summer of 1943, he began and completed *Le Val d'enfer*—the painful story of a middle-aged man who briefly finds love — within six weeks. To top it off, he then made *Cécile est morte* (*Cecile Is Dead*), based on a Maigret novel by Belgian writer Georges Simenon. Tourneur's last film under the Nazis, the crime story stresses character more than drama. Tourneur apparently believed Simenon's insight: "Deep down the policeman understands the criminal because he could so easily have become one." It's an insight that could apply to many of the detective films Tourneur made.

In late 1945, veteran director Maurice Tourneur posted a letter to his American colleagues to let them know he was "still alive, keeping busy, and doing business at the old stand." The French-born U.S.

citizen and creator of stylish Hollywood silents had been away from moviedom's Western capital for nearly twenty years.

The letter quickly turned emotional. "I can't help being moved when I remember past years," wrote Tourneur, "and all the faces, some of them gone.... William Brady, Louis J. Selznick, ... Clara Kimball ... Elsie Ferguson, Olga Petrova ... Marguerite Clark, Vivian Martin, Mary Pickford, and so many others.... I would be very desperate if I thought I would never see New York again."

Maurice Tourneur had demonstrated valor when he remained in the country of his birth during the Second World War. It was a different story from a generation earlier when, at the height of the First World War, he was establishing himself in America and did not volunteer to fight in the trenches of the Western Front.

Now he described the war years in France, 1940–1944: "We escaped complete starvation, being shot, or bayoneted, bombed from above, blasted from underneath, buried in concentration camps, shattered in fragments by V-1 or V-2.... After all, the real important thing is that all the people we love are still alive."

But the director whose atmospheric sets and photography and experimentation with visual composition had placed him in the ranks of D. W. Griffith, Thomas Ince, and Cecil B. DeMille never returned to America. He lived out the postwar years in Paris, directing two final films and afterwards translating American detective novels into French. Although he directed, overall, more than a score of sound films, he never regained the reputation he enjoyed during the silent era, either in America or in France.

Tourneur, who claimed to have "brought stylization to the screen," might have regretted his impetuousness in quitting Hollywood in 1926, as his son, Jacques, once hinted; but, in fact, Tourneur apparently had good reason to change direction in mid-career and end his film career where it had begun.

Tourneur picked up the camera again in 1947-48, a director for hire once more. The man who all his life made celluloid a paying investment for his backers again turned to an adaptation of a play. *Après l'amour* is a well-crafted, intense domestic drama (as are most of his Hollywood works) about a Nobel Prize–winning author and his wife who both carry secrets about love. Tourneur made extensive use of flashbacks to flesh out the story and bring the truth to light.

Tourneur was praised for completing the film for $83,000 and within six weeks—at a time when American and French directors were seeking enormous budgets to make even the most pedestrian films. Tourneur's name was hardly visible on some of the publicity and didn't even appear on the theatre front at the Marivaux in Paris, which, it was said at the time, "leaves him indifferent."

Immediately following that film's release in 1948, Tourneur began *Impasse des deux anges* (*Dilemma of Two Angels*), starring Simone Signoret. Released in November that year, but not shown in the United States, this atmospheric crime drama about a bride-to-be who briefly entertains the thought of running away with a former lover, was photographed by Claude Renoir and has been praised by Georges Sadoul as remarkable in its sense of love lost. It was Tourneur's last achievement and his final statement about love's impossibility under certain conditions.

A year later, the director suffered a grievous accident. He was driving a fully-loaded car when one of his bags fell off the roof. When Tourneur pulled over and set out to retrieve the luggage, he was hit by an oncoming vehicle. He lost a leg. Retiring from filmmaking, Tourneur took up the next best thing: translating his favorite crime thrillers into French. One of these was William O'Farrell's *Repeat Performance* (published in 1942), which Gallimard issued in 1951 under the title *Les Carottes sont cuites / The Carrots Are Cooked*.

On August 4, 1961, at the age of 85, Maurice Tourneur died. He was one of the last of a handful of pioneer filmmakers: He'd outlived and worked longer than the likes of Griffith, Ingram, Ince, and Brenon. He had survived by bringing his French talent to America and then taking his American interests and techniques to Germany and France. In 1920, when the prospect of filming a bad script stared him in the face on a regular basis, he recounted all too vividly the "feelings of gloom and depression with which I have walked away with a script of this sort under my arm, wondering how in the name of heaven I was going to live the next few weeks without committing suicide, or what sort of new stunt I could invent to make it get by."

In his last years in Hollywood, Tourneur was seen as the leader of the "artistic school of director and in many respects ... five years ahead of the rest of the pack," said Tamar Lane. He liked colorful stories which lent themselves to interesting backgrounds and artistic treatment, able to get more drama and beauty out of small sets than others could get "through the burning of Rome or replicas of Fifth Avenue mansions."

Then, after Tourneur left America, Lewis Jacobs wrote that Tourneur's importance in the history of American film was his "suggestiveness to the industry. Much of the atmosphere, design, and pictorial beauty of pictures ... are due to Tourneur's influence." But in his long career, Tourneur, despite his stated unease with stars, had also directed major screen personalities: Mary Pickford, Elsie Ferguson, Olga Petrova, John Gilbert, Marlene Dietrich, Charles Vanel, Harry Baur, Raimu, Fernandel, Pierre Fresnay, Louis Jouvet, Maurice Chevalier, Pierre Blanchar, Marcelle Chantal, Edwige Feuillère, Madeleine Renaud, and Simone Signoret. Many times he collaborated with them more than once. In America and France he often worked with the same scriptwriters, designers, photographers, and musicians. In other words, he knew what he liked and didn't like.

After Maurice Tourneur's death in 1961, his son, Jacques, summed up his father's American days this way: "Father was happy in this country.... The only reason he left was the institution of the producer 'system.' He could not tolerate anyone over him on the set."

The Films in Europe, 1927–1948

Das Schiff der verlorenen Menschen/ The Ship of Lost Souls

(1927). Max Glass Ufa. Assistant Director: Jacques Tourneur. Script: Tourneur. Photography: Nicholas Farkas. Design: Franz Schroedter. With Marlene Dietrich (Ethel Marley), Fritz Kortner (Captain Fernando Vela), Robin Irvine (T. William Cheyne), Vladimir Sokoloff (Grischa), Gaston Modot (Morain), Boris De Fas, Feodor Chaliapin, Jr., Robert Garrison, and Max Maximilian.

From a story by Greek writer Frenzos Kerzemen came the tale of Vela, the cynical, cruel captain of the decrepit and mysterious sailing ship *Galatea*, notorious for selling passage out of Germany to fugitives. On board are men who do little but brawl and work under grim conditions: smugglers, pirates, escapees, criminals.

William Cheyne, a young American doctor, is aboard the ship when it suddenly and without notice heads out to sea. He finds himself shanghaied on a voyage to Brazil. On the way, Cheyne helps rescue the survivor of a watery plane crash. She is the lovely American heiress Ethel Marley — in leather flight suit, goggles, and gloves. She had been attempting to break the European flight record across the Atlantic when her plane developed engine problems. Cheyne and the ship's cook, Grischa, the only other decent fellow aboard, must keep her whereabouts hidden from the captain and his notorious crew. But a brutal incident leads to mutiny, murder, and mayhem, putting the two men and the beautiful pilot in great danger.

Before rocketing to stardom in talkies, Dietrich had already appeared in a score of silents. Tourneur's 97-minute production — the interiors were filmed in Berlin's Staaken film studios and the exteriors at Hamburg and Travemunde — was

Dietrich's last silent film. The film was praised for its photography by Farkas, which was called exquisite, especially the atmospheric lighting, in contrast to the shadows of the cabins. The work also contains beautiful, dramatic shots of the open sea — the kinds of shots for which Tourneur was well-known in numerous American silents. And most revealing of all, critics found Dietrich magnificent in whatever she wore, whether flying suit or male clothing. Extant.

L'Equipage / The Crew

(1928). Lutèce Film–Aubert. Assistant Director: Henry Wulschleger. Script: Joseph Kessel. Photography: Léonce-Henri Burel and Emile Pierre. With Claire de Lorenz (Denise Maury), Camille Bert, Georges Charlia (Lt. Hérbillon), Pierre de Guingand, Jean Dax (Capt. Maury), Daniel Mendaille, Jean Murat, and Charles Vanel.

Adapted from the first successful novel (1923) by Joseph Kessel (1898–1979) and released on the tenth anniversary of the end of the First World War, this was Tourneur's first French film in fifteen years and his last silent. It is a tribute to the Frenchmen who fought and died in the war.

In Tourneur's film three protagonists are silently suffering, their fates bordering on tragedy: two officer pilots in the same squad are in love with the same woman, Denise. Although she's married to the middle-aged lieutenant, her feelings towards him are ones of indifference. Instead, she falls for his protégé, Capt. Hérbillon, who is unaware of her marital status. He is the means through which she believes she will find happiness. In combat, however, her newest love interest is killed and, like most of Tourneur's heroines, she shows her mettle when she has to. She embraces her returning husband, Lt. Maury, who feels first grief, then relief, and finally a sense of happiness.

The 3,100-m film, which was released in the United States under the title *The Last Flight*, ranks alongside three French classics about the Great War, Henri Roussell's *L'Ame du bronze* (1918), Abel Gance's *J'Accuse!* (1919), and Léon Poirier's *Verdun, visions d'histoire* (1928).

"It can be said frankly," wrote *Variety* from Paris, that Tourneur's film is a "good French film. The photographic work is excellent, the aviation stunts interesting and the acting first class." The story was later filmed twice by Anatole Litvak: *L'Equipage* (1935) and *The Woman I Love* (1937).

Tourneur's tale about the earliest air combat (in which Kessel participated in 1916), was called by Georges Sadoul one of a "series of films" by Tourneur that are "largely forgotten today but of often remarkable achievement." Sadoul included in that series *Accusée, levez-vous!* (1930), *Au nom de la loi* (1932), *Les Gaîtés de l'escadron* (1932), *La Main du diable* (1943), and *Impasse des deux anges* (1948). Extant.

Accusée, levez-vous! / Accused, Stand up!

(1930). Pathé-Natan. Assistant Director: Jacques Tourneur. Script Jean José Frappa and Mary Murillo. Photography: Victor Arménise. Design: Jacques Colombier. Music: M. de Lucchesi. With Gaby Morlay (Gaby Delange), André Roanne (André Darbois), Charles Vanel, Jean Dax (stage manager), Suzanne Delvé (Yvonne), Camille Bert, and Alexandre Mihalesco (janitor).

From the story, continuity, and dialogue by the Hollywood veteran Mary Murillo came Tourneur's first sound film. It is a 110-minute social drama about a music-hall performer accused of a vengeful murder. It helped the French film industry in its move to sound films: *Variety* wrote in October 1930, that Tourneur's film "is playing SRO and with heavy advance sales.... It must be considered as the first French screen drama that makes a 100% hit."

The film opens during the rehearsals of a revue at the Folies Montmartre (though it is the famous Casino de Paris that has been reproduced in the film). André Darbois and Gaby Delange are the star attractions in a knife-throwing act. But before their act is to go on stage, Gaby is seen in a heated exchange with Yvonne Delys. Later that evening — after a blackout in the theater and after a shot is fired — Yvonne is found dead of a knife wound. Suspicion immediately falls on Gaby, and she is arrested on the charge of murder.

The second half of the film concerns itself with her trial, during which it appears to be an open and shut case. The proceedings bear a striking resemblance to a famous tale of the era, "The Trial of Mary Dugan." Not surprisingly, the concluding incident exposes the real killer (the janitor).

Tourneur's direction was called "A-1 as also is the photography." "Very effective angles and lighting effects," wrote the critics. The experienced "Morlay's picturization of the innocent woman who finds herself unable to demonstrate her innocence is masterly acted and caught by the camera." Just as significantly, the film was considered an economical demonstration of what Tourneur's "Hollywood experience" had to offer to French procedures. Extant.

Maison de danses / House of Dances

(1931). Pathé-Natan. Script: Paul Reboux. Photography: Victor Arménise and Marc Bujard. Design: Robert Gys. With Gaby Morlay (Estrella), José Noguéro (Luisito), Charles Vanel (Ramon), Edmond Van Daêle (Benito), Christine Virdeau (Amalia), and Delphine Abdala.

Paul Reboux's novel and the 1909 Paris stage adaptation (starring Polaire) formed the bases for Tourneur's dark drama. He fashioned an exotic and biting 85-minute tale whose heroine is another hot-blooded Carmen — but a Carmen living in a hostile world. She does, however, revel in the power to arouse men — a power she will use to win love and freedom.

The tale is set in a port city in Spain's Andalusia, where the ballerina Estrella performs at the House of Dances. The only one with whom the demonic and serpentine woman plays with fairness is a professional dancer as false as herself — a fact which makes him the more fascinating to her. While toying with other earnest admirers she is planning all the while to escape from her native city to Paris.

In the end, the other lovers, who have found her out, cease to quarrel among themselves. Instead, they band together to kill her. A key moment in this tale of dramatic suspense that is vibrant with intense passion takes place in the garden of the House of Dances. Benito, Luisito, and Ramon are ready to strike her down as they would a wild beast. They have overheard an exchange of promises between her and her dance partner; even as Estrella sees death glittering on the very points of their knives she exercises her strange sensual power over them: She subjects them to insults, sarcasm, and mockery, taunting them to strike. And they dare not. They are left crestfallen, ashamed of their weakness, and they fall again to fighting among themselves. Benito winds up killing Ramon, the owner of the cabaret. A 13-year-old girl, who, hidden in the bushes, has witnessed the series of events, exclaims, "So that is love!"

Unlike the ending in Reboux's novel, but like that of the play by Nosiere and Muller, the desirable protagonist of Tourneur's sound adaptation survives. In his silent film along the same lines, *Human Driftwood* (1915), the heroine dies. Extant.

Partir / Departure

(1931). Pathé-Natan. Assistant Director: Jacques Tourneur. Script: Maurice Tourneur. Photography: Georges Benôit and Henri Barreyre. Design: Jacques Colombier. Music: Roland Manuel. With Simone Cerdun (Florence Bernard), Jean Marchat (Jacques Largy), Ginette d'Yd (Odette Nicolai), Gaby Basset, Hélène Robert, Charles Prince, and Gaston Mauger.

The popular 1926 novel by the prolific Roland Dorgelès (1886–1973) inspired Tourneur to film a ninety-minute sea adventure about love on the run. This film imparts the sense that "the idea of a person that one forms in one's heart is so much more valuable than his real portrait."

This is the tale in which "everyone has left his troubles behind at the port, has banished all apprehensions, restraints, disappointments. Besides, it does no good to worry, there is nothing you can do to remedy matters. Let come what may … your carefree heart now beats only for yourself.… Yes, this is good," says a voyager. "Only in my childhood, on the first morning of vacation, have I known such intoxicating joy. The voyage will never last long enough to satisfy my thirst for liberty and adventure. I have departed at last.… For me, the voyage does not lie in the arrival, but the departure."

Accompanying Florence (played by Simone Cerdun, cousin of the famous French boxer), the star of an opera company whose tour is taking them from Marseilles to Saigon, is her friend Jacques. He is a well-dressed young man of about thirty, with a scar on his chin, who has been hired to join the troupe because its tenor died at the last minute. His air of gravity intrigues the passengers, and Florence becomes his lover as they make their way through Port Said, the Red Sea, and the East Indies.

The long, dreamy trip, with its promise of the "lure of tomorrow, the eternal tomorrow," includes a carnival aboard ship, which gives the lovers and other passengers a sense that all is well and that the past is the past. Still, everyone on board this bit of "floating France" harbors secrets.

The young man, it turns out, is in agony, having murdered the man who ruined the life of his mother and squandered her fortune. When his affair with Florence goes sour, he becomes insanely jealous and feels lost. One evening, Odette reveals her love for Jacques, and with her Jacques begins to feel he might be able to start life all over again. But, facing arrest near the journey's end in Saigon, he jumps overboard and drowns.

The boat continues on its way until the last port of call. Odette says of him, "Do not seek amid those deserted paths for the cross of Jacques Largy, the stranger … whom I met one rainy November morning in the Vieux-Port. There are no tombs for phantoms." Extant.

Au nom de la loi / **In the Name of the Law**

(1932). Pathé-Natan. Assistant Director: Jacques Tourneur. Script: Tourneur. Photography: Georges Benôit and Marc Bujard. Design: Jacques Colombier. With Marcelle Chantal (Sandra), Régine Dancourt (Mireille), Charles Vanel (Inspector Lancelot), Jean Marchat (Inspector Marcel), Jean Dax (Commissioner Chevalier), Pierre Labry

Au nom de la loi (1932): Marcelle Chantal (as Sandra) is the woman suspected of, and tried for, murder in Tourneur's well-received French thriller.

(Ludovic), Nestor Ariani (Bullack), and Gabriel Gabrio (Amédée).

Taking a police story by Paul Bringuier, Tourneur shot a crisp 85-minute crime drama, set in Marseilles and Avignon, about a woman suspected by the police of smuggling drugs and committing murder. The film details the harsh methods of the French police, and ends with the woman's suicide.

The story begins when the body of a police inspector is fished from the Seine. His colleagues, Lancelot and Ludovic, vow to find the killer. On the police force is Marcel, who loves the beautiful, adventurous Sandra. But Sandra is also something else: a drug smuggler for the formidable Bullack and his gang for which Amédée is a driver. First the driver comes under suspicion, then Sandra, who is arrested as she attempts to flee to Germany on the advice of Marcel. Though Bullack is finally revealed to be the killer, Sandra ends her life of distress when her lover abandons her as well.

Marcelle Chantal has come up with her "best so far in talkers," wrote *Variety*. Tourneur's American experience has "saved him from wasting footage. Film provides excellent entertainment from beginning to end—latter being rather abrupt, contrary to French habit." Extant.

Les Gaîtés de l'escadron / Fun in the Barracks

(1932). Assistant Director: Henry Lepage. Script: Georges Dolley. Photography: Victor Arménise, Raymond Agnel and René Colas. Design: Jacques Colombier. With Raimu (Capt. Hurluret), Mady Berry, Fernandel (Vanderague), Jean Gabin (Fricot), Henri Roussell (the general), Charles Camus (Adjutant Flick), Paul Azais (Croquebol), Georges Bever (Guillaumette), René Donnio (Laplotte), Julienne Carette, and Pierre Labry.

For the second time in his career, Tourneur remade a film. He had done it America, with two versions of *Sporting Life*, in 1918 and 1925.

Based on Georges Courteline and Edouard Norès's play about enervating and mindless routine in the French military, Tourneur's 85-minute film — one of his most expensive — is less a satire or diatribe than a light, amusing look at a day in the lives of soldiers in Squadron 51. There are plenty of tricks to avoid doing what the Army says you have to do, but the film is less biting than Tourneur's 1913 version — in which Henri Roussell (1875–1946) played the same role. The sound version was a big hit in its day.

Within the barracks of the 51st, life follows the course of … soldiers. Croquebol and Guillaumette carry out their dream, to make for the wall and escape. Fricot and Laplotte, more dirty than clean, are eternal recalcitrants who are forever facing punishment. Vanderague, persecuted, opposes the contradictory commands of his superiors.

Captain Hurluret is master of this domain. He tries to maintain a pretense of a command structure while avoiding the stupid excesses of Adjutant Flick and others. There are also reservists to be taken care of, especially Potiron, a "big mouth."

But what Hurluret especially fears are the rounds of an Inspector General. He hopes that at least on this day his two deserters will have returned.

The worst occurs: The General arrives; the deserters are nowhere in sight. The General knows Hurluret and comments on the irregularities in the barracks. In a beautiful tirade, however, Hurluret expresses his devotion to the men and the army. At this point, Croquebol and Guillaumette make their way back to the barracks. The General acts as if nothing has happened, and ends the inspection.

At the time of its release, the sound film was hailed as an "exceptional smash," hinging on subtlety and with a diffuse storyline, "But [the] treatment has been clever enough to produce continuity which is of a snappy tempo," wrote *Variety*. Despite the clear demonstrations of the petty annoyances, constant inspections, and innumerable trivialities inherent in French army regimen that the reservists have to face, "there is something really great hiding in the military vocation."

That is best expressed by the fatherly figure of Raimu (Capt. Hurluret). His "magnificent acting gets sentimental tears" from many viewers. The only color in the film is that of the red and blue uniforms worn by the men. "For any other picture [this] treatment would have been fatal," concluded the critics, but for this one Tourneur's point was to evoke the slower, more understandable, and more comfortable world of prewar Europe, a world Tourneur had grown up in. Extant.

Lidoire

(1932). Pathé-Natan. Assistant Director: Jacques Tourneur. Script: Tourneur. Photography: Victor Arménise. Design: Jacques Colombier. With Fernandel (Lidoire), Rivers Cadet (Biscotte), Jean Clarens, Germaine

Michel, Paulette Duval, and Jean-François Marcial.

Tourneur's twenty-minute satire is based on a one-act play by Georges Courteline which André Antoine, Tourneur's stage mentor, had produced in Paris in 1891, starring the popular Alexandre Arquillière. At the time it was called a "military scene put on the stage.... It is absolutely true." It was a big hit.

Tourneur's film may be called a military snapshot for the screen and a companion piece to his previous, humorous film on life in the armed forces. This short was filmed at a time when sound shorts were in vogue.

In a soldier's room, with its six to eight beds, only two men are allowed to rest, the others having been punished: the trooper Lidoire—his name is a poem—and the trumpeter Biscotte. Lidoire is a good-natured, resourceful, helpful peasant destined to do everything that no one else will. Lidoire does not like the *caserne* life, but he is conscientious to a fault.

Biscotte, his friend, is the drunken soldier who awakens Lidoire when in distress: to help him into bed in the freezing cold, to put him back into bed when he falls out, to get him a drink, to prevent him from breaking his trumpet, or to make sure by consolation or persuasion that Biscotte is never seen as a "disgrace to the French Army."

For his efforts, it is poor Lidoire who winds up being sent to the brig for the most trifling of infractions: When Biscotte finally falls asleep, poor Lidoire is detected burning a candle and is hauled to the Salle de Police.

Les Deux orphélines /
The Two Orphans

(1933). Pathé-Nathan. Script: René Pujol. Photography: Georges Benôit and Roger Lucas. Design: Lucien Aquettand. Music: Marcel Dellany and Jacques Ibert. With Yvette Guilbert (La Frochard), Camille Bert (the doctor), Rosine Deréan (Louise), Gabriel Gabrio (Jacques), Pierre Magnier (Count de Lignières), Jean Martinelli (Roger de Vaudray), Renée Saint-Cyr (Henriette), Emmy Lynn (Countess de Lignières), and Emile Saulieu (Marquis de Presles).

This old, celebrated classic of a melodrama about the victimized young sisters Louise and Henriette had been made into silent films several times in the United States (most notably D. W. Griffith's *Orphans of the Storm*) and abroad, but "never as well as in this instance," wrote *Variety*. It includes the last, great performance by the legendary Yvette Guilbert; it was the screen debut of Renée Saint-Cyr; and it reunited Tourneur and the silent-screen actress Emmy Lynn, after a 20-year absence.

In his 100-minute rendition about two young waifs who, in typical Tourneur fashion, have hardly a happy moment, Tourneur altered the original story by setting the drama at the beginning of the 19th century, rather than at the start of the French Revolution, as depicted in the novel by Adolphe d'Ennery and Eugène Cormon, *La Frochard et les deux orphélines*. Yet that hardly mattered.

Filmgoers wondered whether there was a god in the heaven of the film to save Henriette, who is kidnapped by the wicked old roué, the Marquis de Presles; and whether anyone could avenge the foul and dastardly crimes of the Frochard family, who have made a beggar of Louise. Those filthy and cruel rascals heap villainy upon villainy, and garnish the whole with treachery, imposture, and cruelty. They seek charity in the name of the blind orphan Louise, who has been left "alone—alone—alone in a great city."

Les Deux orphélines (1933): One of the few light moments — youngsters at play — in Tourneur's 19th-century tale of suffering, perhaps the best screen rendition of the well-known story.

In their odious trade they drive the young girl to ignominy and suffering. But near the end comes Chevalier Maurice de Vaudrey, who disarms and captures the scoundrels and cutthroats. The two sweet innocent orphans are rescued from bitter shame and misfortune and reunited with their family, the Count and Countess de Lignières.

"The outstanding player is Mme. Guilbert," wrote the *New York Times*, "who leaves nothing undone to make her every presence dreaded." To counterbalance the malevolent figure of La Frochard, the film, observed the critics, "has several really beautiful women. That's something new for a French film, and it's probably the Maurice Tourneur influence," said the paper.

The drama is "played here so sincerely and effortlessly" that "it really grips. It is a tearjerker that really jerks," wrote a critic. The director was praised for shooting his period piece in such a way that "audiences forget the period and see only living human beings." What makes the film is the humanity of the characters and situations, and Tourneur's masterly brevity and dramatic succinctness with which the situations and climaxes are worked up.

Filmgoers would have had to search far and wide for another film in which the characters are so varied, true, and vital a factor in bringing about the main plotlines of the tale. As he had learned in Hollywood, Tourneur made sure that "everything comes out wonderfully in the end." Extant.

Le Voleur / The Thief

(1933). Vandal and Delac. Assistant Director: Jacques Tourneur. Script André Lang. Photography: Curt Courant. Design: Jacques Colombier. Music: Maurice Thiriet. With Jean-Pierre Aumont (Fernand Lagardes), Victor Francen (Richard Voisin), Yolande Laffon (Isabelle Lagardes), Madeleine Renaud (Marise Voisin), Simone Simon, and Jean Worms (Raymond Lagardes).

Tourneur's intense sixty-minute exploration of love, jealousy, and insecurity is based on the powerful 1907 play by Henri Bernstein (1876–1953), who was one of Tourneur's colleagues from the early part of the century. It stars the great Madeleine Renaud.

She plays the protagonist Marise, the beautiful wife of Richard Voisin. They are, apparently, deeply in love, their domestic heaven rarely disturbed by so much as a cloud, though the fact that at times she feels less beautiful than better-dressed women is a foreshadowing of things to come. While the couple is staying at the home of the Lagardeses, their wealthy friends, Fernand Lagardes, the young man of the household, falls in love with Marise. At first his passion is rationalized as stemming from an overdose of De Maupassant, and Marise avoids telling her husband of the youth's interest her.

Then Marise commits an act that alters her life. She steals 20,000 francs from her friend Isabelle Lagardes. A detective — a Rouletabille type — is brought in to investigate the theft. Fernand is suspected of being the culprit. After a meek denial, the young man admits to the deed.

Soon after, however, Richard Voisin discovers a large sum of money in his wife's possession, the presence of which she cannot explain. Her confession that she stole the money is followed by denunciation, then forgiveness on his part, and then something else. Richard believes that he has discovered a painful truth: Fernand made his self-sacrifice because of a guilty passion for Marise. Richard remains uneasy with all that has happened, and imagines that his wife has become the young man's lover.

The tale has a dual climax: Fernand is sent to Indochina by his father; Richard and Marise separate. The story on which the film is based, wrote a critic, "is superior to nine out of ten ... that are commonly presented."

Obsession

(1934). Pathé-Natan. Assistant Director: Edouard Lepage. Script: André de Lorde. Photography: Raymond Agnel and René Colas. Design: Jacques Colombier. Music: Maurice Jaubert. Editor: Jacques Tourneur. With Louise Lagrange (Louise Bercier), Jean Yonnel (Raymond Bercier), Charles Vanel (Pierre Bercier), Paul Amiot (the doctor), Georges Paulais (the director), Henri Bonvallet (the attorney), Jean Bara (young Jean) and Louise Marquet.

Based on the 1910 Grand-Guignol play *L'Homme mystérieux*, by André de Lorde and Alfred Binet, the frightening film harkens back to the first films Tourneur directed in France. In this one, love does almost nothing to alleviate a continuous state of terror in the protagonist and his family — until the end.

Also called *L'Homme mystérieux*, Tourneur's 35-minute (1100-m) drama, which contains flashbacks, concerns Raymond Bercier, a man who once tried to kill his wife, Louise. As a result, his wife has committed him to an institution. Raymond's brother, Pierre, and Raymond's attorney pressure her to agree to have him released from the asylum — advice that goes against that of Raymond's own doctor.

At the moment that he gains his freedom, Raymond (played by Jean Yonnel, the well-known performer from the Comédie Française) appears to have justified his brother's faith in him: He acts as if he were sane. But once settled into his comfortable home, Raymond becomes the Raymond of old. He hallucinates about enemies all around, further frightening his already frightened wife. At the point when Raymond is about to strangle her in her sleep, he hears the plaintive voice of their son (played by the excellent child actor, Jean Bara). Lucid and sane for a few moments, Raymond phones his doctor — and asks to be recommitted.

Maurice Jaubert's haunting music adds to the mood of terror. Extant.

Justin de Marseille

(1935). Pathé-Natan. Script: Carlo Rim. Photography: Georges Benôit and René Colas. Design: Lazare Meerson. Music: Jacques Ibert and Vincent Scotto. With Antonin Berval (Justin), Ghislaine Bru (Totone), Pierre Larquey (the Stutterer), Milly Mathis (Mme. Trompette), Line Noro, Paul Ollivier (Achille), Alexandre Rignault (Esposito), José Davert, Armand Lacher (Silvio Néri), Jacques Duluard (Pantalon), Marcel Raine (Brutus), Paul Grail (Félicien), and Tino Rossi (the singer).

One of Tourneur's most highly acclaimed sound films from the 1930s — it is still a favorite today in France — is this beautifully made 95-minute crime drama, which contains a bit of documentary footage of street life. Before Julien Duvivier's *Pépé le moko* (1937), there was Tourneur's film. Initially called *Ma belle Marseilles*, it introduced to filmgoers a young singer named Constantino Rossi. It's a tale less of poetic realism than of enjoyment about Justin and his gang who are in a perpetual state of warfare against a rival group, which is led by a sinister man named Esposito.

In Marseilles, a group of youngsters, led by a vagabond pied piper, parades through the port. Then at the bar at La Pinède, honest citizens gather along with some rather dubious individuals: pimps, their girls, gangsters from Italy and from North Africa. A journalist from the *Parisian Echo* begins to make inquiries into the nature of this picturesque but sometimes disturbing setting, where gang activities have contributed to making France's second city a worthy rival to infamous Chicago. A truck driver tells him that you can't trust statistics.

Two heads of rival gangs reign in this milieu: Justin, a son of the country, is respected by those who know him or have heard his name. Esposito, on the other hand, is a Neapolitan without scruples. Justin is the head of a local black market and the friend of Asian dope dealers. He has in his pockets the local authorities, protecting the weak and maintaining with his men — the Stammerer, Achille, Pantalon, Brutus and others — an orderly climate of confidence in the city. Justin's gangsters know how to live in style, and the most stylish, elegant, and easygoing is the leader of the gang. When Justin is in love, he even breaks into song.

Various episodes, both happy and tragic, make up this display of Marseilles and its colorful inhabitants: warfare between the gangs; the too-easy execution of a Senegalese stoolie; the unloading at the Port of Joliette of a cargo of opium hidden within a coffin, which is a pretext for a prearranged shootout; Esposito's "con-

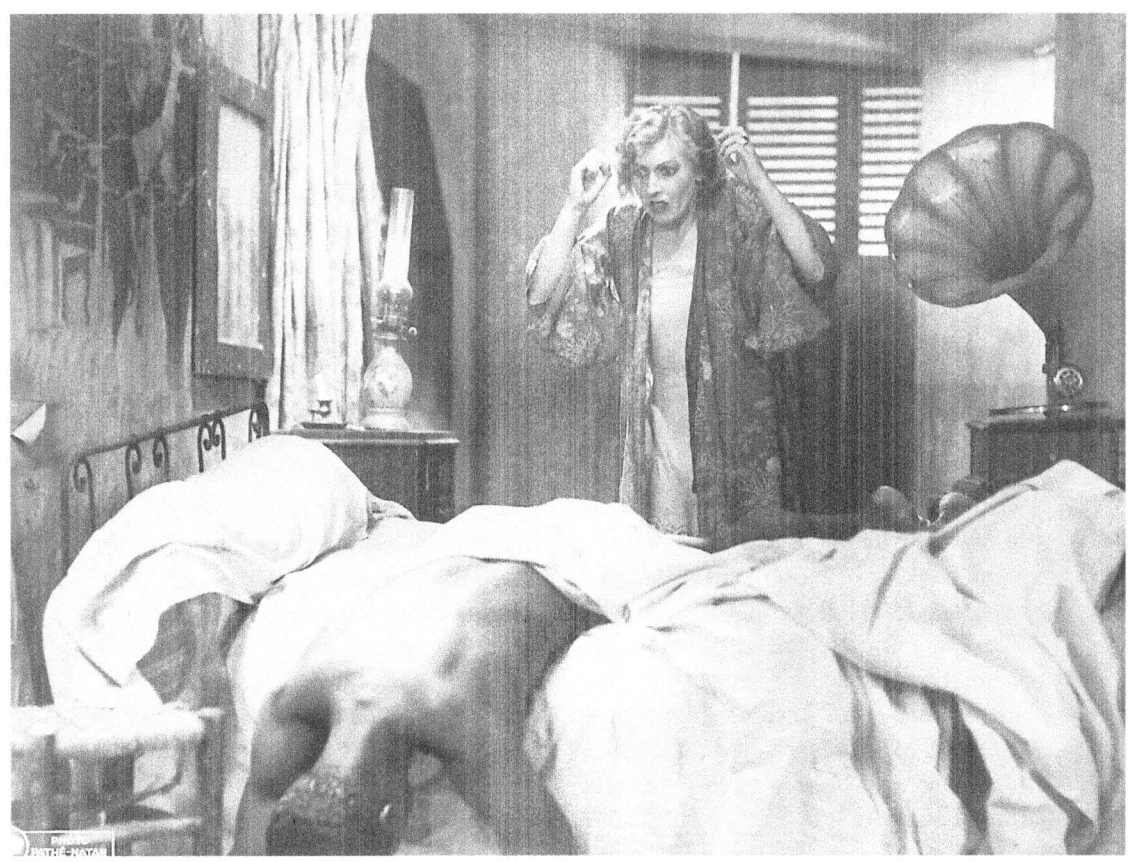

Justin de Marseille (1935): Murder is but one of the elements that take place in Tourneur's entertaining and stylish crime thriller.

tract" on Justin's life; the cheap seduction of Totone and her suicide attempt under a starry sky, thwarted in time by Justin. Esposito, however, will get his comeuppance — and Justin will take Totone to the cinema while running through a list of famous tourist sites in Marseilles.

The tale's most delicate sequence involves the arrival of the coffin bearing the body of "poor Félicien who died in Saigon." This "corpse" is actually a shipment of drugs. Justin and his men are at their assigned posts, wearing mourning clothing, carrying wreaths, and setting themselves strategically around the horse-drawn hearse. Justin succeeds in getting hold of the eighty kilos, but one of his men is killed by Esposito. Then, in a knife fight later on, Justin rids himself of Esposito. At the end, Justin saves the unfortunate Totone from her fate.

The sequence that filmgoers of the era liked best is the one in which the young heroine, who thought she was on the road to happiness, instead finds herself on the road to nowhere. Under the moonlight sky and during the hour in which the Marseilles fisherman are bringing in their nets, she throws herself into the sea. You hear one of the men singing, and it is a voice, wrote a critic, "like nothing you've ever heard." The voice is that of a young Corsican named Tino Rossi, from Ajaccio, the birthplace of Napoléon. Extant.

Koenigsmark

(1936). Roger Richebé Films. Script: Léonce Perret, André-Paul Antoine, and Renée Champigny. Photography: Victor Arménise. Design: Lucien Aguettand. Music: Jacques Ibert. With Jean Debucourt (Lt. de Hagen), Pierre Fresnay (Raoul Vignerte), André Dubosc (the king), Cecil Humphreys (De Marçais), Jean-Max (de Bosse), Jean Yonnel (Grand Duke Rodolphe), Elissa Landi (Grand Duchess Aurore), Antonin Artaud (Cyrus Back), John Lodge (Grand Duke Frédéric), Georges Prieur (the young Prince Tumène), and Marcelle Roger.

Film pioneer Léonce Perret, who in the late 1910s had worked in America, died before the start of shooting of this luxurious sound film. It is a grand remake of his 1923 Pathé film of the same name that starred Huguette Duflos and Jacques Catelain. André-Paul Antoine, the son of André Antoine, coscripted Tourneur's tragic tale, a splendidly atmospheric 115-minute adaptation of Pierre Benôit's 1918 novel of the same name. It was that author's first prose work and one of his most successful. Tourneur took on the director's assignment because of the story and the challenging nature of the production.

The imaginative richness of Benôit's story, his taste for the fantastic, the suspenseful, and the mysterious, and his precise documentation appealed to Tourneur. So did the author's psychological bent, his strong element of fatalism in love and destiny, and the fact that the story hinges on a secret. The director fashioned a sumptuous production of pageantry, exoticism, passion, and intrigue in high circles. The design of the set pieces, notably the grand library of the chateau, represents some of the finest design in any Tourneur film. The story is set in a Ruritanian state, beginning in 1912.

The heroine of this romantic region is a beautiful aristocrat, Aurore (Pierre Benôit favored heroines whose names began with the letter A). Accompanied by her father, Prince Tumène, and a lady's companion, she arrives at the royal chateau of Mégranie. The king, who is the prince's uncle, wants Aurore to marry his heir, Grand Duke Rodolphe. She accepts, but lets the grand duke know that as his wife she can only be a friend to him, not a lover.

Six months later, the king sends Rodolphe on a dangerous mission to equatorial Africa. Before his departure, Rodolphe asks Aurore if one day they might be lovers. She declines, but gives him a medallion with her picture on it. In his absence, she will direct the Duchy of Lautenburg, assisted by Grand Duke Frédéric, Rodolph's brother.

Her settled life changes when her husband suddenly vanishes while abroad. He has been assassinated, and the killer is a member of the royal family: Rodolphe's own brother, Grand Duke Frédéric, who wants to be named regent.

Frédéric hires a handsome young Frenchman, Raoul Vignerte, to tutor his son, the young prince. The tutor and Aurore meet — and he falls in love with her. The young Frenchman is also researching and writing a book about a mystery. During his investigations into one mystery, he uncovers another. In the great library, he comes across information which suggests the existence of a secret hideaway in the chimney of the chateau. Following up on the lead, Raoul comes across a shock.

To his astonishment and amazement, he finds in the hideaway an unrecognizable body covered with lime. With the corpse is something else: a medallion containing a picture of Aurore. It is evidence that points to the murder of Rodolphe, and worse, implies that the killer is a member of the royal family.

While Raoul warns Aurore, Frédéric and his aide-de-camp, de Bosse, who have been alerted by a spy, destroy the chimney and the body. Frédéric arranges it so that de Bosse, an awkward witness, is killed in the explosion. Raoul, however, succeeds in saving the medallion — the key piece of evidence to the assassination.

On July 30, 1914, a general mobilization is issued. War erupts across Europe. Thanks to the help of Lieutenant de Hagen, Aurore manages to get Raoul out of the country. On his return to the castle, Frédéric, greatly confused, commits suicide. And Aurore, refusing to fight against France, abdicates.

Four years later, at the conclusion of the war, Aurore is seen holding in her hands an edition of a book called "Koenigsmark." She places pages from the book on Raoul's tomb. Her only true friend and lover, he perished in 1916. Aurore then dies of a broken heart.

Tourneur also filmed a 95-minute English-language version of this film, with the same cast. Released under the title *Crimson Dynasty* in Britain, it starred the same exemplary cast. *Variety* noted "the remarkable linguistic demonstration" by the performers. "If there were many more players like these the problem of the international talker market would be solved," the trade journal concluded. Extant.

Samson

(1936). Paris Films. Script: Léopold Marchand. Photography: Victor Arménise and René Colas. Design: Guy de Gastyne. Music: Jacques Dallin. With Harry Baur (Jacques Brachart), Gaby Morlay (Anne-Marie d'Andeline), André Luguet (Jerome "Jessie" Le Govain), Suzy Prim (Grace Ritter), Gabrielle Dorziat (the Marquise d'Andeline), André Lefaur (the Marquis d'Andeline), Christian Gérard (Max d'Andeline), and Joffre.

In this fierce 88-minute adaptation of Henri Bernstein's satiric 1908 play, Tourneur repeats themes he favored in Hollywood — and adds a strong biblical bent to the storyline. The ruses of love lead to a terrible retribution and a hint of reconciliation.

There is the mother, who sells her daughter for gold; the titled father, who is selfish enough to agree to it; and the self-sacrificing heroine, who marries without love and is then prepared to take advantage of her husband's first absence from the city to have her "one hour of freedom" with the man she imagines she loves. He is, of course, a scoundrel. There is also the deserted lady from whom he has borrowed money until his friendship with a millionaire places him in a position to win a fortune of his own. She is on hand, however, to betray the villain to the husband at the right moment.

Tourneur's film centers on Jacques Brachart, a brilliant man of finance and the boss of African Coppers. Nothing seems to be able to stop the rise of Jacques Brachart. When a journalist, for instance, tries to print rumors about his checkered past, Brachart purchases the newspaper. But the money is not enough. Brachart also hopes to attain a certain recognition within high society.

During a charity affair organized by Jerome Le Govain, a friendly dandy whom Brachart helped to attain a measure of success, Brachart becomes acquainted with the young and beautiful Anne-Marie d'Andeline. He falls in love with her. The aristocratic d'Andelines, who are noble but penniless, arrange, in effect, to sacrifice their daughter, Anne-Marie, to save the family. Although she doesn't much care for

Brachart, Anne-Marie marries the wealthy man who loves her. But Brachart is a man of few illusions; he knows his wife does not care for him.

Le Govain, on the other hand, has fun and continues to carry on a beautiful, adventurous life, playing with people's feelings and with his mistress, Grace Ritter. He also attracts the attention of Anne-Marie, who more and more often leaves her marital home.

Anne-Marie takes Jerome Le Govain as her lover. Jerome is also a noted duelist and a man of polish and position in society who talks about his honor and has often put it to the test. One evening, Jerome invites Anne-Marie to accompany him to a "pleasure party" among people of good manners. Suspicious, Brachart cancels a trip to London. Shocked by the spectacle of vice at this party, Anne-Marie breaks with Jerome. Although Anne-Marie makes some excuses, Brachart is not easily deceived.

Anne-Marie's family, on the other hand, is anxious about her escapades. They expect the worst and prepare for her divorce. Anne-Marie, however, refuses the rupture to the rough man who began life as a laborer on the docks of Marseilles. Although his nature still disturbs Anne-Marie, she has at least been cured of her illusions about Jerome. When Brachart finds out about the brief affair, he reacts with the only weapon at his command. In the process, he reverts to a type of primitive masculinity and fights with a kind of animal intensity for what he holds to be dear to him.

During this period, Brachart, magnanimous but vengeful, acts. He first comforts Grace Ritter and then commits himself to get even with Jerome. The powerful businessman speculates on the Stock Exchange against his own financial interests! In a few minutes, he loses his fortune and ruins his "friend." Ruined himself, Brachart is on the point of flying to London, in the hopes of making a new life for himself. He is joined by Anne-Marie, who from now on is ready to follow her husband against all winds and tides.

Brachart has brought his own house down. Though impoverished herself, Anne-Marie stays by his side — for love or pity, or perhaps both. There is even a hint that Brachart has it within him to recoup his losses — and that his wife is impressed with great deeds. So this Delilah, at least, does not revel in triumph in his defeat. Her husband must leave Paris for a while, and Anne-Marie will be at his side.

Tourneur's film, said a critic, "shouldn't be criticized too much nor does it merit excess praise." Extant.

Avec le sourire / With a Smile

(1936). Marquis Films. Script: Louis Verneuil. Photography: Armand Thirard. Design: Lucien Carré and Emile Duquesne. Music: Marcel Lattès, Borel Clerc, and Oberfeld. With Paule Andral (Mme Villary), Maurice Chevalier (Victor Larnois), Marie Glory (Gisèle), Viviane Gosset (Suzy Dorfeuil), André Lefaur (Villary), Milly Mathis, Rivers Cadet, Georges Bever, and Marcel Vallée.

One of Maurice Tourneur's finest efforts in his long career is this 98-minute biting satire, based on Louis Verneuil's play. It is a stark and funny lesson in how to get the world to love you. It is also a film that united two Hollywood expatriates. One directed the other in a tale about a man who makes a success of himself — a scoundrel's progress, so to speak, based on charm and likability, and most certainly not on the adage, "honesty is the best policy." The film, with its songs, became one of the classics of 1930s French cinema. It

Avec le sourire (1936): Maurice Chevalier is the man with the unassailable smile and ability to get his way in Tourneur's satiric classic; with Marie Glory.

was Chevalier's first role after returning to France from Hollywood.

Chevalier plays Victor Larnois, a man who arrives in Paris penniless but far from helpless. He's equipped with plenty of confidence, savoir faire — and a great (close-up) smile. He shows what he's made of when he steals a dog and returns it for the reward. His casual pick up of the chorus girl Gisèle leads to love at first sight. Victor then replaces the doorman of the Palace Music Hall, where she works, by making a speech extolling his passionate devotion to door-opening. He progresses in easy stages to the position of secretary to the music-hall manager, a man of character named Villary. After taking a writing course, Victor helps his wife rise to the top by a bit of yellow journalism. He follows that up by buying a partnership in the music hall. Finally, he gains complete ownership of the theater thanks to the clever machinations of his wife, the former chorus girl, who puts Villary in a compromising position.

Lacking one last thing, social connections, Victor turns to what he knows. He blackmails the owner of the Paris Opera — and gains the post of impresario. Life now comes full circle when Villary, his former employer, having lost his wife and served time in jail (thanks to Victor), begs Victor for the job of doorman — the same

The famous Chevalier and his smile.

Chevalier's performance was called "outstanding. He carries the heaviest burden throughout but his work is well-sustained," wrote *Variety*. The *New York Herald Tribune* noted, "If one is equipped with a smile, *Avec le sourire* will prove a saucy, frothy entertainment." Extant.

Le Patriote

(1938). Société des Productions F.C.L. Assistant Director: Henry Lepage. Script: Henri Jeanson. Photography: Armand Thirard and Louis Née. Design: Ivan Lochakov and V. Meingard. Costumes: Boris Bilinsky. Music Jacques Ibert. With Harry Baur (Tsar Paul I), Pierre Renoir (Pahlen), Colette Darfeuil (Lopouchina), Josette Day (Nadia), Geller, Gérard Landry (the Tsarevitch), Suzy Prim (Countess Anna Ostermann), Nicolas Rimsky, Jacques Varennes, and Elmire Vautier (Tsarina).

job that Victor had before making his mischievous climb to the top. Victor installs Villary as secretary, in the process summing up his philosophy of life with all the charm and grace at his command — and with his ever-present, award-winning, hypocritical smile. After having learned how to smile, Villary gives up his principles of morality and integrity and undertakes a new and merrier career.

The *New York Times* called the film, whose theme is akin to Sacha Guitry's *Story of a Cheat* (1936), "one of those gay, Frenchy little satires. After his prolonged absence, we are happy to welcome back Chevalier.... Alas, these French! How wicked they are! But then, how amusing, too. The picture sparkles with little gems of dialogue."

This evocative 105-minute tragedy is based on Alfred Neumann's pseudohistorical novel and the subsequent stage productions in Berlin (1927) and New York (1928, lasting 10 days on Broadway). At first glance the film is a remake of Ernst Lubitsch's 1928 silent (lost) classic starring Emil Jannings; it is one of several remakes that Tourneur undertook in his career.

Yet Tourneur's rendition of the tale about the early 19th-century reign of the alcoholic, violent, and imbecilic Tsar Paul I is also something more. It digs deep into the intrigues of the Tsar's only friend, Governor Pahlen. The film abounds in plotting, roguery, pathos, nobility in service to the state, perils, and violence. It is a film that rose above the commercially routine and assembly-line French and American productions of the era to become an allegory about the madness in high places in late–1930s Europe. To do it justice, to give it atmosphere and depth, Tourneur effectively employed his American experience.

The half-mad, mistress-ridden tyrant, Paul I, the successor to Catherine the Great, brings those about him to such a pitch of desperation that at last a plot is set in motion to replace him. The scheme is headed by the one man who has a chance at succeeding. Pahlen — the patriot — is a shrewd and lucid aristocrat who is military governor of St. Petersburg. Stifling his humane impulses, Pahlen leads the conspiracy against his master and betrays him. He does so by suppressing his conscience and grimly reducing the woman he loves (Countess Anna Ostermann) to a tool in the plot.

There is swift, convincing drama in the way Pahlen makes his way inexorably towards the assassination — and then fulfills a death pact with the actual killer: When Paul is dead and his son is acclaimed the new ruler, both the assassin and Count Pahlen put an end to their own lives. Two pistol shots in the darkness announce two self-inflicted wounds. A subplot centers on the love affair between the young tsar-to-be and a pretty girl.

The drama features Tourneur's longstanding colleague Harry Baur, who, said *Monthly Film Bulletin*, "gives one of his very best performances: he is everything that is required — crazy, overbearing, pathetic, uncontrollable — and gets as near as humanly possible to overcoming the contradictions in the script." Similarly, Pierre Renoir as Pahlen "gives an entirely admirable performance, and succeeds in fully convincing us of the essential patriotism of his motives."

The film was released in the United States in 1941 as *The Mad Emperor*. "At its best," wrote the *Herald Tribune*, the film "is a vivid and poignant portrait of a historical monster." By the same token, old Paul "was a blundering tyro," wrote the *New York Times*, "compared to today's master of the blood purge and the Panzer Blitzkrieg." Extant.

Katia

(1938). Metropa Film. Assistant Director: Henry Lepage. Script: Jacques Companéez, Jean Jacques Bernard, and Henri Deçoin. Photography: Robert Lefebre. Design: Guy de Gastyne and Alexander Arnstam. Music: Roger Fernay. With Danielle Darrieux (Katia Dolgorouki), Marie-Hélène Dasté (Tsarina), John Loder (Tsar Alexandra II), Marcel Simon (Prince Dolgorouki), Aimé Clariond, Thérèse Dorny, Marie Dasté, Paul Escoffier, and Marcel Carpentier.

A huge cast — headed by Danielle Darrieux in her first film after returning from Hollywood — was involved in making this ninety-minute tragedy, which was adapted from the 1938 novel by Martha Bibescu (1887–1973) called *Katia, le démon bleu du tsar Alexandre*. Tourneur's film is history that has been rewritten to suit fiction, about the love affair between the liberal Tsar Alexander II and Princess Katia Dolgorouki. The tale begins in 1859.

While his wife is ill and possibly dying, forty-year-old Alexander II meets the youthful, sweet, and beautiful Princess Katia at her family estate. He ignores the real possibility of scandal by courting Katia, who attends boarding school in Smolny. The Tsar has a harder time ignoring something worse, however. There is trouble on the horizon, signaled by stirrings of widespread discontent within the country. The liberal-minded ruler is intent on making life better for his people. At the same time, the whiff of impropriety forces the charming Katia into exile.

In 1867, the Tsar travels to Paris to attend the International Exposition, and to find Katia. The Empress of Russia has died, and Alexander II seeks a new wife. He brings Katia back to Russia. Katia urges

The youthful Danielle Darrieux as the doomed princess in *Katia* (1938).

Katia (1938): Danielle Darrieux and John Loder are paired as the aristocratic lovers in Tourneur's tragic tale.

him to follow his instincts about something else as well: to create a liberal constitution for the troubled nation. However, before anything can be put into practice, and just before Katia is to be crowned the new Empress of Russia, the Tsar is assassinated by anarchists.

It appears that Katia's openly expressed interests in the welfare of the Russian people may have inadvertently spurred the terrorists to act quickly. The Tsar was going to give Katia credit for being the promulgator of a new constitution. Brokenhearted and alone, Katia ends her days in exile in France.

In point of fact, Alexander II, who took over the reins of power in Russia in 1855, was assassinated in 1881, years after he freed the serfs and instituted a lawful constitution. At the time of his death, he was leaning towards creating a constitutional monarchy. His death at the hands of anarchists was a tragedy for his nation, which returned to autocratic rule under Alexander III. The new tsar undid most of his father's reforms and unleashed the demons of anti-semitism and, eventually, revolution.

Tourneur's fictitious tale bears a strong resemblance to *Mayerling* (1936), the tragic romance set in late 19th-century Austria, along with similarities to Robert Siodmak's *Katia* (1959). Tourneur's film contains the director's favorite mixture of romance, intrigue in high circles, and a sense of fatality in love. The essence of his story, commented *Variety*, "is reproduced splendidly."

"Opportunity is found," wrote the *Monthly Film Bulletin*, "for the introduction of such typically romantic incidents as the Emperor taking his young protégée for a sleigh ride while she is a girl at school, or ignoring Court convention to waltz with her at an Imperial Ball, or disguising himself as a Cossack, while on a state visit to Paris, in order to wander about with her unrecognized." Extant.

Volpone

(1939–40). Ile de France Films. Script: Jules Romains and Stefan Zweig. Photography: Armand Thirard, René Colas, and André Dumaitre. Design: Jean Perrier and André Barsacq. Costumes: Boris Bilinsky. Music: Marcel Delannoy. With Harry Baur (Volpone), Louis Jouvet (Mosca), Charles Dullin (Corbaccio), Fernand Ledoux (Corvino), Jacqueline Delubac (Colomba), Marion Dorian (Canina), Jean Temerson (Voltore), and Alexandre Rignault (Léone).

This is a classic of French cinema, a bawdy, sly, and bold 85-minute adaptation of Ben Jonson's 1606 Elizabethan comedy, and arguably Tourneur's greatest film. Tourneur's evocative style and imagination—coupled with an almost perfect cast, who give their roles the complete Grand-Guignol treatment—are evident in this rollicking, naughty tale of humanity's avarice, treachery, and lack of love, here epitomized by a Levantine merchant of Venice.

The tale is a moral comedy set in motion by a wonderful ruse. Volpone, a commercial Venetian, finds himself in jail because he is unable to pay his debts when one of his cargo-laden ships disappears at sea. There he meets Mosca, a rapscallion whom he makes his confidant. When the ship arrives at port, Volpone becomes a free man. He pays Mosca's debts and then devises a macabre scheme: Volpone pretends to be dying. Since he has no heirs, the plan is to encourage speculators and others to curry his favor—and show their love—by bearing gifts in the expectation of being named in his will. Thus we see Corbaccio the usurer disinheriting his son and naming Volpone as his heir, while

Corvino, the most jealous of husbands, sends his faithful wife to Volpone's bed.

Tourneur's great colleague Harry Baur takes center stage with Jouvet as his helpful but scheming steward. The titanic jest of Volpone, elaborated on and executed with devilish cunning by the wily Mosca is, noted the critics, a masterful stroke of irony, with Mosca enjoying the last laugh. He becomes heir to his patron's gold and turns the old merchant out in the street. After Volpone is declared "dead," Mosca saves the old man from being hanged. At the end, Mosca is throwing gold out the window to the crowds below.

Central to Mosca's fabulous feats, which expose the duplicity and greed of Volpone's friends, are the way he talks the silk merchant Corvino into consenting to send his pretty wife Colomba to comfort the supposedly dying old man; and the trickery he employs to get the aged usurer Corbaccio to name Volpone as the beneficiary of his will.

With its farcical air, the film gets away with lots of hijinks, which in other contexts of the day would have been called bad taste or worse. These include an attempted rape, the dousing of a gondolier serenader with a chamber pot, and other "mentions and unmentionables," but all done in a spirit of fun, Gallic style, "that'll melt the cold tip of a bluenose," wrote *Variety*.

Harry Baur, wrote the *New York Times* in December 1947, when the film was released in a censored version in the United States, "plays Volpone with broad theatrical gestures and some of the most delightful and suggestive facial grimaces you are likely to see in a long time on the screen." Baur, who was Jewish, had died in France in 1943. But towering above all, wrote the newspaper, "is the brilliantly modulated acting" of Jouvet. Tourneur's film, the critic concluded, "has a gusto that is to be admired." Extant.

Péchés de jeunesse / *Mistakes of Childhood*

(1941). Continental-Tobis. Script: Albert Valentin. Adaptation: Michel Duran and Charles Spaak. Photography: Jules Kruger. Design: Guy de Gastyne. Music: Henri Sauguet. With Harry Baur (Lacalade), Pierre Bertin (Gaston Noblet), Alfred Pasquali (Edmond Vacheron), Suzanne Dantès (Louise Noblet), Lise Delamare (Madeleine), Margaret Ducouret (Emma), Jean Bobillot (Lucien Noblet), Jean Buquet (Frédéric), Monique Joyce (Mlle. Florence), Guillaume de Sax (Dr. Pelletan), Jeanne Fusier Gir, and Jacques Varennes.

In May 1941, a year after France surrendered to, and signed an armistice with, Nazi Germany, Tourneur shot this 95-minute nationalist tale, based on the sad story by Albert Valentin. By this point in his career, Tourneur was one of many French performers and writers under contract to Continental-Tobis. Others included Pierre Benôit, Henri Decoin, Georges Lacombe, Georges Simenon, Christian-Jaque, Danielle Darrieux, Arletty, and Spinelly. Tourneur's film is a series of four sketches (along the lines of *Carnet de bal*) that stars the great Jewish actor Harry Baur who had given a towering performance in *Volpone* (released in 1941). In his next-to-last film before his torture and death at the hands of the Paris Gestapo, Baur gave a more restrained performance in deference to the troubled times.

Baur plays rich, vain, old Lacalade, who, in his youth, had engaged in numerous follies. Now living alone, he decides, on the advice of his doctor, to make amends for past misdeeds. He will try to find out what happened to the children he fathered and abandoned. Although Lacalade's voyage of conscience starts out as a selfish attempt to secure love, the effort will change his life.

The first search leads Lacalade to Edmond Vacheron, a fine young man who is the happy owner, along with his mother Emma, of a restaurant. Lacalade is met with disappointing news. The young man tells the old one that he is no longer in need of a father. Lacalade departs empty-handed.

The second of his illegitimate children is Lucien. This man turns out to be a brilliant and talented composer who, at the age of 22, saw his ballet performed at the Paris Opera. Lucien was able to attain a measure of success, he tells Lacalade, because of the sacrifice by his good and caring stepfather. Lacalade again comes up empty.

The third of the children Lacalade tracks down is Frédéric, the son of a Mlle. Florence. She tells Lacalade that the young man is an acrobat in a circus; however, he is not, in fact, Lacalade's son. Disappointed, Lacalade searches for the last child. The fourth and final child turns out to be the one who has suffered the most because of an indifferent world. Abandoned not only by Lacalade but also by his mother, he was reared in an orphanage.

Though Lacalade can do only a little for this son now that he has grown up, he decides on making a grander gesture: Lacalade gains a measure of consolation when he welcomes the children from the orphanage into his home. Extant.

Mam'zelle Bonaparte /
Miss Bonaparte

(1942). Continental-Tobis. Script: Henri-André Legrand. Photography: Jules Kruger. Design: Guy de Gastyne. Music: Henri Verdun. With Edwige Feuillère (Cora Pearl), Monique Joyce (Lucy de Kaula), Guillaume de Sax (Prince Jérôme), Marguerite Pierry, Raymond Rouleau (Philippe de Vaudrey), Noël Roquevert (Criscelli), Aimé Clariond (Duke de Morny), and Nina Sinclair.

This Tourneur work belongs to a genre that was enormously popular in France during the war: the costume drama with a hidden meaning for French filmgoers. It is set in the 19th century, the favored period for such films. Tourneur's film became one of the most popular French films of the time, featuring the beautiful Feuillère (1907–1998), who was called the first lady of French cinema.

Adapted from the novel by Pierre Chanlaine and Gérard Bourgeois, Tourneur's thrilling 100-minute historical fantasy is about a woman who discovers a secret about the man she has fallen in love with: that he is plotting to overthrow the ruler of the nation, Napoléon III — who is her cousin. Her love opens her up to life, but at the same time the conflict this knowledge engenders has fatal consequences.

Cora Pearl, nicknamed Mam'zelle Bonaparte, is a notorious demimondaine and the mistress of Prince Jérôme Bonaparte, cousin of Napoléon III. Because of a carriage accident on the way to Bordeaux, she meets Philippe de Vaudrey, a property owner plotting against the emperor (and the Second Empire) in order to restore the monarchy. Though she falls passionately in love with the charming and irresistible Philippe, Cora hides the facts of her own identity, calling herself merely Madame Jérôme. This attempt to seek and hold onto love will backfire.

When the coup he supports fails, Philippe is wounded in a fight and flees. He takes refuge at Cora's home. Cora's rival for Philippe's attention, Lucy de

Kaula, alerts the authorities to the man's whereabouts—and reveals Cora's identity to her lover. Torn, Philippe gives himself up, while Cora takes revenge by wounding Lucy in a sword fight. Then Cora frantically rushes out to try to obtain a pardon for Philippe. She obtains one, but delivers it too late to the authorities; Philippe has died trying to escape. Cora returns home alone, a courtesan bereft of love.

During the war, in the early part of 1942 in occupied France, *Petit Parisien* called Tourneur's work a "magnificent film with an incomparable refinement and sumptuosity ... Feuillère is more beautiful and more moving than she has ever been ... Rouleau, a partner for the first time, will share with her the triumph that will greet the new couple of French cinema." Extant.

La Main du diable / Hand of the Devil

(1942). Continental-Tobis. Script: Jean-Paul Le Chanois. Photography: Armand Thirard. Design: André Andriev. Music Roger Dumas. With Pierre Fresnay (Roland Brissot), Josselyne Gaël (Irène), Noël Roquevert (Mélissa, the cook), Guillaume de Sax (Gibelin), Palau (little man in black), Pierre Larquey (Ange), Jean Davy (the musketeer), Jean Coquelin, Jean Despeaux (the boxer), Garzoni (the juggler), René Blancard (the surgeon), Marcel (the illusionist), and André Gabriello.

Tourneur's last great work hearkens back to his earliest efforts at Grand Guignol. It is an 82-minute tale of mystery, adapted by Jean-Paul Le Chanois from Gérard de Nerval's story "La Main enchantée." Tourneur carefully created a very distressing atmosphere by means of an expressionistic use of shading and lighting. He presented an astonishing and enthralling history of a curse set in motion by a diabolical pact between a painter and a "little man in black" who wants to take his soul. The *Penguin Film Review* noted that the theme "could not lend itself better to film adaptation."

It begins when Roland, a man in a panic, arrives at an isolated mountain inn. He is carrying only a precious little enigmatic box under his left arm. Thunder resounds, darkness settles in, and when the lights come on, the box has vanished. The man then tells his terrible history of the "hand of the Devil."

In front of the other guests, Roland offers shocking details. He was once struggling to express his feelings on canvas, hoping to win the affections of his beautiful model Irène. He altered his life by purchasing, for a mere cent, a grisly talisman—a hand—from an Italian cook named Mélissa.

This ghoulish memento brings Roland everything he wants—love, marriage, fame, and wealth. Fortune smiles on him. But Roland can only keep the hand for a year, after which he is obliged to sell it for *less* than he paid for it. Otherwise, the Devil—a little man in black—will come looking for him, demanding his due.

Roland has forgotten the expiration date. But the Devil is willing to resell the item to Roland—at a figure that doubles every day Roland delays. The unfairness of it all corrodes his life. His wife, Irène, is then kidnapped and killed. Roland frantically tries to come up with the money. At a carnival one evening, Roland is confronted by seven successive owners of the item: a robber, juggler, musketeer, illusionist, surgeon, boxer, and the cook. On the run no more, Roland has taken refuge at the isolated retreat. Having told his story, Roland goes to the nearby tomb of Monk Maximus Léo, where the Devil had

La Main du diable (1942): The carnival scene is one of the fantastic elements at the core of Tourneur's tale of the grotesque, his last great film.

first concealed the hand 300 years earlier. There he kills himself. His death breaks the long chain of events associated with the hand of the Devil.

Made and released in France during the war, Tourneur's film was the only "fantastic" film produced by Continental during this period. Scriptwriter Jean-Paul Le Chanois transposed to a contemporary universe the romantic account of Gérard de Nerval's story. During these years, French filmmakers produced some fantastic works whose timelessness made it possible to express uncomfortable ideas without risking Nazi censure.

Tourneur's film apparently, then, had a deeper meaning for the French population; that is, it was taken to represent the relationship between France and Nazi Germany. When the film was released in the United States in April 1947 under the title *Carnival of Sinners*, the *New York Times* noted "there may be some hidden significance in this film which is applicable to those citizens of France who bartered their souls during the Nazi occupation."

The direction by Tourneur, wrote *Variety*, "is well paced, has its suspenseful moments, and carries with it a degree of symbolism." One scene in particular stands out. Around a banquet table, Roland's predecessors are gathered, and the image "has a balletlike quality that moves with poetic motion." Extant.

Le Val d'enfer / The Valley of Hell

(1943). Continental-A.C.E. Script: Carlo Rim. Photography: Armand Thirard. Design: Guy de Gastyne. Music: Roger Dumas. With Charles Blavette (Cagnard), Raymond Cordy (Poiroux), Edward Delmont (the old man), Gabrielle Fontan (the old woman), Gabriel Gabrio (Noël Bienvenu), Paul Fournier (Romieux), Lucien Gallas (Barthélémy), Ginette Leclerc (Marthe), Georges Patrix, and André Reybaz (Bastien Bienvenu).

Tourneur's 100-minute film is a sad tale of loneliness, suffering, and acceptance, written by his longtime colleague Carlo Rim (the pseudonym of Jean Marius Richard).

It centers on Noël Bienvenu, a widower and father of a young man who has gotten into trouble with the law. Noël works as a quarry foreman. His career has been one of slaving under the sun and the crushing heat, in the "Valley of Hell." Many workmen labor there under his supervision, which is firm but friendly. He is around fifty, living with his parents who adore him and dream of seeing their son married again. But Noël is working himself to exhaustion to obliterate his loneliness and to forget the fact that his son Bastien, a hooligan, is in prison. The deathbed request of an old friend changes Noël's life.

As he lies dying, Romieux asks Noël, his old comrade, to take care of his free-spirited daughter, Marthe, who, in Paris, lives off her charms. Noël goes a step further: He suggests that Marthe come and live with him. Touched by the tender offer, Marthe accepts. Cherished by Noël's parents, she seems to like her more settled country life, and soon agrees to marry her benefactor. But on the day of her marriage, the very new Mrs. Bienvenu realizes that the world of her husband and that of his workmen—Poiroux, Cagnard, Rodrigo, and others—may not be for her.

Then she starts to receive the knowing glances of Barthélémy, the handsome boss of a tugboat that carts stones from the quarry. Marthe becomes his mistress. That greatly upsets Noël's parents, who eventually are forced to leave for an old-age home. Her husband, unaware of her affair, all the while yields to her whims. But a silent, solitary, and envious workman knows the truth of what the Marthe and her lover are up to.

One day, this man, called the "savage," sets a boobytrap on one of the quarry trails, which leads to a fatal accident: Marthe is killed in an explosion. Noël never finds out that Marthe planned to announce that she was going to leave him. A widower once more, Noël brings his parents back to his home. And when Bastien, who appears to have repented, rings at the gate of his father's home, the good man opens his arms to his son. Extant.

Cécile est morte / Cecile Is Dead

(1944). Continental-A.C.E. Assistant: Jean Devaivre. Script: Jean Paul Le Chanois. Dialogue: Michel Duran. Photography: Pierre Montazel and Roger Dormoy. Design: Guy de Gastyne. Music: Roger Dumas. With Jean Brochard, André Gabriello, Germaine Kerjean (Juliette Boynet), Albert Préjean (Maigret), Santa Relli (Cécile Pardon), Jean Brochard (Dandurand), André Reybaz (Gérard Pardon), Liliane Maigne (Gilberte Pardon) and Yves Deniaud (Machepied), and Marcel Carpentier.

This is an excellently atmospheric and suspenseful ninety-minute adaptation of the crime novel of the same name by Georges Simenon. It is one of three Simenon adaptations in which Préjean plays Maigret. Tourneur's adaptation is full of tricks and deceptions, punctuated at times with humor, but the director avoids the social analysis and psychological interpretation that characterize the crime films of Julien Duvivier and Henri-Georges Clouzot during this period of French filmmaking. Rather, Tourneur does his usual nice job of setting the scenes for the action.

At the Quai des Orfèvres, people smile when they see Cécile Pardon. For six months, indeed, the young woman has been coming to the police station to talk to Police Chief Maigret. Annoyed over the mocking remarks of his colleagues, Maigret pays her little heed. Cécile, however, is sure that somebody is haunting her apartment building, where she lives with her aunt, a miserly old woman named Juliette Boynet. Cécile wants police protection.

Soon thereafter, the police are notified about the decapitated body of a young woman in a hotel. The name of Cécile is scrawled on a wash-hand basin at the scene of the crime. Cécile, seeking to calm her anxiety that night, lends a key to her apartment to her brother Gérard. He is willing to watch over her, perhaps even be paid a bit since his wife is expecting a baby. But Juliette Boynet, the miserly old aunt, refuses to let him in.

The following day, Cécile shows up at Maigret's office in a panic, but Maigret has no time to see her. He has just learned the identity of the dead girl. She is Gilberte Pardon — Cécile's sister — who worked for a man named Machepied, a cousin and associate of Mrs. Boynet. Maigret heads out to find the old woman — and finds her strangled in her bed. On his return to the office, Maigret gets more bad news: Cécile is dead, strangled also, without having been able to speak to him.

The police chief questions a man named Dandurand, a neighbor, former lover, and businessman with ties to Mrs. Boynet. The old woman, Maigret finds out to his great surprise, was the owner of a string of brothels throughout France. Maigret also finds out more: that Dandurand on the previous night had tried to drug Cécile in order to sneak into her apartment. Instead, Gérard drank the drink intended for Cécile who, awakened, heard her aunt and Dandurand speaking of money, lots of money.

Once alone with her aunt, Cécile demanded that the miserly old woman lend money to her brother Gérard. When she refused, Cécile strangled her.

The following day, fearing revelations of his involvement, Dandurand strangled Cécile before she could confess to Maigret. Dandurand is held, but, for lack of evidence, Maigret lets him go. With the burial of the three women, Machepied, who was unaware of the hidden resources of his cousin, meets Dandurand and the managers of her houses. Then Maigret comes upon the truth: Mrs. Boynet had hidden a letter proving that Dandurand had poisoned her husband.

Having discovered the letter, Gilberte Pardon had come to Paris to blackmail Dandurand, who murdered her in her hotel room. The surviving sibling Gérard inherits his aunt's money. He is now free and rich. After his wife gives birth to a girl, Maigret suggests that she be named named Cécile. Extant.

Après l'amour / After Love

(1947). Modern Films. Assistant: Christian Gaudin. Script: Jean Bernard and Jacques Natanson. Photography: Armand Thirard. Design: Guy de Gastyne and Boutié. Music: Roger Dumas. With Pierre Blanchar (François Mézaule), Simone Renant (Nicole Mézaule), Gisèle Pascal (Germaine), Fernand Fabre (Fournier), Germaine

Ledoyen (the sister), and Gabrielle Fontan (Catou).

This work is based on the 1922 short story "Un Soir de pluie"/"Evening Rain" by the highly regarded Henri Duvernois, and on the subsequent dramatization, called *Après l'amour*, by Duvernois and his colleague Pierre Wolff. In 1932, Tourneur's old friend Léonce Perret directed an early sound version, which was more or less a photographed play. Tourneur shot this later, more animated and tender rendition in his usual efficient manner in five weeks and under budget.

The contemporary tale, which has the kind of surprise ending Tourneur favored, retains the brilliant dialogue for which Henri Duvernois became known. It is an intriguing and intense ninety-minutes' worth of an old story. However, here there is a twist.

The crisis of the tale occurs when Prof. François Mézaule is at the height of his glory. He has just received the Nobel Prize in literature. He discovers to his shock, however, that all is not well at home. Even though he and his wife have not slept together for years, he is stunned to find out that his wife, Nicole, has been unfaithful. Feeling angry and betrayed, he has an affair and falls in love with an attractive young student, Germaine.

Nicole soon has a child by her own lover, a journalist named Fournier, on the very same day that Germaine gives birth to a son by the professor. Germaine dies not long after. Nicole's act of taking a lover at first appears to be the thing that sets everything else in motion. But her husband is far from innocent: He has been a womanizer for years. Although exposed and in a desperate situation herself because of an act of indiscretion, Nicole has long had reason to scorn intimacy with her self-absorbed husband.

Six years pass. François has taken another mistress when the events surrounding his affair years earlier with Germaine come to light. The child of that union is about the same age as Nicole's boy, and is being raised by Germaine's sister. François, in a heartfelt moment, suggests that it might be best for both the children if they raised that boy as well. Nicole at first resists the idea.

One mystery at the heart of the tale is whether the child who is in François and Nicole's home is the father's or the mother's. The mystery is cleared up when Nicole eventually agrees to François' idea. They will be the parents of two boys. Only then does Nicole find out that six years earlier, when she gave birth and Germaine died giving birth, François did something extraordinary: he switched the babies. By now admitting to what he did, François faces a harsh truth about himself. At the same time, Nicole learns that the boy she is taking into her home is really her own, the one she actually gave birth to. François' startling confession allows husband and wife to come to some kind of reconciliation.

Tourneur's direction, notably his use of flashbacks to fill in the missing details, was called "skillful," and Armand Thirard's photography was called "impeccable." *Variety*'s Paris reviewer said this of the veteran director: "Maurice Tourneur, who is now 72 and has had plenty of Hollywood experience, enjoys the rare distinction among French directors of never having one of his numerous pictures turn anything but a handsome profit to the producer. He is still the safest and soundest French director.... This is what makes this very modest budgeter well worthy of notice.... Tourneur's name is hardly visible on some of the publicity and doesn't even appear on the theatre front, which leaves him indifferent…. Picture is … type of story the French proletariat loves." Extant.

Impasse des deux anges / Dilemma of Two Angels

(1948). Tuscherer-Sirius. Assistant Directors: Roland Stragliati and Pierre Alkan. Script: Jacques Viot. Adaptation: Jean-Paul Le Chanois. Photography: Claude Renoir. Design: Jean d'Eaubonne. Music: Yves Baudrier. With Paul Meurisse (Jean), Simone Signoret (Marianne), Danièle Delorme, Marcel Herrand (Marquis Antoine de Fontaine), Jacques Castelot, and Jacques Baumer.

This was Tourneur's last film in his long career. He shot it in six weeks, after which he suffered the accident that ended his filmmaking days.

It is a gripping, atmospheric 84-minute psychological tale about a woman who has forsaken her main passion in life, her love of acting and the stage, to marry into wealth. The ruse is exposed for what it is when, out of the past, comes a former lover, who has his own approach to wealth: He steals to get it. An attempted burglary leads to a painful misadventure and an unwelcome awakening for the two of them.

Marianne is going to become the wife of the Marquis de Fontaine. For him, she has vowed to give up her career. On the evening before their marriage, there is a reception to mark the upcoming occasion at the Marquis's beautiful, luxurious home. But a band of thieves is planning to steal a beautiful diamond necklace that the Marquis has given his bride to be. Jean, a smooth, stylish specialist at pilfering jewelry, has taken on the main assignment. He will pretend to be an extra at the affair. There is one hitch, however: After Jean gets his hands on the necklace, Marianne recognizes him. They were lovers long ago, when they were poorer but perhaps wiser.

She and Jean reunite for a brief moment; her feelings of being alive and wanted are revived. Marianne thinks about taking a bigger step: running away with this man. But there is a problem: the other gang members are becoming suspicious. They begin looking for Jean and want the loot. Trapped in the house, with no way out, the two of them deem their love to be impossible, a dead end, and a blind alley. Jean returns the necklace. Marianne returns to her future husband, in the foyer. Then with little left to live for, Jean allows himself to be slain in a shootout with the gangsters.

The young Signoret was credited with being "alive and sincere" in one of her earliest screen roles. Meurisse (Jean) was fresh from his scintillating performance in the exciting crime drama, *Macadam/Back Streets of Paris* (1946). Extant.

SOURCES

Photos and stills were obtained from the Museum of Modern Art, Cinémathèque Française, and the Quigley Collection (Georgetown University).

Reviews are quoted from *Exhibitor's Trade Review, Film Daily, Harrison's Reports, Monthly Film Bulletin, Motion Picture News, Moving Picture World, The New York Times,* and *Variety.*

Selected Bibliography

American Film Institute Catalogues 1911–1920 and *1921–30* (1993).

Catalogue des Films de Fiction de Première Partie, 1929–1939. Paris, Archives du Film de Centre National de la Cinématographie, 1988.

Catalogue des Films Françaises de Long Métrage, 1929–1939. Cinémathèque Royale de Belgique.

Daisne, Johan. *Filmographic Dictionary of World Literature,* 1977.

Griffithiana, May/September 1992.

Histoire du Cinéma Française, 1929–1935.

Mitry, Jean. *Filmographie universelle.* Paris, Institut des hautes études cinématographiques, 1963–1987.

Le Roy, Eric, and Laurent Billia. *Eclair: un siècle du cinéma à Epinay-sur-Seine.* Calman-Levy, 1995.

Thurman, Judith. *A Life of Colette.* Knopf, 1999.

Waldman, Harry. *Beyond Hollywood's Grasp: American Filmmakers Abroad, 1914–1945.* Scarecrow Press, 1994.

INDEX

A.P.R.-Goldwyn 110
Accusée, levez-vous! 134, 142–143
Adair, Belle 33
Agnel, Raymond 5, 11, 12, 16, 17, 146, 149
Aguettand, Lucien 152
Aitken, Spottiswoode 82, 83, 98
Alexander, S. Grubb 91
Alias Jimmy Valentine 38–39
Alkan, Pierre 168
Aloma of the South Seas 29, 126–128
Andriev, André 163
Andriot, Josette 17, 22
Andriot, Lucien 17, 43, 61, 63, 65, 67, 70, 72, 73, 75, 77
Anstey, F.M. 114
Antoine, André 74, 147, 152
Antoine, André-Paul 152
Après l'amour 138, 166–167
Aquettand, Lucien 147
Arménise, Victor 142, 143, 146, 152, 153
Armstrong, Paul 38
Arnaud, Etienne 25
Arnstam, Alexander 157
Arquillière, Alexandre 8, 20, 147
Artaud, Antonin 152
Artcraft 70
Associated Producers 28
Au nom de la loi 134, 142, 144–145
Aumont, Jean-Pierre 149
Avec le sourire 27, 136, 154, 155–157
The Bait 103
Ballin, Hugo 110
Ballin, Mabel 82, 84

Bara, Jean 149
Barbary Sheep 65–67, 79, 80
Barnett, Chester 32, 34, 39, 53, 78
Barreyre, Henri 144
Barrymore, Lionel 29, 128
Barsacq, André 160
Baudrier, Yves 168
Baur, Harry 22, 136, 137, 153, 156, 157, 160, 161
Baxter, Warner 127
Beal, Scott 115
Beban, George 46, 47
Bedford, Barbara 100, 101, 104, 105, 125, 126
Beery, Wallace 85, 87, 104
Bell, Emma 56
Bellamy, Madge 107, 108
Belle, Tula 72, 73
Benôit, Georges 25, 144, 147, 150
Benton, Curtis 120
La Bergère d'Ivry 14
Bern, Paul 110
Bernard, Jean 166
Bernard, Jean Jacques 157
Bernstein, Henri 3, 149, 153
Bertin, Pierre 161
Berval, Antonin 150
Bilinsky, Boris 156, 160
Billings, Florence 78
Binet, Alfred 149
Blackmore, R.D. 107
Blanchar, Pierre 166
Blinn, Holbrook 42, 43
The Blue Bird 27, 73–75, 79, 80
Le Bonhomme Jadis 5, 11
Borzage, Frank 29
Bosworth, Hobart 106
Boudrioz, Robert 9, 20

Bouffes du Nord 3
Bourgeois, Gérard 162
Boutié 166
Bowers, John 107
Brady, William A. 26, 131, 138
Brady World 26, 31, 32, 34, 37
The Brass Bottle 28, 113–114
Breamer, Sylvia 80, 81
Brenon, Herbert 139
Bringuier, Paul 145
Broadhurst, George 32, 60
Broek, John van den 26, 31, 32, 34, 37, 62
The Broken Butterfly 89–91
Brown, Clarence 26, 27, 41, 42, 43, 47, 48, 51, 52, 53, 58, 60, 92, 93, 104, 106, 130, 131
Buchanan, Thompson 41
Bugeaud, Thomas-Robert 15
Bujard, Marc 143, 144
Burel, Léonce-Henri 142
Burgess, Neil 91
Burne, Brian Donn 106
Busch, Mae 110
Butler, David 91
The Butterfly on the Wheel 43–44

Cadet, Rivers 146, 154
Caine, Hall 28
Le Camée 8, 20
Capra, Frank 29
Card, James 1
Carette, Julienne 146
Carré, Ben 25, 26, 39, 48, 49, 51, 52, 53, 56, 58, 61, 63, 65, 67, 70, 72, 73, 75, 77, 78, 82, 85, 87, 89, 95
Carré, Lucien 154

Castle, Agnes 70
Castle, Edgerton 70
Cat People 135
Cécile est morte 165–166
Cerdan, Simon 144
Chaliapin, Feodor, Jr. 141
Champigny, Renée 152
Chaney, Lon 87, 88, 93, 94, 95, 98
Chanlaine, Pierre 162
Chanois, Jean-Paul Le 163, 165, 168
Chantal, Marcelle 144, 145
Charlia, Georges 142
Chautard, Emile 2, 4, 5, 6, 7, 11, 12, 13, 14, 16, 17, 21, 25, 44, 46, 53, 54, 55
Chevalier, Maurice 136, 139, 154, 155, 156
Christensen, Benjamin 128
The Christian 28, 29, 110–111
Christians, Broerken 100, 101
Citroën, André 3
Clark, Marguerite 75, 76, 138
Clerc, Borel 154
The Closed Road 49–51, 93
Clothes Make the Pirate 123–124
Le Coeur d'une gosse 7, 17
Cohl, Emile 4
Colas, René 146, 149, 150, 153, 160
Colette 8, 19
Colombier, Jacques 142, 144, 146, 149
Companéez, Jacques 157
Conrad, Joseph 87
Conscience de l'enfant 5, 12
Continental-A.C.E 165
Continental-Tobis 161, 162, 163
Cook, Warren 55, 56, 58, 61, 72, 78, 80
Cooper, James Fenimore 104
Cormon, Eugène 147
Le Corso rouge 9, 22
The County Fair 91
Courant, Curt 149
Courteline, Georges 146, 147
Creelman, James A. 126
Cronjager, Henry 123, 125
The Cub 41–42

Dallin, Jacques 153
La Dame de chez Maxim 5, 12
La Dame de Monsoreau 7, 16
Darrieux, Danielle 136, 157, 158, 159
Davis, Owen 34
Daw, Marjorie 92
Dax, Jean 142, 144
Day, Josette 156
Day, Marceline 29
d'Eaubonne, Jean 168
Debucourt, Jean 152
Decaux, Lucile 157
Deçoin, Henri 157
Deep Waters 29, 100, 101, 103
Delannoy, Marcel 160
Delluc, Louis 27, 40
Delubac, Jacqueline 160
Delvé, Suzanne 142

De Mille, Cecil B. 138
d'Ennery, Adolphe 147
Deréan, Rosine 147
Le Dernier pardon 8, 20
Derval, Marie-Louise 16
Les Deux orphélines 135, 147–149
Devaivre, Jean 156
Devalence 13, 15, 22
Le Dictateur 16
Dietrich, Marlene 133, 141, 142
Dillon, Robert A. 104
Dix, Richard 110
A Doll's House 70–73
Dolley, Georges 146
Dormoy, Roger 165
Drury Lane 82
Dubois, Philip R. 104
Dulac, Laurence 13
Dullin, Charles 160
Duma, Alexandre 7
Dumaitre, André 160
Dumas, Roger 163, 165, 166
du Maurier, George L. 39
Dunn, Emma 31, 32
Duquesne 15
Duquesne, Emil 154
Duran, Michel 161, 165
Duvernois, Henri 167
Dwan, Alan 28

Eclair 2, 4, 5, 6, 11, 12, 13, 14, 15, 16, 17, 18, 19, 20, 21, 22, 23, 25, 31, 32, 34, 37, 181
Elvidge, June 43, 48, 53, 55
L'Equipage 134, 142
Equitable-World 39, 41, 42, 44, 47
Equitable-World Film Corp 38
Errol, Leon 123, 124
Escoffier, Paul 13
Evans, Madge 38
Exhibitor's Trade Review 58, 62, 65, 70, 80, 84, 87, 96, 103, 109, 111, 112, 115, 116, 119, 123, 124, 181

Fabre, Fernand 166
Fairfax, Marion 117, 123, 125
Faivre, Joseph 12, 17
Farkas, Nicholas 141
Ferguson, Elsie 65, 66, 67, 70, 71, 72, 79, 138
Fernandel 134, 135, 146
Fernay, Roger 157
Feuillère, Edwige 137, 139, 162
Feydeau, Georges 5, 12
La Fiancée maudite 17
Figures de cire 8, 9, 21
Les Filles de la concierge 135
Film Daily 51, 52, 56, 73, 84, 91, 103, 116, 117, 131, 181
First National 28, 104, 106, 107, 111, 113, 115, 117, 123, 125
Fischbeck, Harry 126
Florey, Robert 2
Foolish Matrons 106–107
Forrester, Izola M. 118
France 1, 3, 4, 6, 7, 15, 16, 26, 29, 38, 42, 49, 63, 93, 133, 134, 135, 136, 137, 138, 139, 144, 149, 155, 160, 161, 162, 163

Francis, Alec B. 32, 34, 37, 38, 42, 44, 47
Franklin, Edgar 52
Frappa, Jean José 142
Fresnay, Pierre 152, 163
Le Friquet 7, 8, 16, 19–20
La Frochard et les deux orphélines 147
Furthman, Jules 87, 92, 95, 98
Futrelle, Jacques 80

Gabin, Jean 134, 146
Gaboriau, Emile 9, 22
Gabrio, Gabriel 145, 147, 165
Les Gaîtés de l'escadron (1913) 15–16
Les Gaîtés de l'escadron (1932) 134, 146
Gallas, Lucien 165
Gance, Abel 142
Garat, Jean 13, 15, 22
Gastyne, Guy de 153, 157, 161, 162, 165, 166
Gaudin, Christian 166
Germany 13, 14, 18, 20, 22, 23, 133, 141, 164
Gilbert, John 26, 82, 92, 93, 98, 99, 100, 101, 103
A Girl's Folly 53–54, 130
Gish, Dorothy 123
Gittens, Wyndham 93, 106, 107, 110, 111
Glory, Marie 155
Goldwyn, Samuel 28
Gordon, Huntley 122
Gouget, Henri 11, 15, 18, 21
Grand Guignol 2, 6, 7, 8, 9, 18, 21, 42, 149
Gray, Gilda 126, 127, 128
The Great Redeemer 27, 92–93
Green, Howard 128
Griffith, David Wark 1, 135, 138, 139, 147
Groswell Smith 91
Guilbert, Yvette 147
Guissart, René 25, 78, 80, 82, 85, 87, 91, 93, 95
Gyp 8, 9, 20, 23
Gys, Robert 143

Hall, Emmett Campbell 44, 46
Hamilton, Henry 55, 82
Hamilton, Mahlon 56, 58, 60, 110
Hampton, Hope 102, 103
The Hand of Peril 48–49
Harrison's Reports 91, 93, 95, 109, 111, 116, 120, 128, 181
Hearst, William Randolph 29
Hedman, Martha 41, 42
Hemmerede, Edward G. 43
Hersholt, Jean 117
Hicks, Seymour 77, 120
Hilburn, Percy 128
Hines, Johnny 32, 38, 41, 47, 53
Hodkinson 93
Holt, Jack 85, 87, 89
Hubbard, Lucien 128, 130
Hull, Edith M. 125
Human Driftwood 44–47
Hymer, John B. 127

I Walked with a Zombie 135
Ibels, André 73, 74, 75, 77, 78
Ibert, Jacques 147, 150, 152, 156
Ibsen 72
Ile de France Films 160
Impasse des deux anges 138, 142, 168
Ince, Thomas 28, 138, 139
Ingram, Rex 139
Irvine, Robin 133, 141
The Isle of Lost Ships 28 111–113, 130, 133
Isle of Man 28, 111
The Ivory Snuff Box 42–43

Jacobs, Lewis 30, 139
Jaques-Dalcroze, Emile 5
Jaubert, Maurice 149, 150
Jealous Husbands 115–117
Jean de poudre 6, 15
Jeanson, Henri 156
Jonson, Ben 160
Joseph-Renaud, Jean 3, 15, 19, 20, 23
Jourjon, Charles 25
Jouvet, Louis 139, 160
Justin de Marseille 135, 150–151

Kane, Gail 36, 37, 51
Karloff, Boris 104, 121
Katia 136, 157–159
Kelley, Winthrop 77
Kenyon, Doris 46, 47, 53, 54, 130
Kessel, Joseph 142
Kirk, Charles M. 126
Knapp, Penelope 89
Kock, Charles Paul de 7, 18
Koenigsmark 136, 152, 153
Kortner, Fritz 133, 141
Krauss, Charles 7, 9, 16, 17, 21, 22
Kruger, Jules 162
Kummer, Frederic Arnold 42
Kuter, Léo E. 120
Kyne, Peter B. 121

La Marr, Barbara 114, 117, 118
Lagrange, Louise 137, 149
Landi, Elissa 152
Lang, André 149
Langois, Henri 1
The Last of the Mohicans 1, 27, 104–106
Lattès, Marcel 154
The Law of the Land 60–61
Ledoux, Fernand 160
Lefebre, Robert 157
The Legion of the Condemned 134
Legrand, Henri-André 162
Lehár, Franz 5, 13
Leopard Man 135
Lepage, Edouard 149
Lepage, Henry 146, 156, 157
Leroux, Gaston 6, 13
Liabel, André 13, 16, 17
Lidoir 135, 146, 147
The Life Line 27, 85–87
Lion, Roger 4
Litson, M.N. 63
Loan, H. H. Van 92

Lochakov, Ivan 156
Loder, John 157, 159
Lodge, John 152
Lonergan, Lloyd 80
Lorde, André de 3, 7, 8, 9, 18, 21, 149
Lorna Doone 28, 107–110
Love, Bessie 117
Love, Montague 129
Lubitsch, Ernst 156
Lucas, Roger 147
Lucchesi, M. de 142
Luguet, André 153
Lutèce Film–Aubert 142
Lynn, Emmy 7, 20, 147
Lytell, Bert 120, 121

MacDonald, Donald 107, 108
Mademoiselle Cent Millions 7, 18
Maginot 3
Maigne, Charles 65, 67, 69, 70, 73, 75, 111
La Main du diable 137, 142, 163–164
Maison de dances 118, 134, 143–144
Mam'zelle Bonaparte 137, 162–163
The Man of the Hour 26, 32–34, 41
Manning, Mildred 93, 94, 106
Manuel, Roland 144
Marchand, Léopold 153
Marinoff, Fania 68, 69
Marion, Frances 53, 64
Marmont, Percy 70, 126, 127
Marquis Films 154
Marriott, Crittenden 111
Marshall, Tully 85, 113, 123, 125
Martel de Janville 8
Martin, Charles 56, 58
Martin, Vivian 34, 35, 37, 43, 138
Masi, Philip W. 55, 56
Mason, Shirley 97
Mathis, Milly 150, 154
Mayer, Louis B. 29, 160
McDonald, Jack 92, 93, 98, 101, 103, 104, 107
Meerson, Lazare 150
Meingard, V. 156
Menasco, Milton 107, 111
Mendaille, Daniel 142
Metropa Film 157
Meurisse, Paul 168
MGM 29, 121, 128
Mirabeau, Sibylle Gabrielle Marie Antoinette de Riquetti de 8
Le Miroir d'Ali Maboul 6, 14
Mitry, Jean 25
Moana of the South Seas 127
Modern Films 166
Modot, Gaston 133, 141
Monsieur Lecoq 21–22
Montazel, Pierre 165
Monthly Film Bulletin 157, 160, 181
Moore, Owen 117
Morgan, Ira 121
Morlay, Gaby 134, 136, 142, 143, 153
Morphy, Michel 8, 18

Mortimer, Edward J. 91
Mother 26, 31–32
Motion Picture News 29, 38, 42, 66, 98, 181
Moving Picture World 14, 18, 19, 22, 26, 29, 32, 33, 38, 39, 40, 44, 47, 48, 49, 52, 53, 54, 56, 58, 61, 62, 65, 67, 69, 70, 72, 75, 78, 81, 88, 91, 95, 97, 101, 107, 181
Mueller, Floyd 87, 92, 95, 98, 101, 104
Mullin, Eugène 121
Mumford, Cecil 107
Murat, Jean 142
Mürger, Henri 5
Murillo, Mary 134, 142
Murnau 26
My Lady's Garter 27, 80–81
Myers, Harry 113, 114
Mysterious Island 29, 128–132, 134
Myton, Fred 113, 115, 117

Naldi, Nita 123, 124
Natan 134, 135, 142, 143, 144, 146, 149, 150
Natanson, Jacques 166
Née, Louis 156
Neilan, Marshall 28
Nelson, Frances 44, 45
Nerval, Gérard de 163
Neumann, Alfred 156
Never the Twain Shall Meet 29, 121–123
The New York Herald Trubune 156
The New York Times 2, 29, 30, 79, 81, 84, 87, 88, 93, 99, 111, 113, 114, 119, 123, 124, 126, 148, 156, 157, 161, 164, 181
Nichols, George 87
Nielson, Francis 43
Nilsson, Anna Q. 111, 112
Nixon, Marion 120
Norès, Edouard 146
Norris, Frank 37
Novak, Jane 115, 116

Oberfeld 154
Obsession 8, 135, 149
Occupe-toi d'Amélie 5, 12
Odéon 3
Ogle, Charles 95, 98
Okey, Jack 117, 125
Old Loves and New 125–128
Orphans of the Storm 147
Ortlieb, Alfred 98, 101, 103
Owen, Seena 85, 87, 89

Paragon 26, 48, 49, 51, 52, 53, 55
Paramount 2, 27, 56, 58, 60, 61, 63, 65, 67, 70, 73, 75, 77, 78, 80, 82, 85, 87, 95, 98, 101, 103, 126, 136
Paris Films 153
Partir 134, 144
Pathé 4, 142, 143, 144, 146, 149, 150, 152
Le Patriot 136, 156
The Pawn of Fate 46, 47

Pawn of Fire 130
Péchés de jeunesse 137, 161–162
Peerless 38
Pelley, William D. 117
Perret, Léonce 4, 152
Perrier, Jean 160
Peters, House 48, 49, 51, 52, 92, 93
Petit, Fernande 29
Petrova, Olga 56, 58, 59, 60, 138
Pickford, Mary 2, 26, 61, 63, 64, 65, 138
Pidgeon, Walter 125
Pierre, Emile 142
The Pit 26, 36, 37–38, 130
Poe, Edgar Allan 18
Poirier, Léon 142
Poisson, Philippe 9, 20
Polaire 8, 9, 10, 19, 23, 143
Polito, Sol 43, 44
Pollock, Channing 37
The Poor Little Rich Girl 2, 26, 63–65, 74
Potter, Paul M. 39
Powell, William 127
Préjean, Albert 165
The Pride of the Clan 2, 26, 61–63
Prieur, Georges 152
Prim, Suzy 153, 156
Prunella 27, 75–77, 79, 80
Le Puits mitoyen 9, 20
Pujol, René 147
Puvis de Chavannes, Pierre 3

The Rail Rider 52, 93
Raimu 9, 20, 134, 146
Raleigh, Cecil 55, 77, 82, 120
Reboux, Paul 143
Reed, Katherine 107
Rejane 3
Renant, Simone 166
Renaud, Madeleine 149
Renoir, Claude 138, 168
Renoir, Pierre 156, 157
Rignault, Alexandre 150, 160
Rim, Carlo 150, 165
The Rise of Jennie Cushing 67–70
Robertson-Cole 89
Roche, Charles De 118
Rodin, Auguste 3
Roger Richebé Films 152
Rolanda, Rosa 74, 78
Romains, Jules 160
Roquevert, Noël 162, 163
Rose of the World 70
Rosher, Charles 98
Rossi, Tino 150, 151
Rouleau, Raymond 162
Rouletabille Part I (Le Mystère de la chambre jaune) 13–14
Rouletabille Part II (La Dernière incarnation de Larsan) 13–14
Roussell, Henri 4, 15, 18, 19, 20, 21, 22, 23, 142, 146
Les Ruses d'amour 9, 20–21

Sadoul, Georges 78, 138, 142
Saint-Cyr, Renée 147
Sales, Pierre 9, 23

Samson 136, 153–154
Sauguet, Henri 161
Sax, Guillaume de 161, 162, 163
Das Schiff der verlorenen Menschen 133, 141–142
Schroedter, Franz 141
Scott, Homer 101
Scotto, Vincent 150
Selznick, Louis J. 26, 138
Sennett, Mack 28
Sessell, Charles 123
Sharp, Henry 107
Signoret, Simone 138, 168
Sills, Milton 37, 111, 112, 130
Simenon, Georges 137, 165
Simon, Marcel 13, 157
Simon, Simone 149
Sims, George R. 86
Sintzenich, Harold 82
Sjöström, Victor 29
Smith, Hopkinson 101
Société des Productions F.C.L. 156
Soeurette 9, 14, 23
Sokoloff, Vladimir 133, 141
Spaak, Charles 161
Spence, Ralph 61, 63
Sporting Life (1918) 27, 77–78
Sporting Life (1925) 28, 120–121
Standing, Wyndham 58, 60, 70, 80, 81
Starke, Pauline 85, 89, 90, 129
Sternberg, Josef von 27, 29, 53, 54, 55
Sterne, Elaine 61
Stevenson, Robert Louis 95, 97, 98, 101
Stewart, Anita 121, 122
Stiller, Mauritz 29
Stone, Lewis 125, 126
Stragliati, Roland 168
Stroheim, Erich von 27, 29, 107
Sylvaire, Renée 5, 12, 13, 15, 17, 18, 19, 20, 21, 22, 23
Le Système du docteur Goudron et du professeur Plume 7, 18–19

Tearle, Conway 118
Temerson, Jean 160
Tennant, Barbara 49, 50
Thalberg, Irving 29, 121
Théâtre Antoine 3
Théâtre de Renaissance 4
Théâtre Libre 3
Thirard, Armand 154, 156, 160, 163, 165, 166, 167
Thiriet, Maurice 149
Todd, Arthur 111, 113, 117, 120
Toler, Sidney 103
Torment 117
Torrence, Ernest 113
Tourneur, Maurice 1–2; in America 25–30; American citizenship of 1; at Eclair 3–10; in Europe 133–140; films at Eclair 11–24; films in America 31–130; films in Europe 141–168
Tourneur, Jacques 29, 135, 141, 142, 144, 146, 149
Treasure Island 27, 95–95

Trilby 39–41
Tucker, George Loane 28
Turnbull, Margaret 89
Tuscherer-Sirius 168

The Undying Flame 56 58, 59
Universal 78, 120
Urban, Joseph 121

Le Val d'enfer 137, 165
Valentin, Albert 161
van den Broek, John 38, 39, 41, 42, 44, 47, 48, 49, 51, 52, 53, 55, 56, 58, 60, 61, 63, 65, 67, 70, 72, 73, 75, 77, 78
Van Doren 29
van Enger, Charles 91, 92, 104, 106, 110
Vandal, Marcel 25
Vandal and Delac 149
Vanel, Charles 142, 143, 144, 149
Varennes, Jacques 156, 161
Variety 29, 31, 34, 41, 43, 48, 49, 51, 54, 56, 58, 61, 62, 65, 66, 84, 88, 93, 95, 103, 107, 110, 132, 135, 142, 143, 145, 146, 147, 153, 156, 160, 161, 164, 167, 181
Vautier, Elmire 156
The Velvet Paw 51–52, 93
Verdun, Henri 162
Verdun, visions d'histoire 142
Verne, Jules 129
Verneuil, Louis 154
La Veuve joyeuse 5, 13
Victory 27, 87–89
Viot, Jacques 168
Le Voleur 135, 149
Volpone 136, 160–161

Warwick, Robert 32, 34, 38, 44, 45, 53
Wellman, William A. 29, 134
West, Paul 51
While Paris Sleeps 93, 94
The Whip 55–56, 57, 78, 91
The White Circle 98–101
The White Heather 27, 29, 82–84, 129
The White Moth 117–119
Whittaker, Charles E. 55, 56, 58, 60, 78, 82, 85
Williams, Earle 115, 116
Williamson, J. Ernest 82, 128, 129
Wilson, Janice 99
Wings 134
The Wishing Ring 26, 34–37
Wolff, Pierre 167
Woman 27, 78–80
Woon, Basil 93
World Pictures 26
Wulschleger, Henry 142
Wyllard, Dolf 58

Young, Clara Kimball 39, 40, 79, 138

Zola, Emile 4
Zweig, Stefan 160